G000136149

Tokenomics

The Crypto Shift of Blockchains, ICOs, and Tokens

Sean Au
Thomas Power

BIRMINGHAM - MUMBAI

Tokenomics

Copyright © 2018 Packt Publishing

All rights reserved. No part of this book may be reproduced, stored in a retrieval system, or transmitted in any form or by any means, without the prior written permission of the publisher, except in the case of brief quotations embedded in critical articles or reviews.

Every effort has been made in the preparation of this book to ensure the accuracy of the information presented. However, the information contained in this book is sold without warranty, either express or implied. Neither the authors, nor Packt Publishing or its dealers and distributors, will be held liable for any damages caused or alleged to have been caused directly or indirectly by this book.

Packt Publishing has endeavored to provide trademark information about all of the companies and products mentioned in this book by the appropriate use of capitals. However, Packt Publishing cannot guarantee the accuracy of this information.

Acquisition Editors: Frank Pohlmann and Andrew Waldron
Project Editor: Radhika Atitkar
Content Development Editor: Joanne Lovell
Technical Editor: Nidhisha Shetty
Proofreader: Safis Editing
Indexer: Pratik Shirodkar
Graphics: Tom Scaria
Production Coordinator: Sandip Tadge

First published: October 2018

Production reference: 1041018

Published by Packt Publishing Ltd.

Livery Place
35 Livery Street
Birmingham B3 2PB, UK.
ISBN 978-1-78913-632-6

www.packtpub.com

To my dear wife Tara whose support has made this dream possible and to my children Ekun, Jayee, and Taline. If daddy can do it, so can you

— Sean Au

To Penny Power who has powered me through the last 30 years since we first met by accident on September 1st 1988, supporting and believing in all the risks we chose to take, thank you for creating the next generation of Power's (PowORS) in Hannah 1992, Ross 1994, and TJ Power 1997. To our three little ones I say, remember the six magic words "we become what we think about" and always be Open Random Supportive (ORS)®

— Thomas Power

Thomas and I

"Just share what you know," he said to me as we sat at the back of a meeting room whispering to each other like kids in a classroom. And it was on that morning, on the 5th of June 2015, in a meeting at Canary Wharf, London where he drew the Nike tick and wrote beneath "Just Share It"... and I've been doing that ever since.

I had heard of the name Thomas Power back in August 2014 in conjunction with words like "a social media guru" and "the guy who teaches high profile board members and individuals how to tweet." That sounded silly to me but then, I knew nothing about social media, and to tell the truth, I didn't really care.

My Twitter, Facebook, and LinkedIn accounts where all dormant, gathering cob webs in some dusty attic in cyberspace. I didn't rate them because I didn't understand them. Besides, as an introverted geek, why on Earth would I want to put myself "out there?" Little did I know that going to London for the first time and accidentally meeting Thomas Power would change my perspective and eventually change the way I would see the world.

At the back of that meeting room I hammered Thomas on why social media was a waste of time, questioned the benefits of being constantly present online and how it was a waste of time tweeting about your favorite TV show or what you just ate.

In the next 45 minutes, Thomas talked about being Open, Random, and Supportive, about being willing to serve and about staying hungry. Concepts that were beyond me but not strange to me. I then thought to myself, "maybe he knows something that I don't. Besides, what do I have to lose?"

Upon my return to New Zealand, I created a new Twitter account, dusted the cob webs off my Facebook and LinkedIn profiles, and tentatively tweeted my first tweet. I started using an application called Klout (now shutdown), which measured one's social influence. I had no intention of trying to be popular but what struck me was the tag line. "Be known for what you love." This got me thinking, what is it that I love?

I've been interested in bitcoins since 2014 as well as blockchain technologies and decided to pursue this full time shortly after. It was one of the biggest decisions of my life. I spent an entire year reading everything I could on the internet and probably only scratched the surface! What has transpired is a deeper understanding of how money works, how the world works, and doing things I never thought possible such as co-authoring a book.

The journey of living and not just existing, of creating a dream list and not a bucket list, and the attitude of whether I succeed or fail being able to tell my kids that at least your daddy gave it a go is not for the faint hearted. It puts to the test the very person that you are. It is an arduous journey. One fought with hard work and determination along with more than the occasional inspirational pick-me-up YouTube videos from the likes of Eric Thomas (@Ericthomasbtc), Gary Vaynerchuck (@garyvee), and Jay Shetty (@JayShettyIW).

I challenge those in similar situations to take a chance and explore this new world, but remember that your fundamentals and core values need to be right. Don't just be social for the sake of being social. Be open, random, and supportive. Help others and stay hungry.

Endorsements

Tokenomics is a great book! Sean and Thomas give a fascinating insight into the wonderfully exciting world of cryptocurrencies, tokens, and ICOs and how this technology is going to change the world. It takes the reader on a journey through time, from the first ICO right through to what could happen 5 years from now.

Dickie Armour

CCO, CorreInnovation.com

My mission as City A.M.'s Crypto Insider is to learn and share new knowledge in the fields of AI, Blockchain, Cryptocurrency, and Tokenization. Sean and Thomas's book *Tokenomics* is a must read for anyone wanting to get a valuable insight into the space and I can highly recommend it.

James Bowater

City AM's Crypto Insider

www.cityam.com/crypto-insider

Sean and Thomas demystify the concepts of blockchains, ICOs, and tokenomics and highlight how this technology will have a profound effect in the years to come. We have seen a new asset class created that can help address some of the challenges in our fast changing digital world from raising capital, helping to attract, engage, reward, and retain customers and helping to give control back to individuals!

Jonny Fry

CEO TeamBlockchain Ltd

www.teamblockchain.net

The momentum around cryptocurrency represents an opportunity for companies to engage communities and solve the "chicken and egg" problem of marketplaces in more innovative and impactful ways. Yet, Token Sales and Initial Coin Offerings (ICOs) are still clouded with uncertainty, even after you remove the bad actors. Tokenomics takes a much-needed look into the challenges that accompany the new world of tokens, blockchain, and the potential for token economies.

Vinny Lingham

Co-founder and CEO, Civic

An exciting and inspiring literary journey into the future of decentralization.

Jason Meyers

Founder of Auditchain.com

Blockchain and distributed ledger technologies have the potential to change the ways many industries work. This book does a great job of deconstructing cryptoeconomics, ICOs, and new models for businesses and individuals to thrive.

Nimo Naamani

Co-founder Horizon State

www.horizonstate.com

Sean and Thomas have done a great job of demystifying the concepts of blockchains, ICOs, and tokenomics in an easy to digest manner. Readers will come away realizing that this technology will have a profound effect on our future. A must read for anybody in business.

Mark Pascall

Director, BlockchainLabs.NZ and

President of the Blockchain Association of New Zealand

`mapt.io`

Mapt is an online digital library that gives you full access to over 5,000 books and videos, as well as industry leading tools to help you plan your personal development and advance your career. For more information, please visit our website.

Why subscribe?

- ◆ Spend less time learning and more time coding with practical eBooks and Videos from over 4,000 industry professionals
- ◆ Learn better with Skill Plans built especially for you
- ◆ Get a free eBook or video every month
- ◆ Mapt is fully searchable
- ◆ Copy and paste, print, and bookmark content

Packt.com

Did you know that Packt offers eBook versions of every book published, with PDF and ePub files available? You can upgrade to the eBook version at www. Packt.com and as a print book customer, you are entitled to a discount on the eBook copy. Get in touch with us at customercare@packtpub. com for more details.

At www.Packt.com, you can also read a collection of free technical articles, sign up for a range of free newsletters, and receive exclusive discounts and offers on Packt books and eBooks.

Contributors

About the authors

Sean Au is a blockchain researcher and trainer with a B.E. (Hons) in Electrical Engineering and a Masters in Engineering Management from the Canterbury University in NZ. His masters' thesis 19 years ago was titled "Information Intermediaries," but with the rise of decentralization, that old model has surely crumbled.

With over 15 years of experience in the field of IT, Sean started out as a programmer, and prior to entering the blockchain rabbit hole, he was an integration architect and consultant, joining cloud systems together.

Sean is a Certified Bitcoin Professional (CBP) and designed and delivered NZ's first blockchain training course in association with the Blockchain Association of New Zealand (BANZ). Sean is the immediate past president and current education chair of BANZ and a member of the NZ ISO/TC307 committee on blockchains and distributed ledger technologies.

Sean continues to contribute by building practical applications and sharing it with the local community as the co-organizer of the Wellington blockchain meetup and organizer of the Wellington smart contract meetup. Some of his projects include "Ubering Energy on the Blockchain" and placing his land title on the blockchain.

This book is the culmination of two minds from different ends of the spectrum with over 24 months of research. It was designed to capture a special moment in history and paint a picture of how the ICO craze came about. It is for the generations to come that want to hear and want to re-live the events that launched the token economy.

There are plenty of people who helped bring this book to fruition, and we are grateful to all of them. First of all, this book would not be possible without the great team at Packt who have done a fantastic job. Producer Andrew Waldron, project editor Radhika Atitkar, development editor Joanne Lovell, technical reviewer Reyan Lamrani and Rick O'Neill, founder of Look Touch & Feel, a digital marketing and automation agency for authoring chapter ten and his expert knowledge in the digital marketing space.

A huge thanks to those that Thomas and I have met on this journey and inspired us in one way or another.

- Aaron McDonald, Co-founder and CEO, Centrality, @aaronmcdnz
- Adriana Belotti, Blockchain Pro Podcast creator, Blockchain Professionals meetup organizer, digital marketer, and web developer, @abelotti
- Amanda Au, Blockchain marketing and social media specialist, @amandaau_
- Bokky PooBah, Co-founder and CEO, Bok Consulting, @BokkyPooBah
- Daniel Barr, Co-founder, Tenzorum, @danieltbar
- Dinis Guarda, Founder and CEO, Ztudium and lifesdna
- Jason Goldberg, Founder and CEO, Simple Tokens, @betashop
- Jason Meyers CEO AuditChain, @JasonMeyersNYC
- John Pericos, IT consultant and crypto enthusiast, @JohnPericos
- Jonny Fry, CEO Teamblockchain, Chairman Lifesdna, @jonnyfry175
- Joseph Lubin, Founder ConsenSys, @ethereumJoseph
- Ken Anderson, Chief Developer Advocate, Hedera Hashgraph
- Lingy Au, Innovation consultant and programme director at Creative HQ, @LingyAu88
- Nick Ayton, Founder 21 Million TV, Chain Starter, @NickAyton
- Nimo Naamani, Co-founder, Horizon State, @nimo_ni
- Vinny Lingham, Co-founder and CEO, Civic, @VinnyLingham

Thomas Power is an author of 7 books since 1998 and has made over 1000 speeches in 56 countries covering all aspects of technology, social media, community building, cloud, and SaaS Apps.

Now the world has shifted its attention to Blockchain, Bitcoin, Ethereum, ICOs, Tokenomics, Cryptonomics, Internet of Things, and Artificial Intelligence, and Thomas has shifted with the times, making presentations on these subjects to conferences and board members around the globe.

Thomas is ranked No 11 in the Crypto 100 most Influential People. Thomas is also ranked No 9 in The Blockchain Fintech 100 People.

Thomas has over 290,000 followers on Twitter and is ranked No. 1 in the world on LinkedIn with 680 written testimonials.

Thomas is a board member and Director of six companies, including 9Spokes PLC in New Zealand who supply Barclays, Royal Bank of Canada, and Bank of New Zealand with Cloud SaaS AI solutions for small businesses and Team Blockchain Ltd based in London.

As GDPR kicked in May 25th 2018, Thomas has woken up many executives to the power of Community Building on The Blockchain to avoid the penalty fines of 4% of global turnover.

The next big development is for us all to hold our identity on The Blockchain so we can go through Know Your Customer (KYC) and Anti-Money Laundering (AML) processes with Banks and Financial Services companies in one click like Amazon Pay. This will further allow us all to trade with tokens for products and services from Brands so we are incentivized and rewarded with every interaction... much like the opening show of Black Mirror part three.

And to all those who have been most helpful guiding me either on Twitter, WhatsApp, LinkedIn, Telegram, Signal, Slack, Skype, and Facebook, thank you all very much indeed as it's not possible to do this research and analysis without your insights and your connections.
– Thomas Power

- Adrian Grant Co-Founder 9Spokes, @AdrianDGrant
- Anthony Pompliano Founder & Partner Morgan Creek Digital, @APompliano
- Bob Pickles Canon, @robertpickles
- Brett King, @BrettKing
- Charles Hoskinson, @IOHK_Charles
- Chris Burniske, @cburniske
- Craig Wright, @ProfFaustus
- Dan Dark Pill Art Science Bitcoin, @DanDarkPill
- David Bundi, @DavidBundiRisk
- David Siegel Founder PillarWallet, @PullNews
- Don Tapscott & Alex Tapscott Authors The Blockchain Revolution, @dtapscott, @alextapscott
- Duncan Gledhill CEO Digital Entrepreneur, @digentre
- Florian Seroussi CEO EverContact, @florianseroussi
- Fran Strajnar CEO Techemy Capital, @Techemist
- Gary Nuttall Team Blockchain, @gpn01
- Gary Vaynerchuk, @garyvee
- Ian Simpson, @ian_simpson80
- James Barrington-Brown https://www.linkedin.com/in/james-barrington-brown-1882481a/
- Jamie Roy, @Jamieroy
- Jay Shetty Storyteller & Viral Video Creator, @JayShettyIW
- Joel Comm, @joelcomm
- Laura Shin CEO Unchained Podcast, @laurashin
- Mark Estall CEO & Co-Founder 9Spokes, @markaestall
- Mark van Rijemenam Author "Blockchain: Transforming Your Business and Our World", @VanRijmenam
- Martha Lane-Fox, @Marthalanefox
- Michael Casey, @mikejcasey
- Mike Dudas CEO The Block Crypto, @mdudas
- Naval Ravikant, @naval
- Olga Feldmeier CEO SmartValor, @OlgaFeldmeier
- Oliver Bussmann, @obussmann
- Pat Lynes Founder & CEO Sullivan & Stanley, @patlynes
- Paul du Plessis Development Director OST, @paulduplessis
- Preston Byrne, @prestonjbyrne
- Siam Kidd CEO The Realistic Trader, @SiamKidd

- Simon Esner Director WSH Ltd, @ezziboy
- Spiros Margaris, @SpirosMargaris
- Steve Waldron, @Stevewal63
- Syed Ahmed CEO Savortex, @SyedAhmed
- Tuur Demeester Founder Adamant Capital, @TuurDemeester
- Urs Bolt, @UrsBolt
- Vitalik Buterin, @VitalikButerin
- William Mougayar JM3 Capital, @wmougayar
- Yannick Lescure, @yannicklescure
- Zeeshan Mallick CEO ICO Marketing Solutions, @ZeeshanMallick

---

About the reviewer

Reyan Lamrani is from a traditional finance background and is currently building an economic and financial framework adequate to the Blockchain ecosystem. Reyan primarily works on Token Model Design and Token Valuation for ICOs. He helps the start-ups going through an ICO to define a relevant Token ecosystem to attract rational buyers. He puts the value creation at the heart of its analysis. Reyan is the Founder of Token Capital Market, a consulting firm for the crypto market.

Packt is Searching for Authors Like You

If you're interested in becoming an author for Packt, please visit authors. packtpub.com and apply today. We have worked with thousands of developers and tech professionals, just like you, to help them share their insight with the global tech community. You can make a general application, apply for a specific hot topic that we are recruiting an author for, or submit your own idea.

TABLE OF CONTENTS

Preface

Tokenomics is the economy of this new world. This is a no-holds-barred, in-depth exploration of the way in which we can participate in the blockchain economy. The reader will learn the basics of Bitcoin, blockchains and tokenomics, what the very first ICO was and how over a period of 5 years, various projects managed to raise the enormous sums of money they did. It then provides insights from ICO experts and looks at what the future holds. By comparing the past, current, and future of this technology, the book will inform anyone, whatever motivates their interest.

The crypto shift of blockchains, ICOs and tokens is much more than just buying bitcoins, creating tokens or raising millions in minute in an ICO. It is a new paradigm shift from centralized to decentralized, from closed to open and from opaqueness to transparency. ICOs and the creation of tokens during the craze of 2017 needed a lot of preparation, an understanding of cryptocurrencies, and of emerging legal frameworks but this has spurred a new movement to tokenize the world.

The author gives an unbiased, authoritative picture of the current playing field, exploring the token opportunities and provides a unique insight into the developing world of this tokenized economy. This book will nourish hungry minds wanting to grow their knowledge in this fascinating area.

Who this book is for

With the media hype about bitcoin, this book appeals to anyone, from those with a general interest in anything crypto to those with some knowledge of the nuances between cryptocurrency, ICOs, IPOs, and the token economy.

What this book covers

Chapter 1, *Once Upon a Token*, provides an introduction to tokenomics looking at the meaning of a network of markets and compares the Internet of information versus the Internet of value and what tokenomics is. It looks at the first occurrence of the word tokenomics and discusses tokenization and the benefit it provides.

Chapter 2, A Bit of Coin Theory, lays the foundation, with a bit of coin theory looking at digital currencies before bitcoin and why they failed, and how bitcoin was born, along with some of the founding principles. After bitcoin, we look at the era of alternative coins known as "altcoins" and then take a deeper dive into what a blockchain actually is, including how you can find a Nelson Mandela tribute on the blockchain. We then introduce you to smart contacts and provide an overview of the peak of the ICO craze in 2017.

Chapter 3, The Potential of ICOs, looks at the potential of ICOs, including what an ICO is and the associated and somewhat confusing terminologies involved. We do a comparison between the dot-com bubble and the dot-coin bubble, then we consider the challenges ICOs face, and we finally take a quick look at the new era of ICO innovation that will result from this massive global crypto experiment.

Chapter 4, Token Varieties, takes you on a journey back in time to the very first ICOs on the bitcoin blockchain, then ICOs on custom blockchains, before delving into a number of ICOs on the ever-popular Ethereum blockchain. We also highlight non-blockchain technologies.

Chapter 5, The Need for a Token, asks the question on everyone's lips: do we really need a token? We go through various thought experiments and compare how existing companies versus new companies incorporated tokens into their business model. We present some critical consideration points, to guide you if you are looking to start your own token creation journey.

Chapter 6, Playing by the Rules, introduces you to the concept of security tokens and looks at what they are in the context of ICOs. We then explain the Howey Test and outline the global stances of regulators around the world. We also present several case studies, where the US regulators closed down ICOs for unscrupulous behavior. We also discuss the evolution of white papers.

Chapter 7, The Token Sales Mechanics, explores the often very creative token sales mechanics of several high profile ICOs, looking at the token supply, distribution, presales strategy, and bonuses provided. It considers ICOs that had a hard cap, a soft cap, and even those with no caps and explains the concept of a reverse Dutch auction. Finally, we look at some token mechanic considerations as a guideline.

Chapter 8, White Paper, Website, and Team, looks at the critical components of an ICO, namely the white paper, the website, and the team. White papers have certainly evolved from being technical and mathematical in nature, to being marketing brochures and investment statements. The chapter elaborates on why a well-designed website is very important, along with a great team to boot because quite often, it is not the idea but the people behind the idea that is the difference between success and failure.

Chapter 9, Social Media and Influencers, presents social media and influencers from a different light, exploring the deeper meaning of being social, before explaining what social media is. It then looks at how ICOs use social media, and covers some of the major influencers in the crypto landscape on Twitter and YouTube.

Chapter 10, Marketing and the Launch, covers the marketing and launch of an ICO by describing the state of ICO marketing, examining the messaging and tools used, and, of course, discussing the all-important community aspect. It also explains various marketing strategies, such as bounty campaigns, airdrops, and announcements, which all build up to the launch date.

Chapter 11, Voices of the ICO World, provides a unique insight into several ICO founders: their projects, their tokens, how their ICO went, and general thoughts on the future of ICOs, tokens, and the token economy.

Chapter 12, The Future, looks at the future, highlighting that bitcoin is the only true cryptocurrency without a leader. It takes a closer look at a world full of tokens and what happens when saturation hits. It also covers the rise and importance of privacy coins, quantum blockchains, governments, and societies.

Download the color images

We also provide a PDF file that has color images of the screenshots/diagrams used in this book. You can download it here: `https://www.packtpub.com/sites/default/files/downloads/9781789136326_ColorImages.pdf`.

Conventions used

There are a number of text conventions used throughout this book.

Bold: Indicates a new term, an important word, or words that you see on the screen, for example, in menus or dialog boxes, also appear in the text like this. For example: "To the technical purest amongst us, in an ICO, the coins that investors receive are actually digital tokens, which is why sometimes they are called an **Initial Token Offering**."

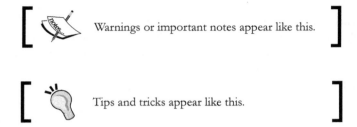

Warnings or important notes appear like this.

Tips and tricks appear like this.

Get in touch

Feedback from our readers is always welcome.

General feedback: If you have questions about any aspect of this book, mention the book title in the subject of your message and email us at customercare@packtpub.com.

Errata: Although we have taken every care to ensure the accuracy of our content, mistakes do happen. If you have found a mistake in this book we would be grateful if you would report this to us. Please visit, http://www.packt.com/submit-errata, selecting your book, clicking on the Errata Submission Form link, and entering the details.

Piracy: If you come across any illegal copies of our works in any form on the Internet, we would be grateful if you would provide us with the location address or website name. Please contact us at copyright@packt.com with a link to the material.

If you are interested in becoming an author: If there is a topic that you have expertise in and you are interested in either writing or contributing to a book, please visit http://authors.packtpub.com.

Reviews

Please leave a review. Once you have read and used this book, why not leave a review on the site that you purchased it from? Potential readers can then see and use your unbiased opinion to make purchase decisions, we at Packt can understand what you think about our products, and our authors can see your feedback on their book. Thank you!

For more information about Packt, please visit packt.com.

1

ONCE UPON A TOKEN

[The future is decentralized and the future is tokenized.]

Out of all the technological advancements that humans have achieved throughout history, the creation of a simple token on a simple digital distributed ledger has the potential to redefine the very meaning of value. This is because the underlying technology, which will be discussed throughout this book, will open up new markets, and these new markets will enable everyone to connect, participate, and exchange value in ways we never thought possible.

We are already seeing snippets of this, such as being able to send value around the world in seconds at a fraction of the normal cost; crypto and token markets trading 24/7 instead of having to close at the end of each business day and all weekend, and, of course, accessing permissionless markets with just a computer and an internet connection.

In this chapter, we start off the journey by introducing some high-level concepts. We will talk about the exciting technology in more detail in subsequent chapters. This first chapter looks at the idea of a network of markets, explains what tokenomics is and paints a picture of a tokenized economy.

These concepts should become clearer as you progress through the book and hopefully, by the end, you can join the network of dots and make your own connections.

We may be surrounded by fancy words, such as "tokenomics" or "blockchain technologies", but beneath it all we are humans trying to connect. We must connect in order to communicate, produce, create, and exchange, all within a market.

A network of markets

Markets have existed for as long as humans have engaged in trade and markets have emerged as a natural process of social coordination. The evolution of markets is constant, through a series of technological discoveries that help these markets to become more efficient.

Money has helped to facilitate trade and make markets much more efficient than bartering. In fact, it was around 5,000 BC that scripts first appeared and then around 2,500 BC when the first coinage appeared. With the onset of the agricultural revolution, and the rise of cities and kingdoms, an economy of favor and obligation didn't work. Therefore, money was invented as a much-needed solution.

Money allows participants within a community to compare quickly and easily the value of different commodities, and to easily exchange one thing for another. Cowry shells were a very popular representation of money used for thousands of years in Africa, South Asia, East Asia, and Oceania (*Sapiens: A Brief History of Humankind, Yuval Noah Harari*). Fast-forward a few thousand years and computers have made updating stock prices much more efficient than using chalk and blackboards, but how have networks and markets developed?

Naval Ravikant, the CEO and founder of AngelList, a website for startups, angel investors, and job-seekers, wrote a very insightful 36-tweet tweetstorm in June 2017 about a network of markets. Here is a summary of Naval's key points:

Blockchains will replace networks with markets. Humans are the networked species. The first to network across genetic boundaries and thus seize the world. Networks allow humans to co-operate and to allocate the fruits of our co-operation. It is this overlapping network that helps to create and organize society. Physical, digital, and mental roads connected us all together. Money is a network, religion is a network, a corporation is a network, roads are networks, electricity is a network, and all these networks must be organized according to rules. They require rulers to enforce these rules against cheaters. (https://twitter.com/naval/status/877467629308395521).

Ravikant further explained the different types of networks, such as social networks, the search network, the telecommunications network, and networks run by the elite, such as the university network, the medical network, and the banking network. The most exciting network mentioned was the blockchain network:

"Blockchains are a new invention that allows meritorious participants in an open network to govern without a ruler and without money. They are a merit-based, tamper-proof, open voting system where the meritorious are those who work to advance the network. As society gives you money for giving society what it wants, blockchains give you coins for giving the network what it wants".

The tweetstorm contained some very deep concepts (you may want to refer back to this when you reach the end of this book) that can be encapsulated by the very first tweet:

Blockchains will replace networks with markets.

Without having to understand what a blockchain is, but accepting that it is some technology that can enable the transfer of value without involving an intermediary, this statement conveys the idea that there is a technology that has come along and, for the very first time, allowed the creation of a network of markets, which is profoundly more powerful than the network of information.

These networks are essentially **Open, Random, and Supportive (ORS)**®, which is a concept expanded on in *Chapter 9, Social Media and Influencers*. Open and random mean permissionless because anyone can join the network at any time. Supportive means that these networks are neutral, censorship-resistant, and democratized.

This network of networks will also have to be interconnected because, as we've seen time and time again, the world will never agree on a single ledger or a single platform, as long as each provider wants to own the network.

Consider this: the largest taxi company in the world (Uber) owns no cars, the largest media company (Facebook) creates no content, the largest accommodation provider (Airbnb) owns no hotels, the largest e-commerce companies (such as Alibaba) own no inventory, and a $130 billion USD currency (bitcoin) has no CEO, no bank branches, and no customer support. What do they all have in common? They all have a network, be it of cars, rooms, suppliers, or trust (https://techcrunch. com/2015/03/03/in-theage-of-disintermediation-the- battle-is-all-for-thecustomer-interface/).

The Internet of information

The internet has allowed access to vast amounts of information and the ability to communicate with anyone in the world from a device in the palm of our hands. It has been a mammoth effort from contributors around the world putting all this information online. Need to know how to cook your better half's favorite dish? The chances are that the recipe will be online and there will probably be a video showing you step-by-step the process of cooking it too. In fact, it was reported that "how to" video searches have surged 70%, with over 100 million hours watched in 2015. (https://searchengineland.com/youtube-how-to-searches-up-70-yoy-with-over-100m-hours-of-how-to-videos-watched-in-2015-220773).

Near instant access to any kind of information was a scene from science fiction movies only several decades ago, but this has now become a reality. The ability to access this information and knowledge, and to communicate, has transformed multiple industries, such as media, telecommunications, and health, and the list goes on. What this information didn't change, though, was how value was transferred because intermediaries were still required.

Take the action of purchasing a pair of shoes online. The payment from the consumer to the producer was not a straight line between two parties but often a zigzag, with multiple intermediaries involved. This was necessary because there was no other way.

Another example is the political system, where when we vote for a representative, we are transferring the rights of our political value to the representative, so that he or she can represent our views for a certain period of time. We have always used intermediation as a tool to scale our society and this was required because there was no better technology to do anything differently.

We have since discovered, or perhaps, more appropriately, we knew all along, that this intermediation is not perfect. Look at financial institutions as an example: it could be argued that banks are the reason that more than half of the world's population has been excluded from basic financial services.

Then comes the predicament where these intermediaries or representatives, once they get big enough and the value they accumulate is large enough, have more incentives to service their own interest than those that they represent.

This leads us to the question: why is the internet that we know and love, that has changed so many aspects of human society, not managed to enable us to transfer value? The reason is relatively simple: information can be almost infinitely replicated without cost. The same music file can be downloaded millions of times, or a digital image can be replicated, shared, and used many times over, all for almost zero cost. This problem didn't have an answer in the decentralized world, until the invention of bitcoin.

Bitcoin, a digital asset, was really a blockchain technology that presented itself as bitcoin. Many people then incorrectly thought that bitcoin was the first application of the blockchain technology. More on this in *Chapter 2, A Bit of Coin Theory*. This is analogous to the development of other technologies, where there was some product that embodied the technology, but as the technology matured, there were different designs aimed at different use cases.

Take, for example, automobile technology, where the goal was to get from point A to point B quicker than on foot or horseback. This technology then developed to getting from point A to point B with a heavy load (a truck), or with a group of people (bus), or even with renewable energy (electric cars). This design-driven approach is focused on one specific use case, rather than a generic design that fits every use case.

Blockchain is similar because there are thousands of token projects searching to find the right use case to focus on and be successful at. The challenge, though, is to look beyond bitcoin because the modus operandi is that we only see what we already know. Many thought PCs were just powerful typewriters and the internet just a place where computer nerds hung out. In fact, Keynesian economist Paul Krugman, who was awarded the Nobel Prize in Economic Sciences in 2008, wrote an article in 1998 on the topic:

"The growth of the internet will slow drastically, as the flaw in 'Metcalfe's law'—which states that the number of potential connections in a network is proportional to the square of the number of participants—becomes apparent: most people have nothing to say to each other! By 2005 or so, it will become clear that the internet's impact on the economy has been no greater than the fax machine's. (http://web.archive.org/web/19980610100009/www.redherring.com/mag/issue55/economics.html)."

We all know now that the internet's impact on the economy is much greater than the fax machine, but it was Krugman's most recent article, in July 2018 in The New York Times, that had many critics up in arms:

"In other words, cryptocurrency enthusiasts are effectively celebrating the use of cutting-edge technology to set the monetary system back 300 years. Why would you want to do that? What problem does it solve? I have yet to see a clear answer to that question" (https://www.nytimes.com/2018/07/31/opinion/transaction-costs-and-tethers-why-im-a-crypto-skeptic.html).

It is almost impossible to see the full potential of any technology from the beginning. Bitcoin may be that powerful typewriter but we must wait for its true potential to reveal itself in the next decade or so. This is because bitcoin is the first network of networks for the transfer of value without requiring an intermediary.

The Internet of value

The Internet of value allows important things in an economy or market to be transferred, instead of just information. The difference between information and value is the scarcity: if you give information to someone you still own it, but if you transfer value to someone, you do not own it anymore. Examples include stocks, intellectual property, art, music, votes, identity, and, of course, money. The Internet of value provides the ability to move value as easily as we move information.

Being able to send the same $1,000 to more than one recipient is not a good idea and this is known as the "double spend problem," which is explained in *Chapter 2, A Bit of Coin Theory*. The problem has previously been managed through intermediaries, such as banks, governments, and numerous other third parties, to establish trust in our economy. They provide the service of identifying people, verifying, clearing, and settling the transaction, and keeping records, so that you cannot spend the same $1,000 twice.

The result, over time, is an increase in cost, a reduction in value, and the exclusion of a large number of people from the global economy. These intermediaries also capture our all-important data. With this new technology called "blockchains", or more accurately "distributed ledger technology", there is a decentralized network where trust is native to the medium. Value can be created, transferred, or exchanged and participants trust the network and the mathematics (believe it or not, the world we live in is governed by the laws of mathematics).

In this Internet of value world, value is represented by none other than a token and the value it represents is governed by the various laws of economics, where the simplest is supply and demand. This has given rise to the concept of tokenomics.

What is tokenomics?

The word "tokenomics" is a portmanteau, or combination, of the words "token" and "economics" and it is a relatively new term that rose to popularity in the middle of 2017. As with anything new, the meaning has yet to be standardized, with many industry leaders attempting to provide their own definition. This is similar to attempting to define blockchains or the internet in the early days, as there are a range of ideas that are encapsulated within the idea of tokenomics.

Tokenomics, however, encompasses the concept of the study, design, and implementation of an economic system to incentivize specific behaviors in a community, using tokens to create a self-sustaining ad hoc mini economy. It includes game theory, mechanism design, and monetary economics.

If we think back to the loyalty points we get from our local supermarket or an airline, when we collect or redeem them some of us analyze the economics. For example, I need to purchase another $50 worth of groceries in order to receive a $15 gift voucher because it only gets paid out after 200 points have been collected, and I'm on 195 points ($10 of spending for one point). Another example is asking how many flights do I need this year to achieve gold status and how many flights do I need to maintain gold status? Anyone who has gone through these scenarios could argue that they were analyzing the tokenomics of the loyalty points system.

Tokenomics was selected as the title of this book because with all the ICOs in the last few years, and this new tokenized economy that is emerging, token supply, inflation rate, and even the various incentive schemes can all be encapsulated into this word.

Micro and macro

In economics there are two major fields: microeconomics and macroeconomics. Microeconomics focuses on individuals or companies, which could mean studying the supply and demand for a specific product or the production that an individual or business can produce. Macroeconomics focuses on the aggregate issues that affect the overall economy, such as the gross domestic product of an economy or the effects of imports or exports.

Tokenomics is similar. Microtokenomics can be considered as features that drive the functions of individual participants within a blockchain economy. Examples include mining rewards and how they change over time, and the mechanics needed to adjust the token supply, demand, and velocity, such as vesting periods, the mining difficulty, and the inflation rate.

Macrotokenomics consists features that relate to the interaction with the wider blockchain economy and they tend to include governance (such as who decides what the next new feature is), the participant interaction within the ecosystem, and also the external factors of the token growth and volatility (such as the utility of the token and the liquidity on exchanges). It is the interaction of all these variables that produces what is known as a 'token economy.'

First occurrence of the word

One of the earliest occurrences of the word was in a tweet with the hashtag **#TOKEnomics**, in March 2012, from DJ Hustlenomics, an American rapper:

Figure 1: One of the earliest uses of the word "tokenomics" by an American rapper.
(https://twitter.com/DjHustlenomics/status/185205191480582144)

'Hustlenomics' was the second studio album by American rapper Jasiel Amon Robinson, who is better known for his stage name 'Yung Joc.' Needless to say, this was probably nothing to do with blockchains or the new decentralized economy.

The next occurrence was from someone on Twitter with the handle @thewayoftheid. Again, we can probably safely assume that Jamie is not talking about blockchains to @Mami_LongLegz:

Figure 2: Another use of the word "tokenomics" on Twitter in December 2013.
(https://twitter.com/thewayoftheid/status/416599434097463296)

Almost a year later, in August 2014, there was a more relevant tweet from Dave Feuling, or @GoodForOneDrink, who tweeted **Enjoying Tokenomics at the good ol Hammond Hotel**. Feuling explained where he heard the word from:

"A local bar (no longer in business) held Tokenomics on Wednesday nights for a certain length of time. It was called this bc (sic) every drink you bought awarded you a drink token that was good for one free drink of equal or lesser value. It was basically a special happy hour" (https://twitter.com/seandotau/status/1024041929158221824).

This tweet may not be directly referencing blockchains or ICOs, but we are getting closer because there is a token involved that can be redeemed for a drink at the Hammond hotel in Wisconsin, USA:

Figure 3: The earliest mention of the word "tokenomics" that has reference to an actual token (https://twitter.com/GoodForOneDrink/status/497159085721391104)

Fast forward to March 2015 and the word "tokenomics" was mentioned again in a tweet by @mmoblogosphere, who was actually referencing @casualnoob blog post titled **Tokenomics**. @casualnoob is a female blogger with the pseudonym "Da Cheng", who is a mage (a magician) character in the computer game **World of Warcraft (WoW)**.

Figure 4: A blog post on tokenomics, analyzing the WoW token

The tokenomics blog was in reference to a WoW token released by Blizzard Entertainment and "Da Cheng" analyzed the economics of the token. Essentially, Blizzard created two in-game tokens. One token could be bought from Blizzard for an initial price of $20 per token and another could be sold to Blizzard to add 30 days of game time to your account. The final tokenomics recommendation from "Da Cheng" was:

"Recommendation: buy Gold WoW tokens on day 1. Buy all you can afford. There will never again be such a concentrated glut of sellers. The price will never drop to 40 000g again. **Don't buy $teel WoW tokens before week 5**, once the upward price momentum of gold tokens is obvious."

The final occurrence before the floodgates opened wasn't until June 2017 (`https://twitter.com/ search?l=&q=%22tokenomics%22%20since%3A2014-07-03%20 until%3A2017-07-04&src=typd&lang=en`) by William Mougayar, a thought leader in tokenomics, who wrote an article titled *Tokenomics—A Business Guide to Token Usage, Utility and Value.* (`https://medium.com/@wmougayar/tokenomics-a-business- guide-to-token-usage-utility-and-value-b19242053416`). Mougayar provided a detailed analysis, where he defined a "token" as just another term for a type of privately issued currency.

Figure 5: The tweet that opened the floodgates on the word "tokenomics."
(https://twitter.com/wmougayar/status/873912937676779522)

The token economy

 Token economy: A system or marketplace where decisions are made driven by economic incentives of digital tokens.

Burrhus Frederic Skinner, or more commonly known as B.F. Skinner, was an American psychologist, behaviorist, and social philosopher who used the term "token economy" in 1972 in a video titled *Token Economy: Behaviorism Applied*" (https://www.youtube.com/watch?v=fyFzPgIy-0g). Skinner used this concept in the context of using physical tokens in a program of therapy for the treatment of criminals and the mentally ill. As a side note, the writer of the famous American animated sitcom *The Simpsons, Jon Vitti*, named the "Principal Skinner" character after B.F. Skinner (The Simpsons season 2 DVD commentary for the episode "Principal Charming" [DVD]. 20th Century Fox).

One of the major teaching techniques was using a token economy with the students. A token economy was very simply a structured learning situation, where tokens, or little plastic chips, were used so that students could earn tokens in a wide variety of ways. This always involved learning more appropriate behavior.

The meaning of a token economy or tokenized economy in 2018 contains the same concepts, but it is applied in a different context. Little plastic chips have now been digitized into tokens and instead of students earning tokens, anyone can earn them and the structured learning environment has now changed into a new digital world, where anyone can participate.

The underlying infrastructure that has allowed this new token economy to flourish is blockchains, which are the equivalent of an ad-hoc miniature economy. In this economy, you have a group of people, or entities, who are all interacting with each other, making decisions, co-operating, and even competing with each other. The driver is an underlying software that enforces the rules created by the original author(s) and it governs how the interactions will unfold.

What is interesting is that all these miniature economies are powered by their own specially created token. Why do these token projects do this? The answer is: because they can. The marginal cost of creating a new token on a platform designed for creating tokens is almost nothing; however, gaining adoption is a totally different challenge.

This leads to the concept of a minimum viable economy, where if traction or critical mass is achieved, the economy can self-sustain and self-govern. Otherwise, it collapses and new ones form very quickly, and it's the low barrier to entry that allows this to occur.

The token is interwoven throughout the business model, providing a way to reward and incentivize the network participants, customers, and stakeholders. This focuses innovation at the token level, as the blockchain infrastructure is already provided, along with other requirements, such as consensus algorithms and the creation of a network.

There are key questions to consider around the tokens with a token economy. For example, is the token tied exclusively to a product usage or a network? The current answer is almost always yes. Other key questions include: does the token provide the owner with special privileges or ownership? Is the token required to run a smart contract or is it used to pay for usage? The answers to these questions are all varied and unfortunately, they depend on the design and context.

The most important question, though, is whether having a token is an absolute necessity in solving the problem. In other words: if digital tokens and the blockchain technology had not been invented, could the problem still be solved?

A unique aspect of the token economy is around the distribution because the key is to get the tokens into the hands of as many users as possible, so they can be used. This is because in this miniature economy, your products or services can only be used or traded with that token, which means that if you provide a valued service or product, that token eventually comes back to you. This circulation between stakeholders is very important. The most successful token projects will be the ones that can solve this challenge or even gamify it.

Marc Andreessen, co-founder of Netscape and venture capitalist firm Andreessen Horowitz, famously stated, *Software is eating the world.* In his 2011 article, he outlined that the world's largest bookseller, Amazon, is a software company; the largest video service by subscriber, Netflix, is a software company; and music companies like iTunes, Spotify, and Pandora are also all software companies. The list keeps going, with the likes of Skype in telecommunications and Pixar for animated movie production and Andreessen added, *Software is also eating much of the value chain of industries that are widely viewed as primarily existing in the physical world* (https://a16z.com/2016/08/20/why-software-is-eating-the-world/).

Nearing a decade on, the manifestation of the physical world is slowly being recreated in the virtual world and the missing piece of the puzzle has been discovered: the ability to transfer value in this virtual world with trust. This is how and why the token economy will continue to grow and develop. The tokenized economy starts with the digitization of the physical world and ends with the realization of the virtual world.

What does the current tokenized economy look like?

A token economy may be hard to conceive because it is not really tangible, like physical assets or your local bazaar, but there are digital tokens being created every day for all sorts of uses. The following image shows only the top 10 out of the thousands available and these thousands will grow further in the coming years. The reason for the growth is because of the new network of markets that is being created.

#	Name	Market Cap	Price	Volume (24h)	Circulating Supply
1	Bitcoin	$132,529,228,796	$7,712.99	$5,168,566,708	17,182,600 BTC
2	Ethereum	$43,518,477,652	$430.70	$1,790,018,335	101,042,019 ETH
3	XRP	$16,978,064,766	$0.431839	$222,377,464	39,315,683,476 XRP *
4	Bitcoin Cash	$13,233,115,417	$766.34	$406,752,302	17,268,013 BCH
5	EOS	$6,582,466,373	$7.26	$688,476,045	906,245,118 EOS *
6	Stellar	$5,131,226,675	$0.273370	$88,200,387	18,770,255,848 XLM *
7	Litecoin	$4,592,668,482	$79.66	$314,754,032	57,651,357 LTC
8	Cardano	$3,681,163,359	$0.141981	$92,357,247	25,927,070,538 ADA *
9	IOTA	$2,599,034,347	$0.935062	$34,472,905	2,779,530,283 MIOTA *
10	Tether	$2,450,867,488	$0.995340	$3,170,488,481	2,462,140,346 USDT *

Figure 6: A list of the top-10 tokens, out of thousands
in a token economy, from CoinMarketCap.com

What is tokenization?

Tokenization is the process of converting the rights of real-world assets into a digital token, stored on a blockchain or decentralized ledger. The simplest analogy is democratizing ownership of real-world assets, where the value stored in some physical asset, such as real estate, is represented as a token. For example, if you had an apartment valued at $1,000,000, one million USD tokens could be created to represent the value of the apartment at $1 per token.

The one million token supply is totally arbitrary. The one million tokens could then be freely bought or sold on an exchange and if you bought 500,000 tokens, you would effective own 50% of the apartment, and the various rights and benefits associated.

This concept is not new, as anyone can create tokens and record the token history using a regular database, managed by a trusted third party, but the novelty now is that it can be done in a decentralized fashion and nobody can "erase" your ownership of these tokens. This is the key tenet of this blockchain technology.

Real-world assets, such as artwork, stocks, and gold, are just the first step because the same thing can be done with digital assets and intangible assets, such as carbon credits, patents, and copyrights. These tokens and their exchange are what creates this token economy. What's more, every brand, every artist, and every community can tokenize its economy with the ability to incentivize early adopters or reward loyal follows within this economy. This is the equivalent of being able to communicate value on a new level. Think of it as loyalty points on steroids.

The tokenization of everything

We've seen the ability to tokenize anything, from the physical and tangible to the intangible. The next logical question is why?

First of all, when assets are tokenized, they unlock liquidity. The value you have in your property is regarded as illiquid because there is no easy or quick way to access the capital stored there. Tokens representing the value of your property can be traded much more easily and hence they are more liquid.

The technology the tokens live on allows greater access to everyone. It may not be to the extent that all you need is a computer and internet connection, but it will be much more democratized than what we have at present.

This increased participation results in greater ease of trade, by bringing in more liquidity and efficiency to a market.

Tokenization enables new economic models, such as fractional ownership (investors can own a certain percentage of a certain asset), therefore users can purchase a smaller, more affordable portion, rather than an expensive whole portion.

Through fractional ownership, more diversification of risk can be obtained. If a valuable piece of artwork was destroyed in a fire, an investor would lose only the proportion of that which was invested.

Tokenization reduces administrative expenses and with smart contracts and an immutable audit trail, auditing and compliance become a lot easier and quicker for regulatory bodies.

It would be presumptuous to assume that tokenizing assets is without its challenges.

The most obvious one is trusting the issuer. Market participants need to be confident that they can redeem their real-world asset at any point in time. Whether it is the ability to redeem the five gold tokens for one ounce of gold, or the 2,000 tokens representing a fraction of a property for USD, if the token is not redeemable or exchangeable, then the token is worthless.

There is still a cloud of uncertainty over the regulations of tokenized assets. Governments and relevant regulatory bodies around the world are closely following developments and currently the default is to apply existing laws to these new scenarios.

Legal enforcement of token ownership and rights has yet to be tested in a court of law, particularly around the recovery of damages and liability. This will no doubt set a precedent if and when it occurs.

Digital identity and relevant **Know Your Customer (KYC)** requirements and anti-money laundering laws need to be met, and most probably integrated into the token platform, to satisfy the requirements of the various relevant regulators and financial market authorities.

Summary

In this chapter, we introduced the concept of a network of markets and considered the fact that blockchains could replace networks with markets. We also looked at how the Internet of information has transformed society, but has fallen short of being able to transfer value because this wasn't possible, until now.

We discovered that solving the "double spend problem" in a decentralized manner has enabled the creation of the Internet of value, which is the missing piece of the puzzle for building internet 2.0. In this new world, tokens will represent this value and they will be created, transferred, and exchanged in new markets making up this new token economy. The digital token economy will continue to grow, causing assets in the physical world to have their digital counterpart in a virtual world.

Now that we have set the scene, let's turn our focus to the all-important theory, setting you up for the rest of the book. It is a light-touch approach for beginners, breaking down several concepts that have become very important in this new decentralized world.

2

A Bit of Coin Theory

Like anything in life, to gain an appreciation of how we got to where we are, it's helpful to understand the background and history of how it all started. To some people, **blockchains** and **cryptocurrency** are just a technology fad, but to the dedicated few, this is a movement of epic proportions, centered around trust and the decentralization of it.

Understanding some of the fundamental concepts of this technology will help to enable all of us to see the potential revolution that blockchains, the wider concept of distributed ledger technologies, smart contracts, and tokens will bring.

In this chapter, we will go back in time and look at:

- ♦ **Bitcoin**: In the beginning
- ♦ **Altcoins**: The alternative to bitcoin
- ♦ **Blockchains**: The immutable database
- ♦ **Smart contracts**: Are they that smart?
- ♦ **ICOs**: The peak of ICOs in 2017

Since bitcoin appeared on the scene in 2009, it has had its fair share of drama. It has become the "crypto gold standard" that everything is measured against, but very quickly, alternative coins were created to copy bitcoin's success. Next came the blockchain era, where everything was being placed on the blockchain.

Smart contracts then became the "in" thing a few years later and that allowed software programs to be created and live on the blockchain. A year later, smart contracts spawned an era of decentralized applications, also known as dApps, on a popular platform called Ethereum. In amongst all of this, tokens were created and a new age of funding was born. Let's dig a little deeper into this by starting at the beginning.

Bitcoin – in the beginning

Money has not had a major innovative disruption in at least several decades, but there have been many attempts in the past, such as **DigiCash** (Chaum, 1989), **e-gold** (Jackson and Downey, 1996), **B-money** (Dai, 1997), **bit gold** (Szabo, 1998), and **Liberty Dollar** (von NotHaus, 1998). It wasn't until the invention of bitcoin that a disruption really started to show, but why did these previous attempts fail?

DigiCash

One of the biggest challenges in creating a cryptocurrency is the **double-spend problem**. This is where the same digital currency is spent twice because it can be easily copied in the digital realm. In fact, it can be spent many times over.

In 1982, David Chaum, an American computer scientist and cryptographer, published a paper on his idea of *Blind Signatures for Untraceable Payments* (http://www.hit.bme.hu/~buttyan/courses/BMEVIHIM219/2009/Chaum.BlindSigForPayment.1982.PDF). Then, in 1988, he co-authored a paper on *Untraceable Electronic Cash* (http://blog.koehntopp.de/uploads/chaum_fiat_naor_ecash.pdf). The concept here was a method of solving the double-spend problem by revealing or exposing the double spender's identity.

In 1989, he took his idea and commercialized it, forming a company called DigiCash. The actual system was called eCash, while the money in the system was called **CyberBucks** (https:// bitcoinmagazine.com/articles/genesis-files-how-david-chaums-ecash-spawned-cypherpunk-dream/). There was significant interest from major banks and other corporations, but for some reason, DigiCash failed to close the deals that would allow the company to realize its full potential.

DigiCash ended up failing due to the lack of adoption because it didn't support peer-to-peer transactions very effectively, and it was very much ahead of its time. This is 1990 we're talking about. The other challenge was that DigiCash required a server to be run by a central authority and for everyone to trust that organization. Chaum eventually exited the company in 1996, DigiCash filed for bankruptcy in 1998, and the company was sold in 2002.

E-gold

E-gold was founded by oncologist Douglas Jackson and attorney Barry Downey in 1996. It had grown to over five million users by 2009, when transfers were suspended due to legal issues. At its peak, in 2008, e-gold was processing more than $2 billion USD worth of precious metals transactions per year.

However, e-gold was indicted (formally accused of or charged with a crime) for money laundering and illegal money transmission, and in July 2008, the directors pleaded guilty to these charges (https://www.justice.gov/archive/opa/pr/2008/July/08-crm-635.html).

B-money

B-money was an idea created by Wei Dai, a computer engineer and cypherpunk, in 1997, that outlined two concepts. The first concept was that *every participant maintains a separate database of how much money belongs to each other* (http://www.weidai.com/bmoney.txt), and the second concept was *the accounts of who has how much money are kept by a subset of the participants.* These were just concepts, though, without actual implementations, primarily because the first concept was impractical, as admitted by Wei Dai:

> *I will actually describe two protocols. The first one is impractical.*

Bit gold

Shortly after the B-money concept was released publicly, Nick Szabo launched a very similar project known as bit gold in 1998. The key concept here was the move away from centralized authorities. It described concepts such as proof of work and digital signatures, similar to bitcoin, but bit gold was never implemented.

Figure 1: Nick Szabo on Twitter comparing his bit gold design to that of bitcoin
(https://twitter.com/nickszabo4/status/846116902833303552)

Liberty Dollar

The Liberty Dollar was an alternate currency created by Bernard von NotHaus, in 1998, for the purpose of combating inflation. Liberty Dollars were backed originally by silver, then later other precious metals, such as gold, copper, and platinum. Von NotHaus introduces himself on his website:

"Hi. My name is Bernard von NotHaus. I was so concerned about what was happening to our country's "money" that I created the Liberty Dollar. For 25 years, I was the Mintmaster at the Royal Hawaiian Mint and devoted those years to the study of money, why it is valuable, and how we use it to fulfill our dreams. I wanted to create a totally new inflation proof currency based on precious metals. That quest was completed on October 1, 1998 when the Liberty Dollar was first issued."

However, FBI agents raided the office of Liberty Dollar in Indiana in November 2007, and confiscated all of its property and equipment. In March 2011, von NotHaus was convicted of making, possessing, and selling his own coins.

Why did Bitcoin succeed?

DigiCash failed because it was centralized. E-gold and Liberty Dollar failed because they broke the law, as well as being centralized. B-money was never implemented because it was impractical, and bit gold was never implemented at all. Therefore, the secret was to create something that was decentralized, leaderless, and practical. Having a decentralized network meant that it could not be taken down, stopped, or disrupted, and not having a leader meant that no government, however powerful, could raid, sue, coerce, or blackmail the company. Being practical meant that the network could be built, demonstrated, and eventually used and adopted by everyone.

The key problem that bitcoin solved that all the previous attempts couldn't, was to prevent double spending in a decentralized manner. The brilliance was that the system was designed to come to an agreement on everyone's bitcoin balance without a central leader, and it even works in the presence of hostile adversaries, so long as they are outnumbered by honest participants. Then bitcoin gained momentum with branding, network effects, popularity, first-mover advantage, investment, exchanges, and applications.

How was Bitcoin born?

Bitcoin came from humble beginnings. A message appeared on a crypto forum mailing list, called `metzdowd.com`, from Satoshi Nakamoto, detailing a new electronic cash system called bitcoin in October 2008.

```
From: Satoshi Nakamoto <satoshi <at> vistomail.com>
Subject: Bitcoin P2P e-cash paper
Newsgroups: gmane.comp.encryption.general
Date: 2008-10-31 18:10:00 GMT (4 years, 8 weeks, 1 day, 8 hours and 48 minutes ago)

I've been working on a new electronic cash system that's fully
peer-to-peer, with no trusted third party.

The paper is available at:
http://www.bitcoin.org/bitcoin.pdf

The main properties:
  Double-spending is prevented with a peer-to-peer network.
  No mint or other trusted parties.
  Participants can be anonymous.
  New coins are made from Hashcash style proof-of-work.
  The proof-of-work for new coin generation also powers the
    network to prevent double-spending.

Bitcoin: A Peer-to-Peer Electronic Cash System
```

Figure 2: Nakamoto announcing the bitcoin idea on a crypto mailing list called metzdowd (https://archive.is/20121228025845/http://article.gmane.org/gmane. comp.encryption.general/12588/)

Mailing list: Facebook for old-school geeks that is completely text based.

The bitcoin white paper detailed a new electronic cash system that claimed to solve the double-spend problem, as mentioned earlier. For the first time, a network was to replace trusted third parties. Many were skeptical and it wasn't until January 3, 2009, when the first bitcoin was created, that many got to see bitcoin in action.

Nakamoto outlined the problem:

"The root problem with conventional currency is all the trust that's required to make it work. The central bank must be trusted not to debase the currency, but the history of fiat currencies is full of breaches of that trust. Banks must be trusted to hold our money and transfer it electronically, but they lend it out in waves of credit bubbles with barely a fraction in reserve. We have to trust them with our privacy, trust them not to let identity thieves drain our accounts" (http://p2pfoundation.ning.com/forum/topics/bitcoin-open-source).

Nakamoto then outlined the solution:

"Before strong encryption, users had to rely on password protection to secure their files, placing trust in the system administrator to keep their information private... Then strong encryption became available to the masses, and trust was no longer required.... It's time we had the same thing for money. With e-currency based on cryptographic proof, without the need to trust a third-party middleman, money can be secure, and transactions effortless."

Trust

This leads us to the first fundamental concept: trust. Users would trust the network instead of third-party centralized intermediaries. Trusting the network provides certain advantages. The network does not discriminate, it is neutral, it is not limited by borders, and it is open to participation by anyone and everyone.

There is also a common misconception that blockchains eliminate trust or allow parties to transact without trust. The truth is that trust is merely converted from one form to another, similar to energy. Instead of trusting banks to verify transactions, with blockchains we trust the technology and the mathematics behind it.

[

Fundamental concept #1
Trust: Removing the need to trust centralized intermediaries and trusting a network instead.
]

Decentralization

The second fundamental concept is just as important as the first. It is decentralization. If we remove the need to trust centralized intermediaries, then who do we trust? We trust a network that is decentralized and participated in by everyone, yet owned by no one.

Decentralization, at first glance, seems very strange. It goes against the popular belief that something has to be owned by someone or at least someone needs to be responsible (or more accurately, held accountable) when something goes wrong. However, in this new world of bitcoin and everything that has stemmed from it, this long-held belief is being tipped on its head.

[

Fundamental concept #2
Decentralization: No single entity is in control.
]

Transparency

A third fundamental concept is transparency, and there is no better example than the open-source nature of the bitcoin software code. Anyone can view the code, understand the rules of game, and choose to participate by their own free will.

[

Fundamental concept #3
Transparency: Open to public scrutiny.
]

These fundamentals are important to keep in mind as we continue along our ICO journey. ICOs that do not earn the users' and community's trust, are centralized in nature, or are not transparent will find themselves not as successful as they could be.

Consensus

Understanding bitcoin and blockchains can be an endless rabbit hole that involves learning more and more technical concepts, such as hash functions, merkle trees, public key cryptography, and the ever-important digital signatures. To the average user, though, all that they need to know is that the underlying mathematics works and when a bitcoin is sent, another copy cannot be created. This is very much like users not needing to understand how the internet works to use the internet.

Having said this, there is one other fundamental concept that is very important to understand: consensus. In a decentralized system with a group of machines, how do the machines agree on something, especially the order of the transactions in a cryptocurrency?

In the case of bitcoin, the whole point is to order a bunch of transactions and the way it works is that anyone in the world can propose a list of transactions to be put into the official list or "chain." If everyone's proposed list was accepted, chaos would ensue. Therefore, a puzzle was invented called proof of work, where the first computer to solve this difficult puzzle would have their version of the list accepted on the official list. Of course, prior to the list being accepted, it would be checked, so if, for example, Alice sent Bob one bitcoin and also sent Charlie the same one bitcoin, only one would be accepted and generally it's the first transaction. Therefore, consensus is very important to understand in blockchain technologies, but there is more than one way to arrive at a consensus. Having a race to solve a mathematical puzzle is only one way.

Consensus: The ability of a group of untrusted computers to come to an agreement. In the case of cryptocurrencies, it is an agreement on the order of a list of transactions.

Other ways to achieve consensus

Another simple way to achieve consensus is for everyone to have a turn at being the leader and having the leader's list of transactions accepted. The problem here is that the leader can be attacked by other computers and prevent consensus from being achieved, stalling the network. If the leader changes, this new leader can be attacked in a follow-the-new-leader scenario. It is also not fair, as the leader has sole discretion on the order of transactions. This is why leader-based consensus is not generally used.

Proof of stake is another consensus algorithm where computers on the network essentially put coins in escrow (staking) and propose a list of transactions. Choosing the winning list can be done in several ways, such as random selection and its variants, or coin age-based selection. Nxt and Blackcoin use random selection and Peercoin uses coin age-based selection.

What is Bitcoin?

To the technical purist, a bitcoin is not really a coin and it is not owned by anyone per se. A bitcoin represents the digital right to transfer ownership of an unspent output of a previous bitcoin transaction, to create an input for the next bitcoin transaction. If that last sentence didn't make sense, don't worry, as it's not critical to understanding bitcoin.

A more common definition of bitcoin is that it is a cryptocurrency that can be used as a form of payment in exchange for goods or services.

Another interesting definition is by Peter Van Valkenburgh, the director of research at Coin Center: "Bitcoin is software running across a network of peers that creates and maintains a shared ledger accounting for holdings of a scarce token."

The unique aspect about bitcoin is that no centralized organization owns it nor has any centralized organization created it. This leads to the question: what is a coin?

What is a coin?

In the crypto world, a coin can be thought of as the native digital asset of a blockchain. For example, a bitcoin is the native digital asset of the bitcoin blockchain, but people usually refer to bitcoin just as a cryptocurrency or a digital currency.

[**Coin**: The native digital asset of a blockchain]

Another way to look at it is that when a network is created and becomes live, the native digital asset or coin is available immediately. Understanding this is important when considering the concept of mining coins.

Mining Bitcoin

Mining is the process of bringing coins into existence over time, usually based on an issuance rate determined by some mathematical formula. In bitcoin, the design was to mimic the discovery or mining of gold, where energy and resources are required to find it and there is a limited supply. This plays to the fact that some people call bitcoin "digital gold."

Mining: The process of using a computer to verify transactions and having them added to the bitcoin blockchain, and bringing more bitcoins into existence.

Bitcoins are rewarded to incentivize people to participate in verifying transactions, and a puzzle is required to be solved to determine who wins this reward because there are many computers attempting to verify transactions.

The formula is quite simple and goes like this: 50 bitcoins are minted on average every 10 minutes and after every four years (approximately), this number halves. When the total supply reaches 21 million, no more bitcoins will be created. Currently, the reward is 12.5 bitcoins before the next halving, at around May 2020.

Minting: often used interchangeably with mining.

Is Bitcoin money?

Learning about bitcoin often leads newcomers to ask the simple question: what is money? While this is an entirely different subject, it is important to note what the functions of money are and how bitcoin compares to money.

Money has three generally-agreed-upon functions: it is a **Unit of Account (UoA)**, a **Medium of Exchange (MoE)**, and a **Store of Value (SoV)**. Nakamoto envisioned bitcoin as operating or functioning as money, as detailed in the bitcoin white paper. However, a bitcoin is not currently a unit of account. We know this because currently, hardly any merchants price their products or services in bitcoin. Merchants may accept bitcoins as a payment option, but prefer to use fiat currencies, such as USD.

In the early days, bitcoin was primarily used as a medium of (decentralized) exchange, making media headlines for being used to buy drugs on the now-defunct *Silk Road* website or being used on gambling sites, such as *Satoshi Dice*. As bitcoin's adoption grew, the value also grew with it, which led many to perceive bitcoins as a store of value. Why spend them today if I believe that they will be worth more tomorrow?

The point here is that bitcoin is constantly evolving and changing. The ultimate goal is to one day visit your local supermarket or grocery store and see bitcoin price tags on the shelves.

Figure 3: Bitcoin price charts started around mid-2010, peaking in December 2017

Open source

Now, because bitcoin was built with transparency in mind, the code was open source. This means that the creator or copyright holder provided the rights to study, change, or freely distribute the software to anyone and for any purpose (*Understanding Open Source and Free Software Licensing, St. Laurent, Andrew M., O'Reilly Media, 2008*). One advantage of open-source software is that it is generally more secure, due to a large community of developers vetting the code and improving it. It is also open to constant attack, as vulnerabilities can be more easily identified if access to the code is available. This is a positive, however, as vulnerabilities typically can be fixed faster than with closed-sourced software.

The bitcoin source code was originally hosted on `sourceforge.net` (`http://www.metzdowd.com/pipermail/cryptography/2009-January/014994.html`), and available for anyone to download and test, and was migrated over to GitHub, where the first commit occurred in August 2009 (`https://github.com/bitcoin/bitcoin/tree/4405b78d6059e536c36974088a8ed4d9f0f29898`). There are currently 548 contributors from around the world, including some of the best and brightest minds.

Alternative coins (Altcoins)

With the bitcoin source code freely available, it wasn't long before someone made a copy and created their own coin. This then led to the era of alternative coins, known as altcoins.

The bitcoin source code has been copied or "forked" 19,358 times thus far. This doesn't mean there are 19,358 different altcoins because many forks will be from people wanting their own copy to learn from or experiment with. As an indication of the active altcoins, there are just over 800 listed at `coinmarketcap.com`.

Forking: A technical term that programmers use when copying code from one application to another. This means the developer does not have to start from scratch.

There are some purists, or bitcoin maximalists, who see bitcoin as the main or supreme coin, and everything else as an altcoin. However, there are some cryptocurrencies that were created from scratch, with their own independent blockchain, and they would take offense at being called an altcoin. They see themselves as independent cryptocurrencies in their own right.

Regardless of their classification, altcoins are often announced and promoted as being better or more useful substitutes to bitcoin. Many altcoins tried to target some of bitcoin's perceived limitations, such as providing a useful service, as in **Namecoin**, reducing the 10-minute mining reward rate, as in **Litecoin**, or providing useful puzzles to solve instead of meaningless ones, as in **Primecoin**.

Namecoin – the first altcoin

The first altcoin to appear on the scene was Namecoin, which was announced in April 2011 on the forum `bitcointalk.org` (`https://bitcointalk.org/?topic=6017.0`). Namecoin was created to *improve decentralization, security, censorship resistance, privacy, and speed of certain components of the Internet infrastructure such as DNS and identities* (`https://namecoin.org`). Basically, it was designed as a place to register internet domain names (.bit) in a decentralized manner, and to challenge the likes of the **Internet Corporation for Assigned Names and Numbers (ICANN)**, the organization that looks after internet domain names.

`Bitcointalk.org` and `Reddit.com` are the main chat forums, typically for crypto-pioneers, where announcements of new altcoins and ICOs are made.

Surprisingly, Namecoin is still alive and kicking today. The source code still receives contributions, the Twitter account is still active, and the Namecoin team are still blogging news updates. However, there has been very little adoption due to a number of factors. Namecoin had a great team of smart developers, but the technology was very clunky to use. In short, they were too early in their ideas. Also, registering a domain name is very inexpensive, which encouraged domain name squatters. In some ways, the first sentence on the Namecoin website says it all, with "experimental" being the key word:

"Namecoin is an experimental open-source technology."

After Namecoin, more and more altcoins appeared, such as ixcoin, i0coin, SolidCoin, GeistGeld, Tenebrix, and Fairbrix. These are all now lying in the digital graveyard at `deadcoins.com`, along with over 800 others, primarily due to a lack of community support. Litecoin is one coin that has stood the test of time.

Litecoin – the silver to Bitcoin's gold

Litecoin was announced on bitcointalk in October 2011 and was forked from the bitcoin source code (`https://bitcointalk.org/index.php?topic=47417.0`). It used various properties of the previous coins listed above, along with the lessons learned from each of those coins' shortcomings. In addition, the supply was increased to four times that of bitcoin, to 84 million, and it could process transactions four times faster, at every 2.5 minutes instead of every 10 minutes. It also changed the puzzle to something slightly different (Scrypt instead of SHA-256 for those who are technically curious).

Litecoin had three critical factors making it the success that it is today. Firstly, it had a very clever marketing strategy in the early years. It was promoted as the "silver to Bitcoin's gold," and this stuck in everyone's mind. Secondly, it had leadership: the creator, Charlie Lee, was very vocal on Twitter and proactively decided to support a new technology called **Segregated Witness** or **SegWit**, which is a technology designed to reduce the size of the blockchain. It was aimed initially at bitcoin but due to indecisions and infighting within the bitcoin community, it was implemented on Litecoin first. So, because of these reasons, Litecoin has consistently ranked in the top 10 in market capitalization.

The crypto community also recognized the efforts of Litecoin to ensure a fair and honest coin distribution when it was launched. This can't be said of many other coins that were pre-mined.

Pre-mining

One of the reasons why many altcoins failed was because they would do a sneaky pre-mine. This meant that if an altcoin was going to mint 40 million coins slowly, over a period of say 80 years, a million or so were pre-mined, usually by the developer or a group of developers. The concern here was that the motive of the developers could undermine the project by making grand promises with unrealistic features, pumping up the price of the coin to say $1, and then dumping all the coins to make a quick $1 million USD and disappearing forever.

Primecoin – finding new prime numbers

Primecoin was launched in July 2013. The main purpose of this coin was to change the meaningless puzzle that miners played when validating transactions to something more useful (https:// bitcointalk.org/index.php?topic=251850.0). The new puzzle would be helping to find new special prime numbers. Prime numbers are very useful in computer science due to the property that it is very hard to factor large numbers back into prime numbers. For example, what are the prime numbers that when multiplied together produce 20? After a bit of pondering, you may deduce that 2 x 2 x 5, all of which are prime numbers, are prime factors of 20. However, given a number such as 1,435,632 the problem becomes significantly harder.

Despite this noble cause, however, the innovation was still not enough, and with an unlimited supply (scarcity is a feature of a coin), Primecoin did not really take off.

Other altcoins

Other altcoins include DarkCoin, FeatherCoin, Worldcoin, Blakecoin, Zetacoin, and even PandaCoin and Potcoin. The template was to fork bitcoin, change a handful of parameters, dream up a name or a word, add the suffix "coin," and hey presto, you had an altcoin!

Lessons learned

The main lesson that can be taken from the altcoin world is that being the first to market in an experimental technology is risky, therefore one must continue to innovate. This can be seen with the number of altcoins that have disappeared from the scene just as fast as they appeared. They were typically the coins that were a simple copy-and-paste of another coin, with a new name. Altcoins that survived often made some subtle change, either in the supply of the coin, in the algorithm used, or even in their usefulness.

Successful altcoin lesson: Innovate, be different to stand out, and have a use or purpose.

The stories of these coins, and the lessons learned, feel like the growing pains of a regular startup company. Just because a fancy technology with a fancy name comes along, it doesn't mean that sound business fundamentals all of a sudden get thrown out the window.

So, while altcoins were appearing like rabbits in spring, in another part of the blockchain universe, there was a group of people studying what was actually powering all these coins, and they discovered that it was a chain of blocks.

Blockchain – the immutable database

The word "blockchain" is a term that many people use but few really understand. The reason it is hard to define is because in such a nascent space, there is no single correct definition. For example, when the internet was invented, some people may remember that it was referred to as "the World Wide Web" or "the Information Super Highway." Such terms are non-existent now and if used, are met with an almost "I know how old you are" look. The same will happen to blockchains 10 or so years down the track.

Along with there currently being no universal definition of a blockchain, there is also widespread disagreement over which qualities are essential in order to call something a blockchain.

Bitcoin was designed to be public. Anyone could join the network, and its blockchain was designed to keep participants honest in the absence of a central authority. The architecture sacrificed efficiency in order to ensure that cheating the system would be costlier than playing nicely within the rules of the system. In order to achieve this, the bitcoin blockchain consists of a digital ledger that records all transactions, from the very first one on January 3, 2009, to the present.

"The Times 03/Jan/2009 Chancellor on brink of second bailout for banks" was a hidden message in the very first transaction, in reference to the numerous worldwide government-initiated, taxpayer-funded bailouts for companies that were considered "too big to fail" during the 2007 **Global Financial Crisis (GFC)**.

Copies of the ledger are not stored in a central place. Instead, they are kept by each computer or node on the network. Some of these nodes are miners and group these transactions together every 10 minutes (on average), and add them to the ledger in blocks, all cryptographically linked together. Miraculously, this system, combined with support from the core bitcoin development team, the users, and the mining community, has functioned for almost 10 years, 24/7, without missing a beat!

The definitions

The following are definitions of a blockchain from three difference sources:

- ♦ "A digital ledger in which transactions made in bitcoin or another cryptocurrency are recorded chronologically and publicly." - Google

- ♦ "A blockchain is a digitized, decentralized, public ledger of all cryptocurrency transactions." - Investopedia

♦ "A blockchain is a decentralized, distributed and public digital ledger that is used to record transactions across many computers so that the record cannot be altered retroactively without the alteration of all subsequent blocks and the consensus of the network." - Wikipedia

While most people would agree that a blockchain is a digital ledger, some blockchains do not have an associated cryptocurrency, such as **Hyperledger**, and an increasing amount are not public but instead private. However, it is common to take the bitcoin blockchain as a reference point, which is what the preceding definitions have done. In doing so, we can describe a blockchain in terms of what it is, what it contains, and the properties that it has:

♦ A blockchain is a digital ledger

♦ It contains or records transactions

♦ It has properties of being distributed, decentralized, public, and immutable or incorruptible

Bringing these concepts together, let's define a blockchain.

 Blockchain: A decentralized, distributed, and public digital ledger used to record transactions on a network of computers, and these transactions cannot be altered without a majority collusion of the network.

This is by no means a formal definition, but there is a group of people looking to develop a blockchain terminology standard for the **International Organization for Standardization (ISO)**.

ISO/TC 307 – Blockchain and distributed ledger technologies

In April 2016, Standards Australia submitted a **New Field of Technical Activity** (**NFTA**) proposal on behalf of Australia, for the ISO to consider developing standards to support blockchain technology.

The proposal was intended to establish a new ISO technical committee for blockchain and distributed ledger technologies. This new committee would be responsible for supporting innovation and competition, by covering blockchain topics including interoperability, terminology, privacy, security, and auditing. This decision resulted in the creation of "ISO/TC 307 – Blockchain and distributed ledger technologies."

There are currently several standards under development, with 38 participating members and 11 observing members at the time of writing. The standards are (https://www.iso.org/committee/6266604.html#liaisons):

- ISO/TC 307/CAG1 – Convenors coordination group
- ISO/TC 307 SG 2 – Use cases
- ISO/TC 307 SG 6 – Governance of blockchain and distributed ledger technology systems
- ISO/TC 307 SG 7 – Interoperability of blockchain and distributed ledger technology systems
- ISO/TC 307 WG 1 – Foundation
- ISO/TC 307 WG 2 – Security, privacy and identity
- ISO/TC 307 WG 3 – Smart contracts and their applications
- ISO/TC 307 WG 4 – Joint ISO/TC 307 - ISO/IEC JTC 1/SC 27 WG: Blockchain and distributed ledger technologies and IT security techniques

Just as we were beginning to understand what a blockchain is, another term has been introduced to add to the confusion: distributed ledger technology.

What is a distributed ledger?

A distributed ledger, sometimes called a shared ledger or **distributed ledger technology (DLT)**, can be thought of as a database where a group of computers need to come to an agreement on the order that certain transactions happen in, in a decentralized manner, using a method of consensus, as discussed earlier. This sounds awfully similar to what a blockchain is, hence the often-widespread confusion. Richard Gendall Brown, the CTO of R3 notes:

"Distributed ledgers – or decentralized databases – are systems that enable parties who don't fully trust each other to form and maintain consensus about the existence, status, and evolution of a set of shared facts."

Therefore, DLT is an umbrella term used to describe technologies that distribute records or information. Blockchains are one form of DLT. Not all distributed ledgers employ a chain of blocks to provide a secure and valid distributed record of transaction; therefore, we can say every blockchain is a distributed ledger, but not every distributed ledger is a blockchain. Clear as mud?

What does a blockchain look like?

Let's now turn our attention to what a blockchain looks like, to help the visual learners amongst us. Anyone can download the bitcoin blockchain by installing the bitcoin software application and joining the over 10,000 other nodes or computers on the network. The software will then download all the bitcoin transactions from the infamous date of January 3, 2009, until the present time, and this is currently about 180 GB in size. This can take anywhere from one week on a powerful computer, with a fast internet connection, to over two months on a Raspberry Pi!

The blockchain will then be displayed as individual .dat files.

Figure 4: The bitcoin blockchain as a series of data files

Opening one of these files will reveal, essentially, a bunch of 1s and 0s because that is how computers understand information, but when displayed to humans, a block looks like a string of random letters and numbers called hexadecimal.

```
:cloudnthings:blocks cloudnthings$ hexdump -n 304 -C blk00000.dat
00000000  f9 be b4 d9 1d 01 00 00  01 00 00 00 00 00 00 00  |................|
00000010  00 00 00 00 00 00 00 00  00 00 00 00 00 00 00 00  |................|
00000020  00 00 00 00 00 00 00 00  00 00 00 00 3b a3 ed fd  |............;...|
00000030  7a 7b 12 b2 7a c7 2c 3e  67 76 8f 61 7f c8 1b c3  |z{..z.,>gv.a....|
00000040  88 8a 51 32 3a 9f b8 aa  4b 1e 5e 4a 29 ab 5f 49  |..Q2:...K.^J)._I|
00000050  ff ff 00 1d 1d ac 2b 7c  01 01 00 00 00 01 00 00  |......+|........|
00000060  00 00 00 00 00 00 00 00  00 00 00 00 00 00 00 00  |................|
00000070  00 00 00 00 00 00 00 00  00 00 00 00 00 00 ff ff  |................|
00000080  ff ff 4d 04 ff ff 00 1d  01 04 45 54 68 65 20 54  |..M.......EThe T|
00000090  69 6d 65 73 20 30 33 2f  4a 61 6e 2f 32 30 30 39  |imes 03/Jan/2009|
000000a0  20 43 68 61 6e 63 65 6c  6c 6f 72 20 6f 6e 20 62  | Chancellor on b|
000000b0  72 69 6e 6b 20 6f 66 20  73 65 63 6f 6e 64 20 62  |rink of second b|
000000c0  61 69 6c 6f 75 74 20 66  6f 72 20 62 61 6e 6b 73  |ailout for banks|
000000d0  ff ff ff ff 01 00 f2 05  2a 01 00 00 00 43 41 04  |........*....CA.|
000000e0  67 8a fd b0 fe 55 48 27  19 67 f1 a6 71 30 b7 10  |g....UH'.g..q0..|
000000f0  5c d6 a8 28 e0 39 09 a6  79 62 e0 ea 1f 61 de b6  |\..(.9..yb...a..|
00000100  49 f6 bc 3f 4c ef 38 c4  f3 55 04 e5 1e c1 12 de  |I..?L.8..U......|
00000110  5c 38 4d f7 ba 0b 8d 57  8a 4c 70 2b 6b f1 1d 5f  |\8M....W.Lp+k.._|
00000120  ac 00 00 00 00 f9 be b4  d9 d7 00 00 00 01 00 00  |................|
```

Figure 5: The bitcoin genesis block with the hidden message on the right-hand side

[💡 **Genesis block**: The very first block of a cryptocurrency coin.]

A very trivial and lighthearted way to visualize a blockchain is as an Excel file. The file is the blockchain, the individual sheets are the blocks, and the rows within are the transactions.

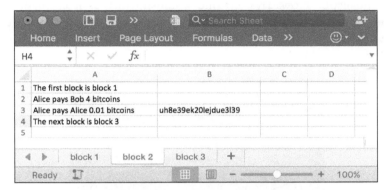

Figure 6: Excel spreadsheet used to represent a blockchain

Storing information on the blockchain

In the early days of bitcoin, various people discovered clever ways to store more than just transactions on the bitcoin blockchain. There is a Nelson Mandela tribute that was created on December 7, 2013, at a cost of 0.1572 bitcoins, which was the equivalent of $90 USD. The Mandela quote can be found at the bitcoin address 8881a937a437ff6ce83be3a89d77ea88ee12315f37f 7ef0dd3742c30eef92dba:

"There is nothing like returning to a place that remains unchanged to find the ways in which you yourself have altered."

An image of Mandela, the bitcoin logo, Rickrolls, emails from Nakamoto, and even Valentine's Day messages have all been found on the blockchain (http://www.righto.com/2014/02/ ascii-bernanke-wikileaks-photographs.html). The original bitcoin white paper was also recorded on the blockchain on April 7, 2013, for presumably posterity purposes.

The disadvantage of putting messages on the blockchain in this manner was that these transactions often clogged the network, and this was referred to as "blockchain bloat" or "blockchain vandalism." Nowadays, no one would do this, as it is financially more sensible to hold or trade bitcoins than spend them, unless you really want to declare your love on the blockchain next Valentine's Day!

Figure 7: This Mandela image is stored on the blockchain

Op Return

Another interesting method of putting information on the blockchain was to utilize something called **OP_RETURN**, which is a special field where around 40 to 80 characters can be stored (more accurately it's 40-80 bytes). Quite often, these would contain the data in a summarized or compressed form, often referred to as a "digital fingerprint" or a **hash**. The "digital fingerprint" would also be stored in a local database, but if there was a dispute of authenticity about a document, the "digital fingerprint" on an organization's centralized database could be compared to the one stored on the decentralized blockchain. If they matched, this would prove that the document was not altered. This concept is often extended to also prove the owner of the document.

[**Digital fingerprint**: A short, unique representation of a digital file.]

Information or files can also be split up and stored on people's computers all over the world, forming a network using clever cryptography and encryption. The advantage here is that these blockchain-type networks are designed to deal with files of all sizes and are more suited to the purpose.

Scaling

One of the main challenges of blockchain technologies is the issue of scaling. Scaling is the ability of a technology or system to cater for a larger number of transactions or activity on a network and still be able to perform its intended function. Comparisons to existing mature payment networks, such as Visa or Mastercard, are often made to highlight the current limitations of blockchains, but this is like comparing apples to oranges. Visa and Mastercard are not decentralized entities and this is the main trade-off that one makes.

[Scalability: The ability of a system to adapt to increased demand without incurring significant performance impact.]

When the internet first took off in the mid-1990s, communication was via text-based emails, quite often using a black screen, where every command line had to be typed.

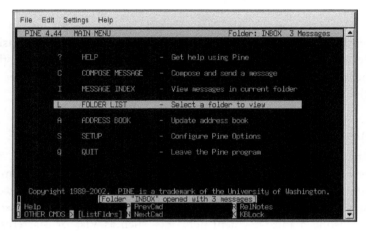

Figure 8: Pine 4.4: How email was accessed back in the early 1990s

Attachments started becoming popular, but the internet was not yet able to handle the increased bandwidth requirements. The network was then upgraded to the point where users could attach files. What happened next? Users started attaching larger files, such as MP3 for music or MPEGs for video. The network improved and upgraded to accommodate this. The Movies then became HD movies and streaming videos, and the cycle repeated. The same can be seen in the mobile world of wireless data transmission, where 1G (first generation), 2G, 3G, and all the way up to the current 5G have developed over the past 30 years.

Blockchain technologies will follow the same patterns of how technology has evolved. There are already proposals where transactions between two parties can occur privately, instantly, and very cheaply, and only after the last transaction is this then broadcast to the blockchain. This technology is known as the Lightning Network on the bitcoin blockchain and Raiden on the Ethereum network.

An analogy of how this works is if you think of running a tab at a bar. Drinks can be constantly purchased throughout the evening but there is no need to swipe your credit card for every drink, which would incur numerous credit card fees. Only when the tab is closed at the end of the night would one transaction be made. Another example would be accepting cash transactions as a merchant and at the end of each trading day, taking a trip to the bank and making one single deposit.

IOTA

Of all the main blockchain platforms out there, a lot of the research revolves around the Bitcoin and Ethereum blockchains because they are the most mature (by virtue of time) compared to the others, and also have a large community support base. Having said this, though, there are new technologies that claim to have solved the scaling issue, at least on paper anyway. One of these technologies is called **IOTA**. IOTA is a blockless distributed ledger. It notes four main features (https://docs.iota.org/introduction):

- **Scalability**: IOTA can achieve high transaction throughput thanks to the parallelized validation of transactions, with no limit as to the number of transactions that can be confirmed in a certain interval.

- **Decentralization**: IOTA has no miners. Every participant in the network, making a transaction, actively participates in the consensus. As such, IOTA is more decentralized than any blockchain.

- **No transaction fees**: IOTA does not have transaction fees.

- **Quantum-immunity**: IOTA utilized a next-generation trinary-hash function called Curl-p, which is quantum immune.

The claims from IOTA are very substantial. If true, they could prove to be a significant step forward for the industry, but many of the arguments have been dismissed by respected cryptographers in the community. IOTA also lacks real use cases at the moment, unlike the concept of coloring bitcoins.

Coloring bitcoins

In the early days, experiments were being conducted on the bitcoin blockchain and what resulted was the concept of colored coins. This meant taking a bitcoin and providing extra meaning to it, leveraging the bitcoin infrastructure and network. An imaginary example of the colored coin concept is if you have a one-dollar bill and written, or stamped, on this bill are the words "one free entry to any Bee Gees concert in the world." Let's imagine that these words were created in some super counterfeit-resistant, holographic, techno-colored ink and 10,000 of these one-dollar bills were dropped from a helicopter. This one-dollar bill has now been given extra meaning: it's been colored. This one-dollar bill is now worth more than a regular one-dollar bill and it's no longer fungible, which is a key property of currency.

Dictionary.com defines fungibility as "being of such nature or kind as to be freely exchangeable or replaceable, in whole or in part, for another of like nature or kind."

Gold is fungible because one ounce of gold is equivalent to any other ounce of gold, but diamonds are not.

Colored coins could be applied to trading, voting, paying dividends, coupons, digital collectibles, and even access and subscriptions to services. Basically, every asset or ownership right could be represented in this way. This was essentially the emergence of programmable money or programmable value, which is where smart contracts enter the discussion.

Smart contracts: are they that smart?

Contracts appear all around us in our daily lives: the agreement to meet for a coffee, to shout a friend lunch, or help pick up your in-laws from the airport during their yearly Christmas visit. Technology has not replaced the notion of contracts but simply changed the interface. The act of putting coins into a street parking meter or swiping your bus transportation card all constitute the act of participating in an agreement.

Take the ever-popular vending machine, for example. When coins are inserted, I expect the can of Coke to be dispensed, along with the appropriate amount of change. Back in the days when these vending machines were invented, they were a revolution. They were also considered smart devices. As technology has progressed, we find ourselves in another age of the vending machine revolution, only this time it involves cryptocurrencies.

"Smart contracts" was a term introduced by Szabo in an article that was published in 1996 called *Smart Contracts: Building Blocks for Digital Markets* (http://www.fon.hum.uva.nl/rob/Courses/InformationInSpeech/CDROM/Literature/LOTwinterschool2006/szabo.best.vwh.net/smart_contracts_2.html). Essentially, they are any sort of contractual clause programmed into some hardware and/or software to be executed. The premise in the decentralized world, though, is that the software executes the contractual clause autonomously and independently, without intervention by any third party, who may have ulterior motives.

[**Smart contracts**: Self-executing contracts that apply specific actions under specific conditions, with the terms of the agreement directly written into software.]

Looking at the basic definition of executing a contractual clause, bitcoin has smart contract capabilities as well.

Smart contracts in Bitcoin

The good old-fashioned cheque book can be thought of as a smart contract. It's a contractual agreement that if a cheque is made out to my name and correctly signed, I can deposit the cheque and access the funds. Cheques can also have a requirement that two signatures must be present or even two out of three signatures, for convenience, in case one company director is away on holiday.

Bitcoin has these capabilities as well. Bitcoin wallets, such as Copay, can be set up so that two people out of three need to click a button in order to authorize the transfer of funds from one account to another. Bitcoin can also be programmed to release the funds only after a certain period of time as well, called a **hashtimelock** function, in the case of a college or pension fund. In fact, bitcoin can be programmed to execute a lot of powerful contracts using a language called Script.

Script

Script is a simple stack-based programming language for transferring bitcoins from one owner to another and should not be confused with Scrypt (pronounced *ess crypt*), which is a mining algorithm that some cryptocurrencies such as Litecoin or Dogecoin use.

It works similarly to reverse polish notation calculators, where "1, 1, +" is entered instead of "1 + 1 =." A trivial explanation of Script is as follows. For Alice to send one bitcoin to Bob, Alice's bitcoin wallet must create a transaction with *bitcoin amount, Bob's bank account number*. To access the bitcoins, Bob adds his super-secret password along with the symbol "=" resulting in *bitcoin amount, Bob's bank account number, Bob's password, =*. If the password matches Bob's bank account number, the bitcoins get released.

Anyone programming contracts in bitcoin had to learn this stack-based programming language. It wasn't that it was hard to do, but the reason why it hasn't become widely popular is that other technologies were invented that made programming money a lot easier. One of those technologies was called **Ethereum**, as we have briefly mentioned.

Ethereum

In 2013 and 2014, as the crypto industry was chugging along, unbeknownst to most people there was another platform brewing in the background. This platform was called Ethereum and it was a culmination of knowledge and ideas from the inventor and co-creator, Vitalik Buterin, who was introduced to bitcoins by his father, Dmitry Buterin.

Buterin started studying the space and was contacted in September 2011 by Mihai Alisie to write for `BitcoinMagazine.com`. This began publishing in 2012 and interestingly enough, Buterin's first article was about bitcoin adoption for teenagers (`https://bitcoinmagazine.com/articles/bitcoin-adoption-opportunity-teenager-1330407280/`). From February 2012 to July 2014, he wrote 269 articles covering a wide range of topics.

Through his research and writing, Buterin worked closely with another project called **Omni** (formally called **MasterCoin**) in October 2013 and saw the potential for improving Omni. He suggested a few new features to make it more generalized and to support more contracts, but when the Omni team decided to go in a different direction, Buterin chose to build upon his idea himself:

"The Mastercoin team was impressed, but they were not interested in dropping everything they were doing to go in this direction, which I was increasingly convinced is the correct choice" (`https://vitalik.ca/general/2017/09/14/prehistory.html`).

Ethereum.org was registered on November 27, 2013, and announced on Reddit on December 14, 2013, and on bitcointalk on January 23, 2014, to not much fanfare. Buterin himself gives a great account of how things started in his blog (http://vitalik.ca/general/2017/09/14/prehistory.html).

Ethereum brought its own blockchain to the party and, as a result, different features to solve different problems. It had several advantages over bitcoin but to say it was better is unfair because Bitcoin and Ethereum serve different purposes. Bitcoin was built to be a global decentralized currency. Ethereum was built with the vision of being a global decentralized computing network. A lot of the concepts that colored coins wanted to achieve could be implemented a lot easier on Ethereum and even extended, with one's imagination.

Smart contracts in Ethereum

Ethereum created a new programming language called **Solidity**, which was loosely based on another language called JavaScript to help to make the transition to learning Solidity easier. Newer blockchain technologies that appeared after Ethereum took this one step further and questioned the need to even invent a new programming language. Blockchains such as **NEM** and **NEO** are written in traditional languages such as Java and C# (pronounced *see-sharp*) and an API can be used to interact with their blockchains.

[**API**: Application Programmable Interface: A generic rule to talk to an independent system such that any programming language can be used, as long as the rules are followed.]

An API makes it easy to interact with smart contracts in a programming language that is familiar to current developers. Instead of learning the concepts of blockchains and smart contracts *and* a new language, only blockchain and smart contract concepts need to be focused on. This is a significant bonus because learning this technology is challenging in itself.

What does an Ethereum smart contract look like?

To those who have never seen a smart contract, it may feel like a super-mysterious mythical creature. To others it looks like this:

```solidity
pragma solidity ^0.4.20;


contract MyToken {
    /* This creates an array with all balances */
    mapping (address => uint256) public balanceOf;


    /* Initializes contract with initial supply
    tokens to the creator of the contract */
    function MyToken(
      uint256 initialSupply
      ) public {
      balanceOf[msg.sender] = initialSupply;

    }


    /* Send coins */
    function transfer(address _to, uint256 _value)
    public {
        require(balanceOf[msg.sender] >= _value);
        require(balanceOf[_to] + _value >=
    balanceOf[_to]);
        balanceOf[msg.sender] -= _value;
        balanceOf[_to] += _value;
```

```
    }
  }
```

Smart contracts are actually rather boring but can be magical when combined with the right mixture of wild crypto enthusiasts, and the excitement of being part of a select few to participate in the first experiment of its kind in history.

The most unfortunate famous smart contract – the DAO

Perhaps the most famous smart contract was the **DAO**, which stands for **Distributed Autonomous Organization**. In May 2016, a few members of the Ethereum community created the DAO smart contract, where anyone could send the cryptocurrency ether to it in return for DAO tokens. These tokens could then be used by token holders to vote for projects that were seeking funding. Should the project become successful, token holders could then share in the rewards.

The DAO experiment was an unexpected success. 12.7 million ether or around $150 million USD was raised. At one point, the price of ether reached $20 USD, making the amount raised just over $250 million USD! No one, though, could have predicted what happened next. A month later, a hacker found a loophole in the code, meaning 3.6 million ether or the equivalent of $70 million USD was taken.

This story highlights two important aspects. Firstly, programming with this new technology is challenging, and secondly, there can be devastating consequences when real money is at stake. The result of this experiment put a philosophical question on the table: should the code be reversed, allowing investors to get their money back, or should the loss be accepted as a consequence of the experiment? Was the DAO "too big" to fail and did it need to be bailed out? It was an issue that divided the community but, in the end, the code was reversed and most investors got their investment back.

Fees in Ethereum smart contracts

In a centralized system, organizations charge a fee to process transactions. These fees are then used to pay staff, rent, and usual company costs. In a decentralized system, network or transaction fees are charged and go to the miners, who are securing the network with physical resources, such as computers and electricity. Fees are therefore an important part of a decentralized network.

Fees are typically in the same denomination as the currency. For example, to send one bitcoin, it may cost 0.0001 bitcoin in fees. This is generally the same for the other altcoins previously discussed. In Ethereum, though, this is slightly different. Ether was designed as a mechanism to pay for computational power to execute smart contracts. The fee is called gas but is denominated in ether. This tends to confuse many people, so let's go through an example.

When a smart contract is executed on the Ethereum network, it is broken down into small instructions, or more accurately operations, such as "add these two numbers together," or "send this transaction to that address." This costs money. If the cost was denominated in ether, the result would be:

Operation	Cost
Adding two numbers together	1 ETH
Send transaction	2 ETH

If the price of ether changed from \$10 to \$20, the cost of adding two numbers together would double. However, using the intermediary unit gas, we can price the operations.

Operation	Cost
Adding two numbers together	1 gas
Send transaction	2 gas

Now, if ether increases in price, it doesn't affect the cost of the operation. Adding two numbers will always cost 0.1 gas. This way gas and ether are decoupled. What it does mean is that obtaining gas to execute the smart contract would be more expensive.

The link between ether and gas is a gas price dictated by the formula:

Ether (ether) = gas (gas) × gas price (ether/gas)

Gas is just a way to express relative cost and you can't send Ethereum gas from one person to another. It is not a sub-currency, like some people tend to think. However, this should not be confused with the NEO blockchain where "GAS" can actually be purchased, traded, and used.

The interesting part is that the person creating the smart contract can set the gas price and the gas limit. This is like if I walk into a store and set the price of a pair of jeans, instead of having the merchant do it, and also setting (or having in my head) the maximum amount I'm willing to pay. Miners can come along and process the operation if they accept the price.

There is a website called `ethgassation.info`, though, that displays the average gas price as an indication and these options are usually automatically provided to help the smart contract developer.

Amount	0 ETH 0.00 USD
Gas Limit	1753590 UNITS
Gas Price	21 GWEI
Max Transaction Fee	0.036825 ETH 22.62 USD
Max Total	0.036825 ETH 22.62 USD

Figure 9: When deploying an Ethereum smart contract, the gas price and gas limit can be adjusted

With an understanding of bitcoin, blockchains, and smart contracts, we will now look at the birth of ICOs and because the majority of them were created on the Ethereum blockchain, how the network managed to cope.

The peak of ICOs

When the ICO wave hit its peak in 2017, there was a mad rush to learn what was going on and how it all worked. Many people followed instructions issued by the company on how to buy into the ICO, but it was a very new and often complicated process. It involved sending bitcoin or ether to a given address that was published on a bitcointalk forum, on a Slack channel, or on the official website.

Take, for example, the Monaco ICO. An investment of one ether would return 150 MCO tokens. Monaco opened the ICO on May 18, 2017, when 1 ether was about $100 USD. This meant that one MCO was the equivalent of $1.50 USD.

The ICO finished on June 17, and about a month later, it listed on exchanges. By the end of August, it had very quickly shot up to $22 USD. The 150 MCO tokens would now be worth $3,300. That is a whopping 1,366% increase.

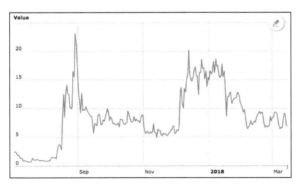

Figure 10: Monaco price chart showing volatile swings
(https://www.worldcoinindex.com/coin/monaco)

The success story being shared was that the tokens would "moon" after listing on exchanges and large profits could be made.

[**Moon or To the Moon**: Increase enormously in value to often 10, 100, or even 1,000 times the original price.]

Monaco was not an exception to the rule. This was common of many ICOs in the early days. Supporters would believe in the project, everything was open and transparent, and there was often a noble cause. This is essentially how the fire started and towards the end of 2017, ICOs were popping up like hotcakes. In the early days, though, participating in these ICOs was a challenge.

Participating in an ICO

The first challenge around participating in ICOs was where to buy the cryptocurrencies from because most ICOs only accepted ether. Initially, this would occur face-to-face, with a willing seller in the local community, but nowadays, there are easier and quicker ways. There are many exchanges around the world that once registered, with some form of driver's license or passport ID, along with a photo of oneself holding a piece of paper with a written statement of some sort, the cryptocurrencies can be purchased. It is important to note that today, ICOs accept all kinds of payment, including bank transfers!

The next challenge was where to store the ether. Typical places would be a mobile wallet, a desktop wallet, or a hardware wallet. A popular wallet for storing tokens was **MyEtherWallet** and many ICOs would recommend using MyEtherWallet, especially due to the usability, accessibility, security, and therefore the popularity.

Tokens would be distributed soon after the ICO had ended and needed to be claimed. This process often involved being provided with the smart contract address and having to add the custom token to MyEtherWallet manually. This was not an easy process for anyone new in the crypto space.

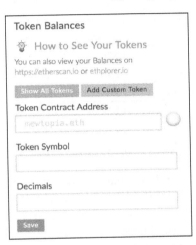

Figure 11: Adding ICO tokens to MyEtherWallet was often
a technically complicated task

The fastest ICO raises

There is a certain thrill in speed-seeking adventures and the same can be said about ICOs raising millions of dollars in seconds. A traditional venture capital raise can take anywhere between weeks to many months of negotiations. In this new world of ICOs, if the fundamentals have been executed correctly, a lot of money can be raised in a very short space of time.

For instance, Brave topped the list, raising $35 million USD in only 30 seconds! That works out to an astonishing $4.2 billion USD an hour. Filecoin managed $200 million USD in one hour and Firstblood and SingularDTV finished their ICOs in 10 minutes and 17 minutes respectively. Some figures can be seen in the following table:

Date	ICO	Raised	Duration	Rate
May, 2017	Brave	$35M	30 seconds	$4,200M/hour
Aug, 2017	Filecoin	$200M	60 minutes	$200M/hour
Feb, 2017	Melonport	$2.9M	3 minutes	$58M/hour
Sep, 2016	Firstblood	$5.5M	10 minutes	$33M/hour
Oct, 2016	SingularDTV	$7.5M	17 minutes	$26.5M/hour
Nov, 2016	Golem	$8.6M	29 mins	$17.2M/hour
May, 2017	Storj	$20M	6 hours	$3.3M/hour
Sep, 2017	KyberNetworks	$48M	24 hours	$2M/hour
Apr, 2014	MaidSafe	$6M	5 hours	$1.2M/hour
June, 2017	Civic	$33M	2 days	$0.69M/hour
June, 2017	SONM	$42M	4 days	$0.58M/hour
Mar, 2016	DigixDao	$5.5M	12 hours	$0.46M/hour

While these numbers may seem impressive and make great click-bait headlines, there are several disadvantages. Firstly, a 30-second sellout tends to mean a few buyers purchasing substantial amounts. There were only around 130 people that managed to buy Brave tokens, with five buyers scooping up half the supply. This is undesirable because these "whales" can later on flood the market and potentially crash the price of the token. This is in contrast to Status or KyberNetworks, which have over 20,000 contributors.

The entire ethos of the ICO community is to allow a large group of genuine users to help support a project they believe in, and become long-term users and advocates. Investors are generally short-term holders looking to make a profit. It's called the flipping game.

To increase the number of contributors, many ICOs put strategies in place. The most obvious method was to limit each token purchase. This was easily circumvented by making lots of small transactions, which then skewed the statistic. It also put unnecessary stress on the Ethereum network and made contribution numbers look higher than they actually were.

Network congestion

Status, a decentralized messaging platform mentioned above, ran an ICO in June 2017 and overloaded the network as thousands of investors, supporters, and contributors wanted to participate. The transaction numbers increased to over three-and-a-half times what Ethereum could normally handle. (`https://www.dashforcenews.com/ico-mania-grinds-ethereum-halt-scaling-issues-not-limited-bitcoin/`). Contributors then resorted to increasing the transaction fees in order to jump the queue. In another instance, a user lost more than $80,000 USD worth of ether in the AirSwap ICO, due to a failed transaction (`https://www.ccn.com/this-airswap-ico-investor-lost-80000-ona-failed-transaction/`). These stories were common during the second half of 2017 and highlighted the challenges of running ICOs with huge user demand tied to FOMO (pronounced *pho-mo*), Fear of Missing Out.

In December 2017, while there was a slight slowdown in ICO offerings, another experiment hit the crypto world: **CryptoKitties**. The concept was that users could not only buy CryptoKitties, which represented a digital asset on the blockchain, but they could actually breed them as well. A CryptoKitty would be generated every 15 minutes for one year and then afterwards, the increase in the population would come from breeding. These CryptoKitties were the first non-fungible digital asset on the blockchain.

Figure 12: Astoundingly, CryptoKitties could be bred
on the blockchain creating more CryptoKitties

There was a concern that the CryptoKitties experiment, essentially a blockchain gamification version of the popular Tamagotchi in the late 1990s, was diverting developer attention away from solving more serious business applications and real-world problems. The creators disagreed and argued in their cleverly titled "White Pa-Purr" that the purpose was that education, accessible user experience, and practical applications were the missing factors for broader adoption.

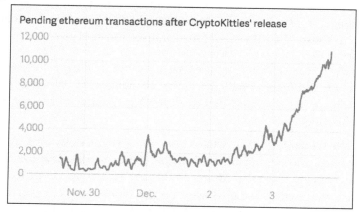

Figure 13: Transaction volumes spike due to CryptoKitties
(https://qz.com/1145833/cryptokitties-is-causing-ethereum-network-congestion/)

Regardless of whether the network was congested with ICOs or virtual CryptoKitties, the fact was that the network was still being experimented on, challenges were being discovered, and potential solutions proposed to improve the underlying infrastructure and network.

The Useless Ethereum Token

The Useless Ethereum Token was the epitome of the ICO hype. Money was being thrown into companies offering tokens by people who were not even reading what the project was about. One project, actually one website called the *Useless Ethereum Token*, was set up in June 2017, allowing people to buy tokens. The website clearly stated that these tokens were not worth anything, didn't represent anything, and if purchased, the funds raised would be used to buy electronics. It even said not to buy these tokens.

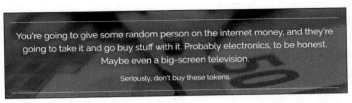

You're going to give some random person on the internet money, and they're going to take it and go buy stuff with it. Probably electronics, to be honest. Maybe even a big-screen television.

Seriously, don't buy these tokens.

Figure 14: A warning from the Useless Ethereum Token website that many ignored (https://uetoken.com/)

What was the end result? Astoundingly, 310 ether, or over $273,000 USD, was raised! The irony is that now, to buy the electronics or a "big-screen television," the 310 ether would need to be sold at an exchange and converted back to fiat currency, and that would involve our dear friends the banks. With all the **Anti-Money Laundering** (**AML**) and **Know Your Customer** (**KYC**) requirements, that will be another challenge in itself. The other option, of course, would be for the person to keep the ether and use it to pay for groceries or utility bills because there are places where you can do this, such as `livingroomofsatoshi.com`.

Ether contributed	Contributions in USD	Tokens issued
310.445	$273753	3965716.097
I had a feeling someone would waste their money.	Enough to buy 228 televisions!	Including 591.000 bonus tokens!

Figure 15: The Useless Ethereum Token ended up raising over $270,000 USD

Network congestion or FOMO meant that 2016 and 2017 were years like no other. There's a movie to be made about this somewhere but in the meantime, all the action can be relived through the bitcointalk forums, provided for over 40 ICOs at theicotrain.com.

Summary

In this chapter, we learned about the various cryptocurrencies that existed before bitcoin and why they failed. We discussed how bitcoin was born and the founding principles it promotes, namely trust, decentralization, and transparency. Three altcoins were examined, out of the more than 1,000 that were created, with Litecoin being the only one that has consistently ranked in the top 10 of all cryptocurrencies.

The various definitions of a blockchain were compared, noting the challenge ahead for the ISO/TC 307 committee in attempting to define blockchains and DLT.

We looked at all the wonderful information people placed on the bitcoin blockchain, such as a picture of Mandela, and explained the concept of coloring bitcoins.

Smart contracts were explored and shown to exist in a simplistic form in bitcoin, but have been drastically improved with the invention of Ethereum, a global decentralized computing network. While the Ethereum platform didn't give birth to ICOs, it dramatically accelerated the growth of them.

Now that we understand the theory, in the next chapter, we will carry on the theme of ICOs and look at their potential.

3

THE POTENTIAL OF ICOS

Whether or not you believe that history repeats itself, there is no denying that there are patterns. Patterns affect other patterns (like a kaleidoscope), patterns are found within patterns (fractals), or are hidden (the value of pi). Much of what we see today, in this new world of cryptocurrencies, blockchain technologies, and the new token economy, can and has been compared to various historic events of the past.

In this chapter, we will take a look at the potential of **Initial Coin Offerings** (**ICOs**) by taking a step back in time, before zooming into the future by looking at the following topics:

- ◆ What is an ICO?
- ◆ The difference between coins and tokens
- ◆ The dot-com versus dot-coin bubble
- ◆ Risk in ICOs
- ◆ A new era of ICO innovation

We will start by explaining what an ICO is and all the associated terminology, before interpreting the days of the dot-com bubble back in the late 1990s/early 2000s and comparing them to what many now call the "dot-coin bubble," where many cryptocurrencies and ICOs are overvalued. So, was the December 2017 crash an actual crash similar to 2000 or are we still at the foothills of the mountains? If it was the bust, shouldn't we start seeing the new era of ICO innovation?

What is an ICO?

An ICO, is a fundraising mechanism where new projects sell an underlying crypto token in exchange for capital. In the early days, the capital was in the form of bitcoin, but over time this increased to other forms of cryptocurrencies, in particular ether. Now that the industry has developed, regular fiat currency is being accepted under certain conditions as well. Accepting fiat currency means the ICO can reach more people.

The term "ICO" was created and popularized to allow comparisons to the term **Initial Public Offering**, otherwise known as an **IPO**. Similar to an IPO, where shares are sold to investors for equity in a company to fund operations, an ICO is where "coins" are created and sold to investors to fund the operations of a company or project.

There are some subtle, but important, differences between an ICO and an IPO. The lack of current regulations and oversight in the ICO space has been seen as an advantage to helping avoid the costly and expensive process of raising capital using traditional methods. Another subtle difference, more relevant in the early days, is that while IPOs deal with investors, ICOs deal with supporters who believe in the cause of the project and are keen to invest, much like a crowdfunding event. The main difference, though, is that these coins do not provide the investor with ownership rights to the company. In other words, they do not represent equity.

To the technical purest amongst us, in an ICO, the coins that investors receive are actually digital tokens, which is why sometimes they are called an **Initial Token Offering**. However, ICO is currently the accepted mainstream terminology.

The ICO acronym

ICO is an unfortunate acronym because, as mentioned in the preceding paragraph, it is actually an **Initial Token Offering** or **ITO**. Another term used was **Token Generation Event** or **TGE**. This is actually a much more accurate description of what exactly is occurring. An *event*, that usually lasts an average of 30 days, is created where cryptocurrencies or regular currencies are received, after which *tokens are generated* and then distributed to those who contributed. This is remarkably different to an ICO, simply because there are no coins and they are arguably not *offered*. What is interesting is that not many white papers reference the term *ICO* and the terminology used varies a lot. In fact, the term *ICO* has been popularized by the media and the wider public.

Date	Company name	Terminology used
Aug 2016	ICONOMI	Initial Coin Offering
Sep 2016	FirstBlood	Crowdsale
Nov 2016	Golem	Crowdfunding
Apr 2017	Humaniq	Initial Coin Offering
Apr 2017	Gnosis	Token Launch
May 2017	Basic Attention Token	Token Launch
May 2017	Monaco	Token Creation Event
Jun 2017	Civic	Token Sale
Jun 2017	OmiseGo	Token Sales
Jun 2017	TenX	Initial Token Sale
Jul 2017	Tezo	Fundraiser
Oct 2017	Horizon State	Initial Coin Offering

Figure 1: Many companies didn't actually use the word ICO in their white paper

TenX uses the term *Initial Token Sale* in its TenX white paper:

"An Initial Token Sale (ITS) is an event in which a new cryptocurrency project sells part of its cryptocurrency tokens to early adopters and enthusiasts in exchange for funding. For the party offering the tokens for sale, this has become a well-documented and well-respected way to raise funds to upscale an existing product or service."

The fact that the word "ICO" is similar to "IPO", which has been around for a long time, provides comfort due to familiarity and we'll continue using the word "ICO" throughout the book for simplicity and brevity. However, we must acknowledge that things change very quickly in the world of crypto and, in fact, new terms such as **Security Coin Offering (SCO)** or **Security Token Offering (STO)** are increasing in popularity. With this said, let's explore the concept and definition of a token in more detail.

What is a token?

Oxford Dictionaries defines a token as:

"A voucher that can be exchanged for goods or services, typically one given as a gift, forming part of a promotional offer, a metal, or plastic disc used to operate a machine or in exchange for particular goods or services."

David Siegel, CEO of Pillar Project and a vocal thought leader in this space, defines a token as follows:

"Fundamentally, a token is an IOU. It is a contract. It represents rights and obligations... with the properties of having an issuer, a substrate (carrier), a system it is meaningful in, a value to someone, and some way to use them." (https://hackernoon.com/the-token-handbook-a80244a6aacb).

William Mougayar, another vocal thought leader introduced in *Chapter 1, Once Upon a Token* defines a token, in the context of this industry and in a more abstract way, as:

"A unit of value that an organization creates to self govern its business model and empower its users to interact with its product, while facilitating the distribution and sharing of rewards and benefits to all its stakeholders."(https://www.slideshare. net/wmougayar/state-of-tokens-by-william-mougayar-april-2018).

Let's start with traditional physical tokens, as we introduced in *Chapter 1, Once Upon a Token*. Examples include milk tokens, which were used back in the good old days when milk was delivered to your doorstep in glass bottles, or arcade tokens that you would have to buy to play your favorite game, such as Donkey Kong, or Street Fighter, at your local arcade hang out.

Taking the concept of an IOU from above, that arcade token is an IOU for access to a game and the milk token is an IOU for a bottle of milk. If we analyze these physical tokens further, what we see is that we have a company that issues the token and we have the perceived value to the holder of the token, due to the promise that the token can be redeemed based on certain terms and conditions. A token in this context is an in-house representation of some amount of real money that now only has some utility value.

Fast-forward in time and let's compare this to frequent flyer miles or "airpoints", which are given by almost every airline in the world. As previously mentioned, these frequent flyer miles are just another form of token. There is an issuer and there is perceived value to the holder, due to a promise that they can be redeemed based on certain terms and conditions.

Then we start moving into the numerous loyalty cards, including the Starbucks loyalty card. The card and the stamp represent the token and ensure that if 10 stamps are collected, the next coffee is free. Note that the stamp alone is not worth anything because if you stamp it on any random piece of paper, my bet is that Starbucks won't be giving you that 10th coffee for free.

This brings us to an interesting point where tokens quickly evolved to inherit anti-counterfeiting technologies. The level of investment made into anti-counterfeiting measures generally reflects the value being protected. There is no point in producing holographic tamper-resistant Starbucks cards where the reward is an extra coffee worth $4.50. A $100 USD bill, though, is an entirely different story.

In the blockchain world, tokens can be considered as the non-native digital asset of a blockchain. They are non-native because tokens can be created on any blockchain technology. These tokens can then be programmed to have meaning. In a sense, they can be considered smart tokens that are powered by smart contracts.

The difference between coins and tokens

Recapping the definition of a coin from the previous chapter, the following table shows the difference between coins and tokens. As of June 2018, CoinMarketCap lists 839 coins and 795 tokens:

Coins	Tokens
Native digital asset of a blockchain.	Non-native digital asset of a blockchain.
Coins are digital currencies in which mathematics is used to regulate the generation of the currency and verify the transfer of funds. Coins belong to and move within decentralized, cryptographically protected blockchains.	Tokens are a representation of a particular asset or utility that usually resides on top of another blockchain. Tokens can represent basically any assets that are fungible and tradable, from commodities to loyalty points, to even other cryptocurrencies!
Examples include Bitcoin, Dash, Litecoin, and Monero.	Examples include OmiseGo, TenX, Augur, and Humaniq.

Figure 2: The difference between a coin and a token

Different types of tokens

Currently, there is no global unified classification of tokens. However, there are attempts being made by various regulatory bodies around the world. The US **Securities and Exchange Commission (SEC)** and the Swiss **Financial Market Supervisory Authority (FINMA)** have divided tokens into three broad categories, which we will return to in *Chapter 6, Playing by the Rules*.

Cryptocurrency coins or payment tokens

These coins or tokens are intended to provide similar functions to currencies, such as the US dollar, euro, or Japanese yen, but they do not have the backing of a government. Bitcoin, Bitcoin Cash, and litecoin are examples of cryptocurrencies whose function is purely to operate as a means of payment.

Utility tokens

These are the most popular types of tokens being promoted, rightly or wrongly, in an ICO and they represent future access to a company's product or service for a customer. Sometimes they are referred to as "user tokens", "appCoins", or "appTokens" (application coins/tokens). The most important feature of a utility token is that it is not issued as an investment asset, which exempts it from having to comply with the relevant regulations.

Security or asset tokens

These are "digital assets" that represent or are backed by "physical underlyings, companies, or earnings streams, or an entitlement to dividends or interest payments. In terms of their economic function, the tokens are analogous to equities, bonds, or derivatives, (https://www.finma.ch/en/news/2018/02/20180216-mm-ico-wegleitung/)" as defined by the FINMA (https://www.finma.ch/en/news/2018/02/20180216-mm-ico-wegleitung/).

Sometimes referred to as "equity tokens", they can provide investors with some amount of ownership and rights to the profit generated by the company, much like traditional stocks. The main point here is that these tokens are subjected to security laws and regulations in the relevant jurisdiction. For example, the tokens for the ICO for tZERO, which is a portfolio company of Overstock Inc, promise to provide quarterly dividends derived from the profits of the tZERO platform to its investors.

LAToken aims to connect cryptocurrencies to the real economy, by allowing crypto holders to diversify their portfolios with access to tokens linked to the price of real assets. The company launched a trading platform for hard assets, such as real estate and gold. LAToken trades in assets, such as shares of blue chips (Apple, Tesla, and so on), and commodities (oil and gold). This classification is not exhaustive, and ICO token types can change over time.

Common ICO terminologies and acronyms

With the rise in popularity of the crypto space, there has been an increase in new terms or terms that were once only popular within a small community. Here are some common terms associated with tokens:

- ◆ **Airdrop**: A strategy to facilitate the wide distribution and use of project tokens. Project creators give away tokens, sometimes randomly, but mostly to avid supporters or potential supporters of the project.

- ◆ **ATH (All Time High)**: This refers to the price of cryptocurrencies or tokens that reach their highest historical price.

♦ **Bounties**: Incentivized reward mechanisms offered by companies to individuals. Many companies incorporate a bounty program as part of their ICO campaign. The reward is usually in the form of cryptocurrency or, more commonly, the ICO tokens themselves. Popular bounties include bug reporting bounties and translation bounties in particular for white papers.

♦ **Burning**: Removing tokens from the total supply by deleting them, if the smart contract allows it, or making the tokens permanently un-spendable by sending them to an address with no known private key. This is usually done when not all tokens are sold in an ICO. The effect is to reduce supply.

♦ **FUD**: Fear, uncertainty, and doubt. A strategy of spreading negative, dubious, or false information to influence perception.

♦ **Locking/freezing**: Preventing the tokens from being used for a set period of time. Early investors' tokens are often locked at specific time intervals to prevent them from selling all their tokens immediately and negatively affecting the price. Pillar Project didn't burn but locked up its unsold tokens and froze them for 10 years.

♦ **Meta coin**: Similar to coloring a coin, where extra meaning is given to a coin to increase the function and hence the purpose. This term has been superseded by the term "token."

♦ **Shilling**: Tricking as many people as possible to invest in a coin or token that may be valuable in the future but in 99% of cases won't be. A shill attempts to spread excitement by endorsing the product or service in public forums with the pretense of sincerity, when actually they are being paid for their services.

♦ **White paper**: Very loosely, it is essentially a prospectus that outlines the technical aspects of the product, the problems it intends to solve, how it is going to address them, a description of the team, and a description of the token generation and distribution strategy (more on this in *Chapter 8, White Paper, Website, and Team*).

ERC20/EIP20

ERC20 deserves a special mention because most of the ICO tokens are classified as ERC20 tokens. **ERC** stands for **Ethereum Request for Comment** and is used for creating standardized smart contracts.

It was proposed in November 2015 by Fabian Vogelsteller and defines a set of rules, or, more specifically, functions that Ethereum tokens should contain (https://github.com/ethereum/eips/issues/20). The six functions are `totalSupply`, `balanceOf()`, `transfer()`, `transferFrom()`, `approve()`, and `allowance()`, along with two events: `Transfer()` and `Approval()`. The ERC20 standard has simplified the process of the creation of tokens and as of June 2018, there are 91,247 ERC20 token contracts listed on `etherscan.io`.

As a side note, an ERC is actually a subtype of **EIP**, which stands for **Ethereum Improvement Proposal**. An ERC is the original proposal, although perhaps not complete, and with further input it is refined to something most participants will agree is useful, that then becomes an EIP. Therefore, ERC20 should really be referred to as "EIP20" but with widespread use of "ERC20", both terms tend to mean the same thing.

Changing the promise

So why is there so much excitement about blockchains and ICOs? The answer is that the promise made is game-changing. The promise is to create, or design, a system, or a platform, that will disrupt the disruptors. The promise is made to decentralize centralized organizations and remove intermediaries that clip the ticket but provide no extra value whatsoever. The promise is made to revolutionize how data is owned and value is stored. There have been attempts in the past to do something similar, but nothing on the scale we are seeing currently. These goals all involve utilizing the disruptive blockchain technology, and ICOs lend a hand by disrupting the funding mechanism. The catch is, ICOs also utilize blockchain technologies.

Some of these promises touch and appeal to our humanitarian emotions, such as helping displaced refugees with aid by tracking donations on the blockchain, or providing a means of personal identification on the blockchain so that no single entity can accidently, or with willful intent, change.

Others see a way of doing old things better. Uber challenged the existing taxi conglomerates by providing a more streamlined and efficient approach to personal transportation. Why not decentralize Uber? With autonomous or driverless cars coming to a town near you within the next decade, there is a paradigm shift coming, involving not just peer-to-peer electronic payments, but peer-to-peer decentralized autonomous transportation. It is these promises, and more, that have the growing community of tech geeks excited.

As the ICO craze caught on, there was a mad rush to buy these tokens in order to participate. This was a contributing factor leading to the increase in demand for bitcoin and ether, which helped to fuel the incredible gains observed in the past few years. These gains have led to what many have called a "speculative bubble."

Next, we look at whether we are indeed in a speculative bubble. Are cryptocurrencies and tokens overvalued? Is this the digital version of Tulip mania or the South Sea Bubble?

The dot-com versus dot-coin bubble

The most common comparison to what is happening now in the cryptocurrency world is made with the dot-com bubble, where between approximately 1997 and 2001, a period of excessive speculation and exuberance, coupled with a significant growth in the usage and adoption of the internet, fueled a frenetic feeding frenzy. Investors and venture capitalists poured money into companies, many of which operated at a net loss, to harness the network efforts and to build market share. The network effort was a great sell because the more something was used, the more value it had due to the users on the network. Any company with a domain name ending in .com, or with the promise of eCommerce, was having money thrown at it, even if the business model was flaky, sketchy, or even nonsensical.

Compare this to early 2014 to 2016, where companies only had to mention the word "blockchain" in their pitch deck to have investors throwing cash at them. Existing companies would pivot from traditional software companies to becoming blockchain companies and overnight, hundreds of self-titled "blockchain experts" or "blockchain consultants" appeared on LinkedIn. As for the network effect, what better story to sell than the more people using a cryptocurrency or a token, the more value it has?

According to the New York-based securities data firm Commscan, web companies raised a total of $1 billion USD in 34 IPOs in 1997, rising to $2 billion USD in 45 deals in 1998, and then exploding to $24.1 billion USD in 292 IPOs in 1999 (`http://money.cnn.com/2000/11/09/technology/overview/`).

The market value of Nasdaq technology companies peaked at $6.7 trillion USD in March 2000 (`http://articles.latimes.com/2006/jul/16/business/fi-overheat16`). The market capitalization of the current cryptocurrency market fluctuates greatly between $200 to 600 billion USD. A common way to show the value of these two markets is as circles drawn side by side in a crude attempt to not just compare, but also to somewhat indicate the potential room for growth of the cryptocurrency and token, or ICO, markets.

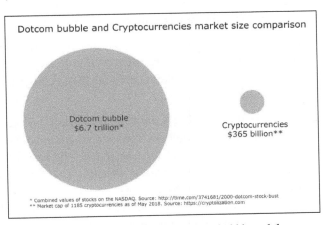

Figure 3: Comparison of the dot-com bubble and the
current cryptocurrency market size

This graphic needs to be taken with a grain of salt, though. The market capitalization or "market cap" of cryptocurrencies is taken as the circulating supply of a cryptocurrency, or token, multiplied by the current market price, and this can be deceiving.

Market capitalization

Traditionally, market capitalization measures the equity value of a business or what investors are willing to pay for its future profits. Visa, for instance, has a market cap of $300 billion USD as of May 2018. (https://ycharts.com/companies/V/market_cap). Bitcoin had a market cap of $300 billion USD at its peak in December 2017 and currently sits at around $136 billion USD as of May 2018. However, bitcoin isn't a business and has no profits. In some ways, we are not comparing apples with apples. Perhaps we should be comparing total assets or perhaps transactions per day. In this case, bitcoin has around 200,000 (https://blockchain.info/) per day versus approximately 345 million on Visa (https://www.reddit.com/r/nanocurrency/comments/824380/visa_is_capable_of_performing_24000_transactions/). Using this comparison, compared to the global financial institutions, bitcoin is still very insignificant.

Now, because the software code of nearly all cryptocurrencies is open source, anyone can create their own cryptocurrency, such as MyCoin, or their own token, such as **My Unique Token (MUT)** in a matter of hours.

Let's imagine that MUT has an arbitrary supply of one billion tokens that somehow managed to increase in price to $1. All of a sudden, the market cap has increased to a billion dollars, all from an idea, a white paper, and a website. Take this example and multiply it by 1,000 coins and we get to the magic market cap of $1 trillion USD out of nowhere. Unfortunately, until there is a better way, the market cap seems to be the easy figure to quote to indicate the potential of the ICO market, however inaccurate it may be.

Circa 1994 and email

If we compare the early internet days circa 1994 to the current progress of blockchain and ICO developments, and believe the far-reaching technological impact they could have, it is obvious that there is a lot of potential ahead. A common understanding in the crypto industry is that bitcoin is just the first application utilizing the blockchain technology and there are many more exciting applications yet to be invented. Some argue that the current "killer application" is these tokens, which have just started to revolutionize the funding industry.

This is similar, though, to how email was the first, and for a long time the only, "killer application" of the internet. Email was invented in 1972 by Ray Tomlinson and it wasn't until the mid-1980s, some 20 years later, that commercial use grew (http://www.nethistory.info/History%20of%20the%20Internet/email.html). In the mid-to-late-1990s, email really started to take off. To get to that point, the technology had to be stable and have features that were valuable to users. User interfaces had to be developed, so it wasn't just a black window full of text (engineers refer to this as a **Command-Line Interface (CLI)**) and a user base had to grow over time, referring to the network effect mentioned earlier.

The same comparison can be made with bitcoin. It was very much for computer geeks and engineering hobbyists in the early days, but now more and more features, services, and products are being developed in and around the crypto space. What needs to be taken into account, when comparing bitcoin's adoption rate with the adoption rate of email and the internet, is that with the current technology suite, adoption times are now compressed.

Instead of taking 20 years for the commercial adoption of email, bitcoin or cryptocurrency will take less. Payment gateways and merchant services appeared very early on. Some websites provided bitcoin addresses for payment to be made or the same address, but represented as a QR code:

Figure 4: A bitcoin address represented as a QR code

Celebrities

When celebrities, such as socialite Paris Hilton, boxer Floyd Mayweather, the rapper The Game, and DJ Khaled, start endorsing ICO projects, you know we are in the midst of a potential bubble. With many projects promoting similar ideas, having celebrity endorsements is one way to get attention and large sums of money have been raised in some of these ICOs.

Hilton tweeted, "Looking forward to participating in the new @LydianCoinLtd Token!" The company is claiming users will be able to trade Lydian tokens for the company's data-driven digital marketing services. The irony is that many of these celebrities probably have no clue what cryptocurrencies are.

Paris Hilton ✔ @ParisHilton · 3h
Looking forward to participating in the
new @LydianCoinLtd
Token! #ThisIsNotAnAd
#CryptoCurrency #BitCoin #ETH
#BlockChain

💬 215   🔁 346   ♡ 960   ✉

Figure 5: Hilton's tweet in September 2017, which was deleted shortly afterwards

The numbers

Statistics on the number of ICOs and the total amount raised
in each year vary depending on the source but, ignoring outliers,
they are all in the same ballpark. There were less than 10 ICOs
in 2014 and 2015 and around 40 in 2016. This jumped almost
10 times in 2017, to just under 400, and although the verdict
is still out in 2018, it is on track to surpass the 2017 numbers.

	2014		2015		2016		2017		2018*	
	#	$USD	#	$USD	#	$USD	#	$USD	#	$USD
coinschedule. com	-	-	-	-	43	$95M	210	$3.8B	420	$9.8B
coindesk.com	7	$30M	7	$9M	43	$256M	343	$5.5B	271	$7.0B
icodata.io	2	$16M	3	$6M	29	$90M	871	$6.1B	846	$5.3B
coinist.io	5	-	4	-	35	$284M	303	$5.9B	-	$3.3B
Tokendata /Fabric Ventures	-	-	-	-	-	$240M	435	$5.6B	-	-

Figure 6: ICO data from various sources showing the number
of ICOs and the amount raised. 2018 figures as of June 2018

The amount raised increased from tens of millions in 2014 and 2015, to hundreds of millions in 2016 and around $6 billion USD in 2017. That is a greater than 10-fold increase each year. One of the reasons for the enormous rise was the ease of creating tokens. As mentioned earlier, it was essentially a cookie-cutter approach where anyone could take some open-source code, replicate the token creation process with very little effort, and then spin up a marketing campaign around it. In fact, the technology was not the challenge: it was all about marketing.

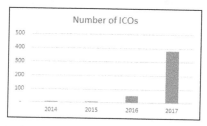

Figure 7: The average number of ICOs from 2014 to 2017

The growth in ICOs came from the emergence of platforms such as Ethereum, Nxt, and Waves. More and more platforms are being created because investors are seeing that the value is not just in the token, but in the platform where tokens can be created from. As these platforms continue to develop, more and more tokens will be invented, spurring on the tokenized economy. When talking about Bitcoin, Ronnie Moas, founder of standpointresearch.com and a prominent stock analyst, has said:

> *"I don't know how much gold there is in the ground, but I know how much bitcoin there is, and in two years there will be 300 million people in the world trying to get their hands on a few million bitcoin."*

Moas claims that currently there is about $230 trillion USD invested in stocks, cash, bonds, and gold and argues that if 2% of that $230 trillion USD finds its way into cryptocurrency, that would be a $4 trillion USD market valuation. Recalling the current $365 billion USD market cap, that would represent 11 times where we are today. The cryptocurrencies Moas talks about include all the ICO tokens as well. So, this is not just about converting frequent flyer miles or supermarket loyalty points into tokens but tokenizing everything from council rubbish bags and Manuka honey, to local sports group membership and Pokémon cards. The potential for tokens in this new economy is tremendous.

Continuing with bitcoin as an example, back in April 2013, many bitcoin detractors called it a "bubble", citing the meteoric rise in price from $20 USD to $200 USD:

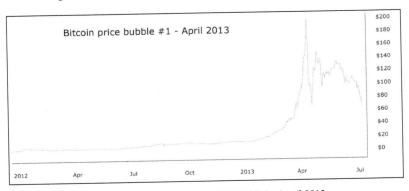

Figure 8: Bitcoin peaked at $200 USD in April 2013

However, during October 2013, just six months later, there was another so-called "bubble." This time, there was a meteoric rise from $200 USD to $1,100 USD, that made the April bubble appear like a small blip in comparison. Again, the detractors cried foul on this, calling it speculative, volatile, and an experiment.

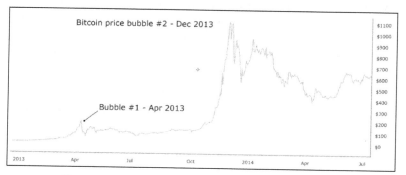

Figure 9: In 2013 to mid-2014, bitcoin peaked at $1100 USD

In December 2017, there was yet another bubble, this time rising from $1,100 USD to just under $20,000 USD:

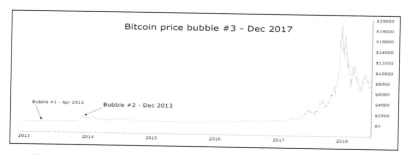

Figure 10: In 2017 to mid-2018, bitcoin peaked at just under $20,000 USD

What we are seeing here is the phenomenon called "scale invariance." In other words, the graph looks similar at different scales, or, more formally, it is any object or function that doesn't change when the scales are multiplied by a common factor.

However, all the other cryptocurrencies and ICO tokens can be observed as following a similar trend. In fact, when bitcoin experiences growth, all other tokens grow along with it. The aphorism "a rising tide lifts all boats" is often seen reverberated in the Twittersphere. Of course, the opposite is true as well.

Bitcoin versus the Nasdaq

Another popular comparison commonly made between the dot-com and dot-coin boom is the growth of the Nasdaq composite index (http://www.macrotrends.net/1320/nasdaq-historical-chart) in conjunction with the price of bitcoin (https://charts.bitcoin.com/chart/price). Compare the rise from 1990 to 2000 for the Nasdaq against a similar rise for bitcoin, but from only April 2017 to January 2018. The comparison also seems to justify the fall in bitcoin's value.

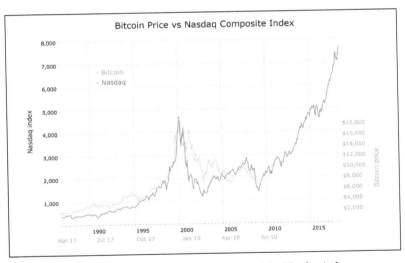

Figure 11: Comparison of bitcoin price and the Nasdaq index (non-inflation adjusted) showing similarities to the dot-com boom and bust

There are two important points to consider when viewing eye candy such as this. Firstly, the time frame of bitcoin is very small. In this case, it is only nine months. A small time frame is similar to conducting statistical research with a small sample size. Therefore, the results are more susceptible to volatility or outliers. Secondly, when overlaying the charts, depending on the scale or zoom factor, the bitcoin chart can be made to fit almost any time frame. It's almost a case of making the data and evidence fit the hypothesis.

The following chart shows an overlay across a larger number of years, effectively taking a zoomed out view. It actually makes the bitcoin rise more dramatic and makes a stronger case that bitcoin and the crypto space is a bubble (please note that although the Nasdaq period from 2000 to 2018 is presented, it is in no way intended to be an extrapolated view of the potential of the price of bitcoin).

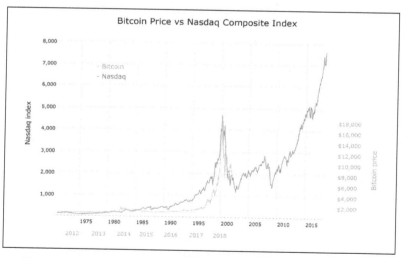

Figure 12: The bitcoin price versus the Nasdaq index over a six-year period

These patterns may or may not be coincidental but combining the knowledge that new blockchain technologies are currently being developed and deployed, and that the awareness of blockchains is growing amongst institutional investors as more and more tokens are created, it is not hard to see the immense potential of blockchains, ICOs, and the new tokenized economy.

The bust

> *"I have not failed. I've just found 10,000 ways that won't work."*
>
> *- Thomas Alva Edison*

To innovate, one must experiment. To experiment, one must continually find new ways of doing things. The catch is that not all of these new ways of doing things will succeed, as Thomas Edison found out. The sensible conclusion to draw is that out of all the thousands of ICOs created so far, most of them will fail. In fact, many have. White papers and GitHub source code repositories have been deleted and any remnant of LinkedIn profiles for the ICOs removed, that is, if they were real in the first place.

The rise of speculators and opportunists is of no surprise to those in the industry and it shouldn't be a surprise to anyone else. It happened in the dot-com bubble, the housing bubble, and even the various gold rush eras throughout the world. However, as the clampdown begins in 2018, from regulators and governments, and closer scrutiny is placed on ICOs, we will start to see a wave of new ICOs that work a lot closer with these regulatory bodies (more on this in *Chapter 6, Playing by the Rules*).

The irony is that these regulators will need to learn and understand this technology in the first place. They often try to wrap it up in a neat and tidy box to categorize it in the existing system of laws and frameworks. This is where the problem lies. Cryptocurrencies and tokens created through ICOs don't fall neatly into any existing categories. New definitions need to be created and new boxes need to be made for cryptocurrencies and tokens.

The dot-com crash resulted from the inflated share prices of technology companies losing significant value over a short period of time, when startups promised the world but all they could deliver was a simple web interface and a credit card form that required manual processing in the back-end. Does this sound familiar?

In the ICO world, we have seen very creative and innovative propositions, such as Augur/Gnosis, a decentralized prediction market; **Basic Attention Tokens (BAT)**, where attention span becomes the traded commodity and Civic, a digital blockchain-based secure identity ecosystem. We may not see it, or even agree with it, but they are the equivalent of the HTML web page of the late 1990s. There is no doubt that digital identities will be a necessity as we all become digital citizens, but there are many questions yet to be asked and so many answers yet to be discovered.

Risk in ICOs

One issue with many of these ICOs is that the tokens are purchased by supporters, users, and investors before the platform is even launched. If the platform has not been launched yet, how are tokens valued? How is this different to someone selling the vision of an unknown product for a certain amount of money, hoping that it will be worth something in the future?

Tremendous faith is put into the team to deliver something potentially six-to-18 months away, where anything could happen, such as the infighting between the Tezos (a blockchain with in-built governance) founders and the foundation it created.

The industry is slowly changing to become a place where many companies build proof of concepts, test their business model and, with more understanding of what tokens are and how they work, offer better and more innovative ideas towards solving real-world problems.

Infrastructure

Infrastructure was a problem for the internet back in the 1990s because you couldn't launch a high-speed video streaming service when the majority of users were still on dial-up modem. The difference now, though, is that the internet infrastructure is there and the users are there also. In a global, interconnected world, where the best minds can work collaboratively with the power of the internet, this blockchain infrastructure can be built much faster. This is what continues to support the potential of blockchain technology and the tokenized economy.

There are several things holding blockchain technology back, though. First of all, scalability is a constant challenge. Although the basic infrastructure, such as access to the internet and computers, and powerful mobile devices, is there, the infrastructure of the blockchain technology itself is still immature. The internet infrastructure of Facebook may be able to support one billion plus Facebook users, but blockchains cannot yet support a billion users on a decentralized version of Facebook. The bitcoin blockchain is said to process only around seven transactions per second. This is a very crude estimate but is reflective of the scalability issue. However, these issues will be solved. The internet didn't manage to support a billion Facebook users overnight and blockchains won't either.

Education

Next comes the complexity problem. It should come as no surprise that humans have evolved into creatures seeking instant gratification: wanting things now and wanting things simple. We have a magic button to cook dinner in four minutes, a magic pill to lose weight in four weeks and, of course, with one click of the mouse we can have our favorite pair of shoes delivered to our doorstep.

In this new crypto world, where we become our own bank and there are no third parties, intermediaries or toll-free customer support lines to call upon, we need to learn and understand how this stuff all works. We cannot shift responsibility to someone else because there is no someone else. Understanding basic concepts, such as public and private keys, and the fact that if you lose your private key you lose all your cryptocurrencies, sounds scary at first, but it is no different to losing your wallet in the back seat of a taxi after a night out in town. Complexity is relative to the amount of effort spent learning and understanding this new and innovative technology. The potential for blockchains and the tokenized economy carries with it the enormous potential for learning.

ICO road maps

All ICO projects have a road map. It is almost a mandatory requirement to show not only the potential of the project, but the timeline as well. There is no point in designing flying cars if the delivery date is a hundred years out. What we are slowly starting to see is projects that did an ICO in early 2017 beginning to miss or delay milestones six-to-nine months later. Smaller ICOs have simply faded away, but bigger ICOs will face intense scrutiny.

The key is that it takes a couple of years for investments into ICOs to see significant tangible results. This follows the trend of investment into blockchain technologies, such as the Lightning Network and Segregated Witness (both introduced in *Chapter 2, A Bit of Coin Theory*) back in 2014, which saw tangible outputs several years later and eventual promotion to production in 2017. Therefore, while many ICOs are still in the honeymoon phase of how to spend the millions that has just been raised, some road maps look very optimistic.

TenX, for example, gets full credit for providing a 12-month and a 36-month road map in its white paper, but looking at the projected growth rate of users, from one million in 2018 to 10 million 12 months later, and then 50 million in 2020, that is some projection. TenX raised $80 million USD and seems to have significant resources to execute its plan, but it doesn't take a rocket scientist to appreciate that out of all the many ICOs that make similar predictions, not all of them can come true, simply because not all projects can achieve 50 million users within three years.

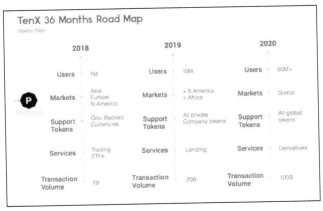

Figure 13: TenX's ambitious 36-month roadmap

Essentially, it comes down to being able to deliver a conceptual idea within a timeline. This is not new. These ICOs are software projects with road maps, milestones, resource requirements, and a budget. What is new is the technology being deployed and in some cases the software language being used.

Working with new technologies

Speak to any software developer at the coalface of developing blockchain technologies, or smart contracts, and you will understand their frustration. An example includes removing certain functions and then delaying the updating of the documentation (https://github.com/ethereum/go-ethereum/issues/3793). This can set back even the best project with the best developers. New ICOs have caught onto this and designed platforms that use existing programming languages and technologies, making them interlocking in an effort to combat the yet-to-mature frameworks out there.

If software projects weren't already difficult to build, in the blockchain world they are made more challenging with the additional concept of economic incentive schemes, in the form of tokens, to incorporate into their design. In the future, programmers may need economics degrees to write software code, just like how lawyers may need to learn programming code to interpret smart contracts.

Token saturation

Logic would tell us that there are only so many loyalty tokens, so many provenance tracking systems tokens or so many personal identity tokens that the market can tolerate before saturation. The smart ones will pivot before saturation hits. The clever ones have already pivoted.

They have pivoted away from just providing a loyalty token, to providing a loyalty platform where loyalty tokens can be created in a very simple, non-technical drag-and-drop manner on the blockchain. However, even most of these will fail too. The reason being that the real innovation is yet to happen, as Mougayar succinctly summarizes:

> *"Tokens 1.0: copying what we see.*
> *Tokens 2.0: inventing what we don't see."*

Take, for example, personal identity on the blockchain. How many personal identities will one have or need? The most logical answer is one. If there is more than one, say per country, then we may end up in a situation similar to that of instant messaging systems. WhatsApp, Skype, WeChat, Viber, Signal, Telegram, Messenger, Slack, LinkedIn Chat, and Google Chat are just a few of the chat services available. We are spoilt for choice and end up saturating our phones and scattering our time. At the moment, all we are doing is building and tokenizing existing systems as it is far easier to copy than to create. If these competing applications don't consume each other, the next big "killer app" that everyone is waiting for will.

Community saturation

Application saturation is not the only reason that many of the ICOs will fail. Communities are being saturated with marketing activities attempting to grow groups of supporters, programmers, and influencers. Large marketing budgets are typically set aside with bounties, which pay people to become supporters or to raise awareness. The company gets everyone excited about using its product on its blockchain. What tends to happen is that the fundamental technology seems to get lost in the noise and hype that is generated.

National or international "community managers" spend the marketing budget that was raised in the ICO to spread the good word in an evangelical manner, explaining why their blockchain platform is better. The fight for this territory will become fiercer because the space is becoming overcrowded.

Greater fool theory

The general concept of this theory is that there's always someone, an even greater fool, that will overpay for something, in this case ICO tokens, that are already overpriced. This can often be seen in a heated or overheated bull market.

Applying this to ICOs, many investors are blinded to the fundamentals and real value that an ICO provides by the marketing hype around how it will change the world. Everyone jumps on the ICO train with the belief not that the value of the technology will increase, but that the price of the token will increase based on media-announced partnerships. It has become a game that has shifted away from how the technology can change the trust relationship, to one of finding another buyer who will pay a higher price for the same token.

What lies in waiting is a bust, as highlighted earlier: a digital graveyard of broken promises, dormant or abandoned Twitter accounts, 404 page not found websites, and the remnants of chat logs in now-empty Telegram groups or Slack channels. Images of empty towns from old Wild West movies, with digital tumbleweed rolling by, come to mind.

In many ways, a clean out will be healthy in the ICO world. There is currently so much noise that it is hard to distinguish between the legitimate ones and the unscrupulous ones. The key to success, though, hasn't changed just because a new three-letter acronym has arrived in town. Business models need to be sound, continuous research, and innovation is required and having a solid team of people is, and always has been, key to any company's success.

A new era of ICO innovation

ICOs may be a relatively new and complex phenomenon but with all the talk of doom and gloom, this hasn't prevented ICOs from continuing to innovate. There will be diamonds in the rough. There are two levels of innovation: firstly, the ICO mechanism itself and secondly, the blockchain-based technology where innovative products and services are created, with almost always a token in tow.

In fact, if you cast your mind back to March 2006, when Twitter first appeared on the scene, or even back to February 2004 if you are a Facebook fan, it wasn't until around three-to-four years later that these companies really found their groove and user adoption started. Now, Twitter and Facebook are household names worldwide.

Facebook and Twitter didn't have all the answers when they first started and neither do all these companies trying to tokenize everything in their path. However, the potential for a handful of companies somewhere out there to discover real applications is exciting. Whether it is through decentralized digital identity, the tokenization of all human interaction in a virtualized world or just the realization of Satoshi Nakamoto's original goal of a peer-to-peer electronic cash system, the future is there to be created.

Innovation in the ICO mechanism

ICOs, in the early days, only accepted bitcoins. Examples included Omni, Counterparty, Ethereum, and Factom. When ICOs started to be built on the Ethereum platform, it was only natural for ether to be included as a payment option.

Then there was a brief period where a multitude of cryptocurrencies were accepted, such as the TenX ICO where bitcoin, ether, litecoin, and dash were accepted. It quickly became a lot of work managing multiple cryptocurrency wallets, along with potential fluctuations in price. So, startups tended to generally opt for payments in ether in 2017. The price of bitcoin also saw large increases, which made people hold Bitcoins rather than spend them.

In the latter half of 2017, it became almost a game of who would take out top gong and raise the most money. Bancor raised the bar to $153 million USD in June, Tezos raised $233 million USD in July, and Filecoin took the cake for 2017 and raised $253 million USD in August. These ICOs will be analyzed in more detail in the next chapter.

Going private

For the Filecoin ICO, around $52 million USD was sold to private investors including Sequoia Capital, Andreessen Horowitz, and Union Square Ventures. Then, the next round was only to accredited investors. An accredited investor was deemed to have a net worth exceeding $1 million USD and/or the ability to demonstrate an annual income of over $200,000.

It then became evident that to raise hundreds of millions of dollars in an ICO, the ICO would have to be bolstered by some form of private money. This private pre-sale provided the added advantage that if well-known investors backed the ICO early, this was a positive signal for public investors.

Well-known advisors

This was particularly evident with Vitalik Buterin, where ICO projects would scramble to have his name associated with their projects. Only a handful succeeded, such as OmiseGo and Fenbushi Capital. OmiseGo also has a lot of other high-profile names endorsing it, such as Gavin Wood, the co-founder of Ethereum, and Joseph Poon, Plasma, and Lightning Network's co-author. Fenbushi Capital, on the other hand, invested in blockchain companies such as Bloq (enterprise grade blockchains), Filament (a decentralized Internet of Things platform), and Tierion (data verification on the blockchain).

Creative discounting

Along with getting big names on board as advisors, and large upfront investments to signal the positive potential of the project, ICO smart contracts incorporated discounted token rates for investors. For example, participating in the pre-ICO would attract a 10% token bonus. Creativity was also extended to the price discovery method of determining a fair price of an ICO. A modified reverse Dutch auction was used by Gnosis (predictions market).

Second round

Some ICOs took on the challenge of doing a second round ICO, which currently is not standard practice. Storj (decentralized file storage) and Synereo (a blockchain-enabled attention economy solution) attempted this with interesting effects. Generally, ICOs should only perform an ICO once. The reason is that there is a common understanding that an ICO's token supply is known and that it is fixed. The belief is that with a limited supply, the value will increase over time.

Whether it is 100 million or one billion tokens, there will be no more. There are various ways around this however, such as creating a family or suite of products, and having an ICO for each of these, or creating a secondary token with a variable exchange rate to convert between the two tokens. Centrality had such a large demand that it provided a further announcement to its investors:

"After completely selling out our token in record time, we know that there are investors who missed out. We're now encouraging those with funds remaining in the Blockhaus sales app to leave them there, as the announcement of our next big token sale is only weeks away."

Innovation in ICO ideas

Although creativity, innovation, and a marketing story were required to increase the success of an ICO, the purpose of the ICO itself was where the real innovation took place. Many of these ICOs were presenting ideas that were very bold and grand, and this was observed across many different industries.

What is interesting to note, also, is that many of these concepts arose several years earlier when blockchain was the buzz. For example, Genomecoin, Healthcoins, Learncoin, Journalcoin, and Campuscoin are only a few mentioned in book *Blockchain: Blueprint for a New Economy, Melanie Swan,* first published in *February 2015.* While it may seem that the only thing that has changed is the word "coin" moving to "token", there is a lot more awareness of this industry, which has brought in a lot more ideas.

Health tokens

No matter where you are in the world, there is a constant battle to aggregate and integrate personal health data between all sorts of different health providers, so that there is a single view of patient information that is accurate, up to date, and reliable.

This means that information from your physiotherapist, your general practitioner, your hospital, and even your chiropractor can be stored on the blockchain, encrypted of course, and you are the only person that can access and allow access to that information.

Blockchain technology is the touted savior where this health information can be stored on a distributed and decentralized network. The difference now is that there is not a generic Healthcoin or even health token, but there are many tokens that have become very specific.

Patientory uses the blockchain along with its own specific token to secure medical records along with Medicalchain, Medibloc, and Solve.Care. There's Dentacoin, a blockchain solution for the global dental industry, MediShares for health insurance, and Nursetoken to apparently solve global nurse shortages. These are just a few random examples of the hundreds out there. This naturally leads to the question of digital identity.

Digital identity

There are ICOs that purport to be working on providing digital identity on the blockchain. This is where cryptography is used to create a super-secret password that only you know and then your personal data is attested by a third party.

A simple example would be your local birth, death, and marriage government department that would attest to your date of birth. In fact, one could foresee a future where the obstetricians or nurses could digitally attest the date and time of the delivery, along with even GPS coordinates, with their mobile device minutes after the actual delivery. This information could then be combined with your super-secret password and placed on the blockchain.

You would then control this data, deciding where, when, and who to release it to. To prove that you are over the minimum age to vote or to drive, you could show evidence by having a recognized third party attest that you meet the criteria, without having to reveal your date of birth.

A similar scenario can be walked through using your name. The difference with a name is that it can be changed at any point in time. This change can be recorded on the blockchain and because it is an update-only database, a record or digital paper trail will be available for audit purposes.

Digital identity can be taken a step further when combined with genomics, the science around the function, evolution, and mapping of genomes. Instead of a doctor stating the claim that your eyes are brown, blue, or green, this can be inferred directly from your genes. In fact, your genome, that is your complete set of genetic material that represents who you are, can be stored on a distributed and decentralized database where, again, you are the only person that can access the information or allow others to access it.

TheKey, Authorian, and KYC.Legal are again a random selection of the many companies out there that have a token that is required to be purchased to be used in their identity verification system.

Supply chain

There are also many examples of ICOs attempting to solve the "supply chain and provenance of food" problem on the blockchain. Many ask the questions: do you know where that piece of beef you had for dinner last night came from, or was the fish you bought sustainably caught? Existing systems can record this information, but are they trustworthy? Who is to know if the data was corrupted or, worse, doctored?

ShipChain, WaltonChain, SmartContainers, Ambrosus, and Sweetbridge are all building the so-called next evolution of logistics enabling privacy, scalability and security for the supply chain, unlocking the value trapped in assets, and payment delays, helping countries and individuals to find a better way to trade and innovate. Enterprises can eliminate traditional supply chain barriers and integrate actors big and small into an efficient, transparent, and secure global network.

The preceding description was a sentence taken from each of the above supply chain ICOs to highlight how many companies are working on very similar ideas in slightly different ways. This is a huge positive as long as there is collaboration and sharing involved. Let's hope that happens.

Energy

Energy is another large area where companies such as SolarCoin, Power Ledger, Grid+, and Global Grid are attempting to disrupt the energy market in energy trading, generation, transmission, and retail. Each ICO has its own token that will be used in its network to represent energy of some form, such as a watt (a unit of power) or even down to the electrons generated from a solar panel or wind farm. These tokens can then be used to represent the amount of energy generated and sold either directly to a consumer on a local micro-community grid or on a decentralized marketplace.

The energy concept can be taken a step further where electric vehicles can plug into a charging station and have tokens automatically transferred from their smart wallet to the wallet of the charging station provider. In fact, with induction charging of mobile phones, the kind where the phone charges simply by being placed on top of a surface, electric cars could be recharged while remaining stationary through a car wash. Tokens can be used as a form of payment, automatically, seamlessly, and even to the nearest minute.

It all seems very futuristic and like science fiction, but there is a prevailing pattern here. The potential of ICOs is tremendous because the tenet of the technology is to decentralize centralized systems and to provide a tokenized medium of exchange. The tokens can be used for anything valuable and exchangeable, therefore, no industry can hide from this innovative disruption. These ICOs are raising capital by creating tokens in a tokenized economy to build the next generation of "entities", that are vastly different to what we are used to.

Summary

The ICO phenomenon has sparked a creative and innovative flair in those young and old. The young are jumping in with naïve, but unlimited, energy and disrupting everything in their path, and the old are radiating caution and timing.

In this chapter, we learned what an ICO is and explained the concept of a token, along with some associated terminology. Several bitcoin bubbles were highlighted, only to discover that subsequent bubbles rendered the previous bubbles insignificant in comparison.

Several challenges were highlighted, such as the need for the development of infrastructure and increased education.

Finally, we learned about the new era of ICO innovation and what the future could bring.

Now that we have an insight into the potential of ICOs and blockchain technologies, we next look at the various token varieties and ICOs that have occurred over the past four years, starting with the very first one: Omni.

4

TOKEN VARIETIES

Nowadays, there are tokens everywhere, purporting to do everything from replicating loyalty programs and gaming credits, all the way to acting as payment systems within messaging apps and even using token platforms to create more tokens. There are a dizzying number of tokens available at present, all claiming to provide exceptional world-changing utility and value.

The question is: do these tokens really offer what they claim? In this chapter, we'll take a closer look at tokens, particularly:

♦ Tokens on the bitcoin blockchain (Omni/Counterparty)

♦ Tokens on custom blockchains (Nxt/Waves)

♦ Tokens on the Ethereum blockchain (Augur/ICONOMI)

♦ Tokens on non-blockchain technologies (IOTA/Hashgraph)

We'll take a step back in time to see how ICOs were done back in the good old days, on the good old original bitcoin blockchain, then on other blockchains such as Nxt and Waves, before jumping into the ever-popular Ethereum blockchain. We will also round off by introducing relatively new, non-blockchain technologies, such as IOTA and Hashgraph.

ICOs on the Bitcoin blockchain

Before Ethereum existed, and ERC20 tokens were the buzzword, ICOs were known as crowdsales or fundraising events. Platforms based on the bitcoin blockchain were invented to enable the creation of tokens linked to a bitcoin address, much like how ERC20 tokens are linked to an Ethereum address. Omni (formerly known as MasterCoin) was such a platform. Counterparty was another and so was Factom.

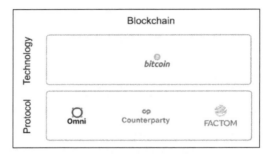

Figure 1: Omni, Counterparty, and Factom were the early adopters
that built on top of the bitcoin technology

These platforms also included rules or "protocols" on how other tokens could be created and are generally referred to as "protocols" for this reason.

 Protocol: A rule or way of doing something or, informally in the software world, a standard language that lets a bunch of people on the internet work together on a specific problem.

Omni (OMNI) (formerly MasterCoin)

Omni is an open-source, fully-decentralized asset platform on the bitcoin blockchain and was created by J.R. Willet when he published a paper in mid-2012 infamously titled *The Second Bitcoin Whitepaper* (https://github.com/OmniLayer/spec#development-mastercoins-dev-msc). Omni claimed in its white paper that *the existing bitcoin network can be used as a protocol layer, on top of which new currency layers with new rules can be built without changing the foundation.*

What this meant was that other currencies could be created using the Omni protocol that ran on the bitcoin blockchain. For example, to create a new currency, Omni stated that, *The user must decide on the ticker symbol, a short name, a long name, a short URL pointing to more information about the currency along with various parameters governing the currency's behavior.*

The goal of the fundraiser was stated in the Omni white paper: *Initial distribution of MasterCoins will essentially be a fundraiser to provide money to pay developers to write the software which fully implements the protocol* (https://e33ec872-a-62cb3a1a-s-sites.googlegroups.com/site/2ndbtcwpaper/MasterCoin%20Specification%201.1.pdf).

In July 2013, the fundraiser ended up collecting 5122 bitcoins, or the equivalent of $500K USD at the time, at the bitcoin *exodus* address 1EXoDusjGwvnjZUyKkxZ4UHEf77z6A5S4P. The exodus address was a play on the bitcoin genesis block terminology.

 In ancient times, books were written on scrolls and were a standard size. Five of these scrolls were used to record the Torah, which is the basis of the Jewish religion and faith. The word *genesis* is the English translation of the title of the first scroll, meaning beginning. *Exodus* is the title of the second scroll, meaning leaving (in reference to the Jewish people leaving Egypt where they were slaves.

The initial 2012 white paper covered a stable coin concept, where a coin would be split into two components: a stable component and a volatile component. It also talked about conditional transfers and distributed exchanges. Interestingly, these concepts rose to popularity several years later, and now many companies are researching and experimenting with stable tokens, and more and more decentralized exchanges are coming to the market.

There was a section in the white paper titled *The Trusted Entity* that was about controlling the initial distribution of MasterCoins and the development of the software. It was later removed from the white paper but its presence can be seen in today's ICOs, as they are all governed by a *trusted entity*, whether they are companies, startups, or not-for-profit foundations.

The terms of the sale were that one bitcoin would obtain 100 MasterCoins. There was also a pre-sales bonus explained in the white paper:

"Early buyers get additional MasterCoins. In order to encourage adoption momentum, buyers will get an additional 10% bonus MasterCoins if they make their purchase a week before the deadline, 20% extra if they purchase two weeks early, and so on, including partial weeks. Thus, if I send 100 bitcoins to the exodus address 1.5 weeks before August 31st, the protocol recognizes my bitcoin address as owning 11,500 MasterCoins (10000 + 15% bonus)."

What made this a currency instead of a token, where all the supply was created at once, was that for every 10 MasterCoins sold, one additional Development MasterCoin called a *Dev MSC* was created. This would then be released into the system using the formula:

$$Dev\, MSC = 1 - (0.5)^y$$

y represents the years since the sale of MasterCoins. This translates to 50% of the Dev MSC released into the supply after year one, 75% in year two and so on. This structure was used as an incentive for developers to continue to maintain, improve, and add features to the protocol and was controlled by the MasterCoin Foundation.

Typically, coins or tokens are created so that they can be used within a platform as a medium of exchange. However, because the MasterCoins idea was a protocol and MasterCoins (the coins) were sold as a means to fund the development of this protocol, you couldn't use MasterCoins (the coins) on the MasterCoin platform because it was a protocol. Confused? Let's explain that again using the new name, Omni.

So, because Omni was a protocol and not a platform, and MasterCoins were sold as a means to fund the development of Omni, you couldn't use MasterCoins anywhere, although they could be traded on an exchange back to USD. This is one of the reasons why Omni is not used anymore because digital assets without features tend to have no value. An interesting experimental proposed feature, though, is to use MasterCoins as an escrow fund to provide price stability for other coins built following the Omni protocol.

Omni's protocol was highly technical and knowledge of the inner workings of the bitcoin blockchain was required to create applications, that users could use to then create new currencies on. However, when the fundraiser opened a year later, and people actually sent Bitcoins, this was the response from J.R. Willet:

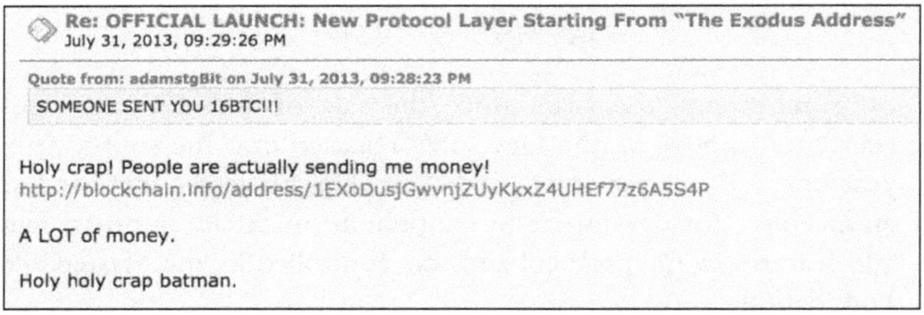

> **Re: OFFICIAL LAUNCH: New Protocol Layer Starting From "The Exodus Address"**
> July 31, 2013, 09:29:26 PM
>
> Quote from: adamstgBit on July 31, 2013, 09:28:23 PM
> SOMEONE SENT YOU 16BTC!!!
>
> Holy crap! People are actually sending me money!
> http://blockchain.info/address/1EXoDusjGwvnjZUyKkxZ4UHEf77z6A5S4P
>
> A LOT of money.
>
> Holy holy crap batman.

Figure 2: J.R. Willet's reaction when Bitcoins were first sent to his ICO (https://bitcointalk.org/index.php?topic=265488.msg2842681#msg2842681)

Another comment in the bitcointalk forum, one day into the fundraiser, noted:

"Wow you're [sic] funds have just shot up from 35 to 1,257 BTC while writing this so you must be doing something right!!" (https://bitcointalk.org/index.php?topic=265488.msg2847476#msg2847476).

Omni was quite forward thinking at the time, considering that it was still early days in 2013, and a few other companies ended up using the platform to create tokens of their own. One of them was MaidSafe.

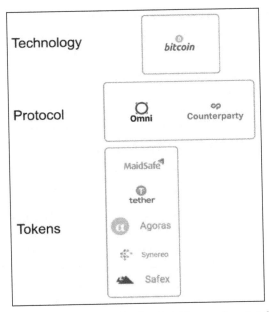

Figure 3: Tokens using the Omni platform and protocol

MaidSafe (SFE) on Omni

The vision of MaidSafe was to create a cheaper, more efficient, and more secure data-storage infrastructure for the internet. The company was founded in 2006 by Scottish engineer David Irvine and it was an acronym for "Massive Array of Internet Disks, Secure Access for Everyone." The project was ambitious and raising funds with an ICO was great timing because the company had a solid eight-year history, with almost $5 million USD in funding prior to the ICO. (`https://metaquestions.me/2014/05/01/surviving-a-crowd-sale/`).

The purpose of the **Safecoin (SFE)** was to access and utilize services on the SAFE network, such as storing data or making **VoIP (Voice over Internet Protocol)** calls.

The total number of Safecoins that could exist on the SAFE network was 2^{32}, or just under 4.3 billion. 5% was allocated to compensate early investors who backed the network over a long period of time, and only 10% was made available in the ICO.

MaidSafe's ICO of Safecoin was launched in April 2014 and ended up raising $6 million USD in five hours, which was huge back in 2014 (https://blog.maidsafe.net/2014/04/23/maidsafe-sells-6-million-of-bitcoin-2-0-software-in-five-hours-press-release/). The MaidSafe team did overlook one small aspect. The original plan was to only accept MasterCoins for 10% of the crowdsale, since there was not much market liquidity for MasterCoins. Bitcoin would then make up the rest of the sale. The allocation of Bitcoins to Safecoins was 1:17,000 and MasterCoins to Safecoins was 1:3,400.

However, what MaidSafe didn't realize was that people could buy far more SafeCoin tokens if they paid with MasterCoins than if they paid with Bitcoins. This resulted in MaidSafe ending up with MasterCoins making up around 50% of the sales. The price of MasterCoins soared in the days leading up to the MaidSafe ICO. As soon as the ICO was over, the major source of demand for MasterCoins was suddenly gone, and the price collapsed.

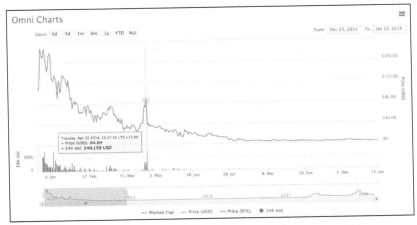

Figure 4: The price crash of Omni immediately after the ICO [1]

Irvine stated:

> *"Ok it was over, we had screwed up and screwed all our supporters who were BTC holders. We had bet the business on this sale and spent months working towards it, sacrificing everything to make this happen."*

(https://metaquestions.me/2014/05/01/surviving-a-crowd-sale/).

There are some valuable points to learn from the MaidSafe ICO. First of all, from Irvine:

> *"We knew MSC could be used directly and automatically issue MaidSafeCoins, this was how the protocol worked. This gave us cause for concern, but experts in the field reassured us the MSC part of sale would be minimal. This was comforting, but relied on us using advice and not setting a rule (this was our big mistake)."*

(https://metaquestions.me/2014/05/01/surviving-a-crowd-sale/).

Nick Lambert, COO of MaidSafe noted:

"A lot of people questioned why we would use two currencies, and looking back we [should] have used one."

(https://www.coindesk.com/maidsafe-lessons-learned-crowdsale/).

In the end, Irvine said,

"So the oodles of cash, the pile of loot, what happens to that? This part is easy, it is much more equivalent to $3M in today's cash if we were to convert it, so there is a long-term position required. It will keep the MaidSafe staff paid and housed for three years as stated."

(https://metaquestions.me/2014/05/01/surviving-a-crowd-sale/).

MaidSafe ended up with anywhere around $3-6 million USD, according to various reports from its ICO. What the ICO did highlight, as explained on MaidSafe's website, was that things can still go wrong, even for a team of *thinkers, inventors, tinkerers, PhDs, engineers, and designers* (https://maidsafe.net/company.html).

Accepting two currencies made it more complicated and as noted above, taking advice and not setting a rule, that could have been incorporated into the code, meant that the balance of the two currencies was far from what was expected.

Tether on Omni

In mid-2014, a few months after MaidSafe's ICO, a company called Tether used the Omni platform to issue tokens. This was not a typical ICO, where one bitcoin could buy a set number of tokens with a goal of say $10 million to bring an idea to the market. It was simply an issue of Tether tokens at a one-to-one ratio for USD. This was called **USDT (United States Dollar Tokens)** and these US Tether tokens could then be used at various exchanges to purchase other cryptocurrencies.

The way that Tether worked was that instead of depositing USD into an exchange's bank account to buy bitcoin, users would deposit it into Tether's account. Tether would then issue USDT. The user would then send the USDT to the exchange and buy cryptocurrencies.

The exchanges liked this idea because it meant that they did not have to have a bank account. The risk of having a bank account is that there are a lot of regulations and compliance rules that need to be followed, and even if they are adhered to, there is nothing stopping the bank from changing its decision at any point in time, and shutting down the bank account.

Cryptopia, a cryptocurrency exchange based in New Zealand, experienced this first-hand when it was notified that its bank intended to close its New Zealand accounts. Cryptopia made a news announcement:

"Unfortunately, our current bank has notified us that they intend to close our NZDT account on 9 February. Due to this, we are announcing an immediate halt to NZDT deposits from COB today and we are asking all customers to cease sending NZD deposits to our NZDT account." (`https://www.cryptopia.co.nz/News`).

Tether sounded like a great idea, especially since on the website (`www.tether.to`) it states:

"Every Tether is always backed 1-to-1, by traditional currency held in our reserves. So 1 USD₮ is always equivalent to 1 USD... our reserve holdings are published daily and subject to frequent professional audits. All Tethers in circulation always match our reserves."

The challenge that Tether has is that the supply of Tether has skyrocketed from 14 million at the start of 2017, to 2.2 billion a year later:

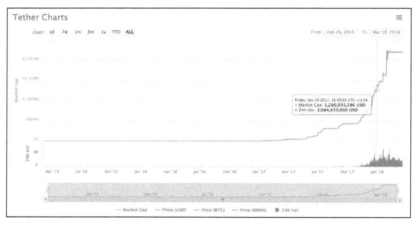

Figure 5: The supply of Tether tokens has drastically increased [2]

In theory, then, Tether should have $2.2 billion in its bank accounts. Some people are questioning this and would like to see an audit to maintain confidence in Tether. Unfortunately, obtaining an audit is not as straightforward as one would think because large auditing firms are understandably cautious and risk adverse when putting their name and reputation on the line to support a cryptocurrency initiative.

There are also a number of other issues that cloud the Tether token. Tether and Bitfinex, one of the world's largest exchanges, appear to be closely associated with common shareholders and potentially the same CEO. Bitfinex and Tether have both been hacked in the past and some banking relationships have soured, for example with Wells Fargo (https://www.coindesk.com/ bitfinex-tether-break-silence-go-media-offensive/). Having said this, though, this is not uncommon in the unregulated world of cryptocurrencies.

What Omni did was to provide a platform for innovation, but it wasn't the only one. Counterparty was another company that used the bitcoin blockchain and built a platform for others to create their own tokens.

Counterparty (XCP)

Counterparty is a platform to manage cryptographic assets. It extends bitcoin's functionality by writing in the *margins* of regular bitcoin transactions.

Counterparty did not hold a crowdsale or ICO, but did issue XCP, about six months after Omni in January 2014, to the bitcoin address 1CounterpartyXXXXXXXXXXXXXXXXUWLpVr.

2130 bitcoins were received and then subsequently *burned* and destroyed using a technique called *proof-of-burn* to avoid pre-mining. The terms of the swap were that one bitcoin burnt would garner between 1000 and 1500 XCP, as stated by Counterparty on bitcointalk:

"No more than 1 BTC may ever be burned by any address, and the number of XCP received per BTC is between 1000 and 1500, with more XCP being rewarded the earlier in the burn period the burn takes place." (https://bitcointalk.org/ index.php?topic=395761.msg4271279#msg4271279).

In the end, the total supply created from the 2130 bitcoins was 2.65 million XCP tokens. These tokens were used to run Counterparty smart contracts on the bitcoin blockchain (`https://coinsutra.com/counterparty-xcp-cryptocurrency-everything-need-know/`).

This was a unique approach to provide maximum legitimacy of the project from the start. Counterparty justified it:

"By opting to distribute all XCP by proof-of-burn, the Counterparty developers eliminated any speculation that they planned to get rich quick or redistribute risk unequally. On the contrary, they put themselves in the same position as everyone else, backing their ideas with destroyed bitcoin to obtain XCP in the hope of eventually benefiting financially from their own project and hard work." (`https://counterparty.io/news/why-proof-of-burn/`).

These bitcoins were valued at $1.8 million USD at the time. Ouch!

Although proof-of-burn is still a technique used to remove coins or tokens from a system and to control supply, it is not used anymore to provide projects with legitimacy in the way that Counterparty did. However, Counterparty is proud to say that it is a community-funded project and has never raised funding or held an ICO.

Focusing on the Counterparty community, the company has a number of projects building on the platform and lists over 70,000 assets or tokens on its website (`https://xchain.io/`):

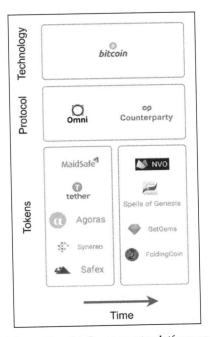

Figure 6: Tokens using the Counterparty platform and protocol

Out of all these Counterparty projects, the most interesting one is actually not on the list. It is called Storj (*pronounced storage*), which provides decentralized storage to compete against the likes of Dropbox, Google, and Amazon. The reason why Storj is interesting is because it ran an ICO on the July 18, 2014, using Counterparty and then did a second ICO on May 19, 2017, on the Ethereum platform!

Storj (SJCX)

The concept of Storj was that if users had spare disk space on their computers, they could rent it out, much like renting a room with Airbnb. It was a way of monetizing excess disk space. Instead of using bitcoins, users would use the SJCX token to pay for storage and receive SJCX tokens in return. Storj was its own little economy with its own price and supply.

Storj issued 500,000,000 SJCX tokens, using the Counterparty platform.

PHASE 1 - 10% Increase	0 - 1,800 BTC	38,500 SJCX per BTC
PHASE 2 - 5% increase	1,800 - 4,800 BTC	36,750 SJCX per BTC
PHASE 3 - Standard rate	4,800 - 9,800 BTC	32,480 SJCX per BTC

Figure 7: Storj terms of sales

The table above shows that for the first 1,800 bitcoins received by Storj, 38,500 SJCX would be allocated. The next phase would receive a little less SJCX tokens, and the last phase would receive the standard 32,480 tokens for each bitcoin received. There was a cap of 9,800 bitcoins, so anything over would not be accepted and would be refunded back to the sender. Storj also disclosed a pre-sale of 40,250 SJCX tokens for up to 200 bitcoins.

The crowdsale address was 132aBrspLgL54cm9eQf GNFLGqXwBRQrugc where it can be seen that 910 Bitcoins were received. This was worth around $460,000 USD as bitcoin, back in July 2014, was around $500 USD.

What is interesting with Storj is that the company moved away from the Counterparty platform to the Ethereum platform and did a second ICO! We'll explore this in more detail in the *Ethereum* section a little later on, but yet another platform called Factom was also built using the bitcoin blockchain.

Factom (FCT)

Factom is a practical blockchain solution for those seeking a collaborative platform to preserve, ensure, and validate digital assets. Factom provided a great analogy on bitcointalk:

"It is most easily understood as a protocol that provides unlimited books of blank paper. Users of the protocol can take a book, label it with the title of their choice, open the book, and write on a page. When that page is submitted to Factom it cannot be altered or deleted. Nobody can back-date a page. All the data written into the book is preserved in the order it was presented to the Factom protocol." (https://bitcointalk.org/index.php?topic=850070.0).

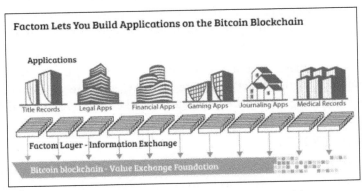

Figure 8: Uses of the Factom blockchain in the Factom white paper

Factom was born out of a conversation between Paul Snow (current CEO) and David Johnston (current chairman of the Factom board) on January 25, 2014, and an ICO was held just over a year later on March 31, 2015.

Factom was offering 2000 factoids for every bitcoin, reducing by 100 factoids every seven days. Factom ended up raising only 2,278 bitcoins at the address 35gLt5EgB367enjSjyEDahhWWcy6p1MGf6, which was the equivalent of $540,000 USD.

Then, several months later, in July 2014, Factom went on to raise a further $1.1 million USD on the crowdfunding website *BnkToTheFuture* for around 8% of the company's equity (https://www.financemagnates.com/cryptocurrency/news/factom-hits-1-millioncrowdfunding-goal-on-bnktothefuture/). Factom continued to raise funds in the traditional manner, with an additional $4.2 million USD raised in Oct 2016 and a further $8 million USD in April 2017.

In the early days, Factom boosted and blogged about the numerous partnerships it had with the likes of the Honduras Government, Coinapult, and Tether, among others. Building on the existing bitcoin blockchain was clever, in that it would strengthen the bitcoin technology and therefore strengthen the value. A user base was already established, so there was no need to promote an entirely new blockchain or build a new community, and it provided speed to market.

While these arguments were valid, others in the industry were thinking of the exact opposite strategy, and the challenges of building a bigger and better custom blockchain were too enticing.

Ripple (XRP)

Although Ripple was not built on the bitcoin blockchain, nor was it an ICO, it deserves special mention because it has a history that preceded bitcoin. To understand Ripple, it is important to go back and see how it all started.

The original concept behind Ripple started with Ryan Fugger back in 2004, when he was working for a local exchange in Vancouver. He created a credit network called Ripplepay, where the premise was to enable individuals to extend credit lines to friends and family (https://xrphodor.wordpress.com/2018/04/09/a-history-of-xrp-ripple-part-1-2011-2013/).

How did Ripplepay work?

Consider a situation where your friend Alice owes you $10. Without Alice having to pay you back, you could get creative and pass this debt on to someone else who knows and trusts Alice, in exchange for something you want. For example, you might be able to get a book you want from Bob, who also knows Alice. Instead of money, you can use Alice's IOU to pay Bob. Alice acts as an intermediary between you and Bob.

The Ripple pay service does the same thing, only it takes the idea one step further. What happens if you want to get a haircut from Carol, who doesn't know Alice at all? Your $10 IOU from Alice isn't useful because Carol being owed money by Alice doesn't mean anything to Carol. However, suppose you had a way to find out that Bob, who knows Alice, also knows Carol. You could talk to Bob and arrange for him to take Alice's IOU in exchange for giving his own IOU for $10 to Carol. Since Alice owes him exactly what he owes Carol, Bob is even on the deal. Both Alice and Bob act as intermediaries between you and Carol (`https://classic.ripplepay.com/about/`).

When was Ripple created?

Jed McCaleb, famously known for creating the bitcoin exchange Mt. Gox, and selling it to Mark Karpeles in February 2011, which then famously collapsed in 2014, started working on a new digital currency around May 2011 that was slightly different to bitcoin.

The key difference between the bitcoin network and the Ripple network is that all transactions happen between parties that know each other. Also, all parties on the Ripple network have a relationship of trust that doesn't exist on the bitcoin network, where parties trust the network but do not necessarily trust each other. So, because Ripple uses a network with a trust relationship, that is blockchain-based, banks can use it to move funds very quickly, yet there's still accountability of the participants of the network. In a way, this is how the modern banking system works already.

Arthur Britto, founder and chief strategist at Ripple, and David Schwartz, the chief cryptographer at Ripple, were also part of the team and they were joined by Chris Larsen, the current chairman of the board. Fugger agreed to support this new effort and the team founded a new company called OpenCoin in September 2012.

Funding

The company received several rounds of angel and seed funding in 2013, from the likes of Andreessen Horowitz, Lightspeed Venture Partners, Google Ventures, and IDG Capital Partners, totaling $9 million USD. OpenCoin then changed its name to Ripple Labs and made its entire source code open source. The latest raise was $55 million USD, which was series B in September 2016, bringing the total raised to $93 million USD. (https:// ripple.com/ripple_press/ripple-raises-55-million-series-b-funding/).

XRP coin

The biggest contentious issue is the 100 billion XRP coins that were created from day one. The initial distribution was 80 billion to the company and 20 billion for various founders. Then on February 20, 2013, Ripple started a promotion on the bitcointalk forum titled *Ripple Giveaway!*. It allowed anyone who had a bitcointalk account created before February 19, 2013 to claim 1000 XRP for free up to October 2013.

In 2017, Ripple decided to place 55 billion XRP into a cryptographically-secured escrow account with 55 contracts of one billion XRP each, that will expire on the first day of every month. As each contract expires, the XRP will become available for Ripple to use. Any unspent XRP will be returned back to the escrow queue. This was Ripple's attempt at forcing an issuance rate on a pre-created coin, removing uncertainty for users and avoiding speculation that Ripple could flood the market with these coins and thus completely devalue them.

The purpose of XRP

The key question remains: what are XRP used for? To answer that, Ripple's offering needs to be discussed. Ripple has three products: xCurrent, xRapid, and xVia.

xCurrent is the main payment network product built on a distributed ledger called Interledger, and the main goal is to provide interoperability between any and all currencies, not just cryptocurrencies. It doesn't operate on the same technology as XRP, which uses a separate system called XRP Ledger. Therefore, it does not use XRP coins.

xRapid, a liquidity solution, where companies can swap assets in and out of XRP, in order to move it through Ripple's xCurrent payment protocol faster, does use XRP, but this is not available yet. There is a "request for early access" application process on the website.

xVia, a payment interface designed to make the user experience of xCurrent and xRapid more intuitive, does not use XRP by default either and it is also at "request for early access" stage.

Particularly revealing is Ripple's FAQ page answering the question *why does Ripple utilize XRP holdings?*:

"Ripple XRP holdings incentivize the company to make Ripple as useful as possible. XRP exists as a native asset on Ripple for anti-spam transaction purposes, and for currency bridging only if beneficial to users. Otherwise, the use of XRP in transactions is completely optional." (https://ripple.com/technical-faq-xrp-ledger/).

A comment from David Schwartz also revealed the purpose of the XRP coins:

"Ripple's targeted use case for XRP is settling international payments. This will require a significant expenditure of money to make it happen. A key reason nobody has done something similar to date is simply that there was no good way to make money at it.

Because Ripple holds so much XRP, Ripple can capture a significant fraction of the value of any future increases in the price of XRP. This gives Ripple a revenue model to justify the expenditures needed to position XRP as a settlement asset.

Ripple's 60+ billion XRP is Ripple's secret sauce, the thing it has that its competitors don't have, that will allow it to spend tens of millions of dollars and attract top talent to build a high-speed, low-cost, cross-currency settlement system." (https://www.quora.com/Why-is-Ripple-holding-50-billion-XRP).

In summary, the XRP coin has limited utility value. It primarily functions as spam prevention and a revenue model to fund the business. Ripple also lack decentralization, holds enormous amounts of coins, and employs a questionable strategy around how it is being marketed and sold to investors. However, the ledger-based payment network technology, targeting banks as the main customers, seems to work and is a very smart move, and the company is well-funded to achieve its goal.

ICOs on custom blockchains

While Omni and Counterparty were busy building new features, based on the existing bitcoin blockchain, and providing services to companies such as MaidSafe, Tether, and Storj, others in the crypto space saw the limitations of the bitcoin blockchain technology. First of all, there were technical limitations in terms of speed, performance, and scalability. The programming language script was not widely used, and it was limited in features; progress and innovation were dependent upon the bitcoin developers. From all of this, several projects emerged, such as Ethereum, Lisk, Waves, and Tezos:

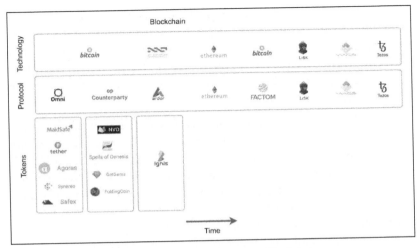

Figure 9: ICOs developing custom blockchains

The first project, though, was Nxt, which appeared very early on in 2013.

Nxt

Nxt (pronounced "next") calls itself a "cryptocurrency constructed from scratch using open source Java" and states in its white paper:

"A total quantity of 1 billion available tokens were distributed in the genesis block." (`https://www.dropbox.com/s/cbuwrorf672c0yy/NxtWhitepaper_v122_rev4.pdf`).

The ICO was very low key, being announced on the bitcointalk forum in September 2013. There was no associated website or traditional white paper, or anything that we are used to with ICOs nowadays. The ICO closed in November 2013, raising only 22 Bitcoins or the equivalent of $14,000 USD. The tokens were proportionally distributed to 99 participants based on their contributions (`https://bitcointalk.org/index.php?topic=303898.msg3641968#msg3641968`). That's a lot of tokens!

What Nxt attempted to provide was the next generation in blockchain technologies. In its white paper, Nxt talked about a payment system, along with other features, such as voting and polling, asset issuance and management, as well as a marketplace of digital goods. The Nxt token would be used for all these purposes.

Although the ICO may not have raised a large sum of money, Nxt is fascinating in terms of how it has structured its company and its products over the years. Nxt created Ardor in mid-2016, which is a blockchain platform marketed as the new and improved version of Nxt. It claimed scalability and new additional features, like messaging and voting. Nxt then announced the incorporation of Jelurida, which holds the intellectual property rights of the Nxt software and the Ardor platform (https://nxtplatform. org/introducing-jelurida/). Ignis is the first application on the Ardor platform, described as the *first child chain* of Ardor.

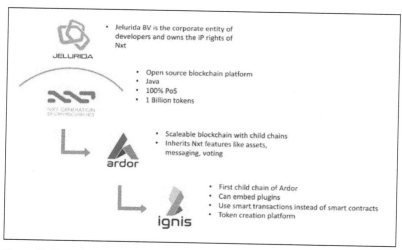

Figure 10: The relationship between the various entities under the Jelurida umbrella

This all gets very complicated very quickly and ignores the fact that Jelurida, Ardor, and Ignis have their own tokens, namely JLRDA, and ARDR, IGNIS! Let's put all this on hold for now.

Ethereum

On July 22, 2014, the Ethereum ICO took place and raised a staggering 31,550 bitcoins, worth $18.4 million USD. This ICO was a huge success and ended up topping the charts in 2014, raising over three times more than its closest rival.

The sales term was explained as:

"The price of ether is initially set to a discounted price of 2000 ETH per BTC, and will stay this way for 14 days before linearly declining to a final rate of 1337 ETH per BTC. The sale will last 42 days, concluding at 23:59 Zug time September 2." (https://blog.ethereum.org/2014/07/22/launching-the-ether-sale/).

In other words, one bitcoin would obtain 2000 ether for the first 14 days. Afterwards, it would drop at a constant rate, down to 1337 on the 28th day.

What is interesting to note is that the number 1337 is a code word for *elite* in hacker speak, used to describe formidable prowess or accomplishment. Elite is pronounced as "eet". "E" is often written as "3", as it resembles the letter when reflected vertically, "l" becomes the numerical number "1" and "t" becomes "7", hence elite => leet =>1337.

Ethereum officially launched on July 30, 2015, at Ethereum block number 1,028,201.

Computer programmers love numbers. 1,028,201 was chosen because it is both a prime number and a palindrome. A palindrome is a word or number that reads the same backwards as forwards. For example, madam.

No one could have predicted the success that Ethereum would experience in the coming years, especially since other blockchain platforms were constantly sprouting up. Two further platforms that had an ICO in 2016 were Lisk and Waves.

Lisk (LSK)

Lisk is an another blockchain platform, that uses a programming language called JavaScript. This was chosen because JavaScript is an extremely popular language for web-based technologies. The platform is not as interesting as its history, though. Lisk actually started out as a blockchain platform called Crypti, that was launched on the bitcointalk forum in June 2014:

"Crypti is a next generation platform that allows for the development and distribution of JavaScript based decentralized applications with an easy to use, fully-featured ecosystem. Through Crypti, developers can build, publish, distribute, and monetize their applications within a cryptocurrency powered system that utilizes custom blockchains, smart contracts, cloud storage, and computing nodes, all from within one industry solution." (https://bitcointalk.org/index.php?topic=654463.0).

The concept here was similar to Ethereum, but a different programming language was used, along with a "modular cryptocurrency" concept. This modular approach uses a concept of sidechains to infinitely extend the scalability of a digital asset ecosystem, without impacting the speed or performance of the core blockchain.

Interestingly, Crypti did an ICO using the terminology "IPO" throughout all of its discussions in the forums (https://bitcointalk.org/index.php?topic=654463.msg7777041#msg7777041). It started in early July 2014 and finished around eight days later, raising 750 Bitcoins (https://bitcointalk.org/index.php?topic=654463.msg7908754#msg7908754).

However, there were disagreements and two of the original team members, Max Kordek and Oliver Beddows, decided to leave the team and fork (make a copy) of the Crypti code and rebrand it to Lisk. This was announced in a blog at the end of January 2016 and they conducted their ICO just three weeks later in February 2016 (https://blog.lisk.io/olivier-and-max-leave-crypti-to-establish-lisk-3fd60eb0808f).

The Lisk ICO raised $5.7 million USD and provided an exchange rate for those holding Crypti to convert to LSK. The Lisk ICO created 100 million coins initially and using Lisk terminology, "forged" 12.6 million new coins in the first year, set to decrease after that to 3 million LSK every year from the year 2020 onwards. (https://www.reddit.com/r/Lisk/comments/6ro198/anyone_know_the_max_supply/).

Lisk is used in the digital asset ecosystem to pay for fees to access various services. There are fees for making transactions, creating delegates, voting, building on the platform and so on. Although LSK is not limited to fees, there is still a lot of confusion, which led to the founders writing a blog post titled *What Is Lisk? And What It Isn't* to help to clarify (https://blog.lisk.io/whatis-lisk-and-what-it-isnt-e7b6b6188211).

Waves (WAVES)

Waves appeared on the scene in early 2016 and only two months after Lisk, on April 12, 2016, Waves ended up raising 30,094 Bitcoins, worth $16 million USD. This was the highest ICO raise in 2016 according to *Coinschedule*.

Waves is defined as a versatile 2.0 platform that allows users to trade tokens of value on a fully-decentralized network. Some of the features it provides include a multicurrency wallet, decentralized exchange, crowdfunding, or *crowdstarting* in Waves terminology, decentralized voting and also an encrypted messenger service. The WAVES token is required to utilize all these features.

> **2.0**: A popular term (pronounced *two point oh*) used as a suffix to indicate a next version, which is better than the last. This is very similar to **NG** meaning **next generation** or **next-gen**.

Waves only created 100 million tokens. No more tokens will be created, and they were all distributed on day one. That is, there will be no minting or releasing of the WAVES tokens slowly over time into the ecosystem. The most interesting part to note is that Waves launched a new asset called **Miner Reward Tokens** (**MRT**) in March 2017, about a year after the ICO, which is used to incentivize miners on the network (https://blog.wavesplatform.com/incentivizing-pos-mining-b26f8702032c).

Total WAVES To Be Produced

The Waves ICO period was from April 12, 2016 – May 31, 2016. During this ICO, $16,436,095 was raised (equivalent to 30,096.7 BTC).

ICO Investors	85 Million Allocated
Pre-ICO bounties	1 Million Allocated
Post-ICO bounties	1 Million Allocated
Strategic partners and backers	4 Million Allocated
Development & Marketing	9 Million Allocated
In Total	100 Million

Figure 11: Waves token allocation [3]

What is even more interesting is that Sasha Ivanov, the founder, introduced this as a "temporary solution" and miners can use this token to vote for certain network parameters, similar to what is done in bitcoin. The Waves mining calculator increases the confusion because it shows WAVES tokens being minted alongside MRT, which suggests that WAVES tokens are not capped at 100 million.

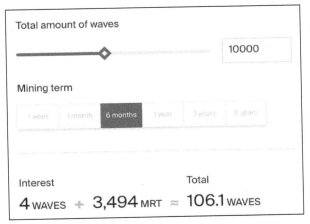

Figure 12: Reward calculator for earning WAVES and MRT [4]

Finally, Waves added a **Waves Community Token (WCT)** to the mix, to provide a tool for the community assessment of crowdfunding campaigns and to incentivize long-term holding by providing an additional income stream. Moreover, WAVES, MRT, and WCT are all tradable tokens with a price, albeit on Waves' own decentralized exchange.

Tezos (XTZ)

Tezos is a new decentralized blockchain that governs itself by establishing a true digital commonwealth. A commonwealth is a group linked with common objectives and interests. What this really means is that Tezos wanted to avoid the conflicts and problems in first-generation blockchains, such as Bitcoin and Ethereum, where the decisions on where to take the technology were primarily given to the core development team and the miners. There was no formal governance or rules in place to resolve conflict and Tezos wanted to change this.

An example would be when a developer offers a protocol upgrade. If it is included in the upgrade, they would be compensated for their work with tokens. This approach provided a strong incentive to improve the core development of the Tezos blockchain, and naturally decentralizes the maintenance and upkeep of the network.

The founders, Arthur and Kathleen Breitman, had been developing Tezos since 2014 and Arthur released a "position paper" on August 3, 2014, under the cheeky pseudonym of "L. M. Goodman", a thinly-veiled reference to the *Newsweek* journalist Leah McGrath Goodman, who incorrectly identified the creator of bitcoin.

 Position paper: An essay that presents an arguable opinion about an issue – typically that of the author or some specified entity.

The token, named *Tezzies*, will drive the Tezos platform, which was built from the ground up, and will be required for running smart contracts, storage costs, compensating developers as mentioned above, and also allowing votes on changes to the protocol. Decentralized governance is at the core of the project.

The ICO started on July 1, 2017, lasting 13 days, and followed the example set by the Ethereum Foundation, with no cap on the amount of contributions that was accepted. This was explained in the Tezos white paper:

"Participation is not limited only to insiders or the "fast-fingered." The Tezos development team believes that an un-capped fundraiser will promote a widespread distribution of the tokens, a necessary prerequisite to launching a robust network. (https://www.tezos.com/static/papers/Tezos_Overview.pdf)."

Tezos ended up raising a whopping 65,703 Bitcoins and 361,122 ether, totaling around $233 million USD! This ended up being the second largest raise in 2017. Unfortunately, Tezos has been marred with controversy since its ICO, over infighting between the founders and the Swiss foundation that they were working with. The infighting has been made quite public and has resulted in delays and broken promises. With a project that raised so much and promised even more, the story of Tezos is still evolving.

NEM (XEM)

NEM is a peer-to-peer crypto platform and is written in Java and JavaScript, with 100% original source code, which means it has its own blockchain. It launched on March 31, 2015 and its primary function is the implementation of what NEM calls the *Smart Asset System*. This system gives users the ability to implement a customized blockchain for their own specific smart contract.

One major difference between Ethereum and NEM is how they handle smart contracts. Ethereum has smart contract functions coded right into the blockchain, whereas NEM doesn't have a concept of a smart contract. It expects applications to hold the functions necessary to manage the token logic and only has the ledger managed by NEM.

The announcement of NEM on bitcointalk, though, was a little confusing. On January 19, 2014, NEM was announced on bitcointalk:

"A groundbreaking cryptocurrency that gives control of their economy back to the people and establishes them as sovereigns over their own destiny. A currency is an expression of a political ideology and social attitude. Do not mistake us as just another cryptocurrency. We are more than a cryptocurrency, we are a New Economy Movement." (https://bitcointalk.org/index. php?topic=422129.0).

In this announcement, NEM stated that it was initially designed as a fork of Nxt, utilizing proof of stake as its consensus algorithm, with a total supply of four billion coins. However, six months later, on June 16, 2014, it was then re-announced that its blockchain would be built from scratch using a proof-of-importance consensus algorithm instead (`https://bitcointalk.org/index.php?topic=654845.0`). The supply was also changed to 8,999,999,999 XEMs or one XEM short of nine billion.

NEM didn't do an ICO. It did a *call for participation* where bitcointalk users had to register their interest in order to receive XEMs. It received approximately 66 BTC and 419,697 NXT, which was anywhere between $65,000 USD and $100,000 USD. (`reddit.com/r/ethereum/comments/6zfihg/ethereums_erc20_token_standard_has_been`):

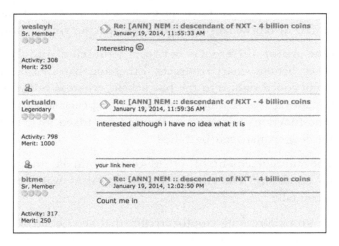

Figure 13: Bitcointalk users registering their interest in order to receive XEMs
(https://bitcointalk.org/index.php?topic=422129.80)

Side note – proof of importance

One unique aspect of NEM is how the network agrees or comes to a consensus. NEM uses an algorithm called proof of importance, which is a modification of the proof-of-stake algorithm. It determines all the transactions over 1000 XEMs made in the last 30 days, sent to other eligible users, and allocates an outlinking score. It uses this outlinking score to determine another score called NCDawareRank (Nearly Completely Disposable), which is a formula to determine how important a node is in the network. This is similar to Google's PageRank for determining how important certain webpages are and what order to display them on the search results page. Then the network calculates the final score using the total vested amount, the outlinking score and the NCDawareRank, plus a weighting factor.

Let's now take a breather from all these custom blockchains, with their own cryptocurrencies or tokens, and focus on one custom blockchain called Ethereum, which has really been the standout in the past few years.

ICOs on the Ethereum blockchain

Towards the end of 2015, a handful of companies started using Ethereum to raise funds for their projects, but no one could have predicted the success that it was about to have. What Ethereum did was take the blockchain cryptocurrency concept to the next level. It not only provided faster transaction speeds, but it added flexibility, and essentially brought a new meaning to programmable money.

Creating tokens on the bitcoin blockchain was somewhat problematic. The bitcoin blockchain was essentially the technology layer; Omni, or Counterparty would be the protocol layer; and applications such as MaidSafe would then represent the token layer. That is a lot of complexity, not to mention a lot of layers. Why not just use one layer to build applications on top of? The thinking at the time was that the bitcoin blockchain was the largest and most secure network, so why not make use of that? What Ethereum did was to reinvent the wheel. It was a risk, but one worth taking:

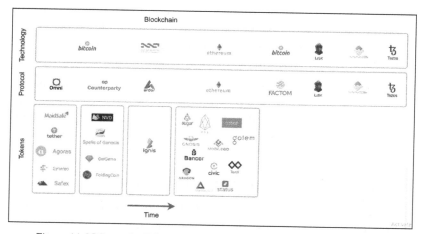

Figure 14: ICOs on the Ethereum platform. Technically, some of the ICOs, such as EOS, Bancor, and Golem, are protocols themselves but they launched ERC20 tokens on the Ethereum platform.

Augur (REP)

Augur was the first to use Ethereum to create a token, in September 2015, and can be defined in several ways. From its white paper:

"Trustless, decentralized platform for prediction markets. It is an extension of bitcoin Core's source code which preserves as much of bitcoin's proven code and security as possible."

From its website:

"Augur allows users to trustlessly create prediction markets on the outcome of any future event."

From Wikipedia:

"A trustless, open-source, decentralized oracle, and prediction market platform built on the Ethereum blockchain."

Augur was based on ideas from Truthcoin, created by Paul Sztorc, and was originally going to use the bitcoin blockchain, as indicated from its original white paper in mid-2014. (`http://bitcoinhivemind.com/blog/case-against-augur/`). The team then changed to the Ethereum blockchain and explained their decision in a blog post in February 2015 (`https://web.archive.org/web/20150216124251/http://www.augur.net/blog/why-ethereum`): Ethereum provided smart contract features, as well as faster iteration cycles.

The theory behind prediction markets is that if you ask enough people something, their average answer is usually far more accurate than that of any expert, in a concept known as the wisdom of the crowd. Previous prediction markets were centralized and relied on a small group of individuals to report on events that occurred. In a decentralized system, thousands of users can report on events and anyone in the world can create a market by asking a question. Anyone can then buy and sell shares in the outcome of that market.

 Wisdom of the crowd: The collective opinion of a group of individuals, rather than that of a single expert.

Another way to understand Augur is that it's a way of people voting or guessing on things that will happen in the future. Some also call this gambling. People are voting with their money that something will occur. The pitch from Augur, though, is not gambling but the ability to Google the future via the wisdom of the crowd. The incentive is that if people correctly predict an event, by putting their money on the line they will get more money in return or, in this case, more tokens.

The token name is **Reputation** or **REP**. Think of casino chips but swap out the casino for a virtual decentralized world, where it is not a black or red number on a felt table but any question that anyone wants to ask.

Augur's ICO started on August 17, 2015 and ended on October 1, 2015. It lasted 45 days and collected 18,000 Bitcoins and 1.1 million ether, which at the time represented $5.2 million USD. The supply was 11 million REP tokens, of which 80% or 8.8 million tokens were up for public sale. (http://augur. strikingly.com/blog/the-augur-crowdsale).

ICONOMI (ICN)

Out of all the 50-plus ICOs in 2016, Waves topped the list with the most raised, as mentioned, followed by ICONOMI ($10.4 million USD (https://www.smithandcrown.com/ICONOMI-raises-10-million-ico/)). ICONOMI is a decentralized crypto-fund platform. There is a semi-social dimension too, since you can follow your favorite asset manager.

The team created a Digital Asset Management Platform, the purpose of which is to allow anyone to invest in and manage digital assets. In other words, the purpose is to allow beginners to invest in multiple cryptocurrencies or tokens, which we'll call digital assets, all at once.

ICONOMI launched with two flagship funds, which is comparable to an index fund and a performance fund. Essentially, this means that an investor can buy into a basket of digital assets, instead of buying them individually. The performance fund is similar to a hedge fund, where they are managed more aggressively, with the ability to make money when the market is falling, and they are typically targeted towards more sophisticated investors.

ICONOMI's ICO ran for five weeks, from August 25, 2016, to September 26, 2016, and accepted investments in crypto and in fiat. What ICONOMI raised can be broken down as follows:

◆ 6,901.2770 BTC, around 4,210,883 USD

◆ 199,205.8296 ETH, around 2,557,802 USD

◆ 3,995,992.5646 LSK, around 895,897 USD

◆ 2,329,478.91 EUR, around 2,599,018 USD

◆ 131,454.20 USD

It was interesting to see ICONOMI accept Lisk as a payment option. This would have created more demand for LSK as well. Max Kordek, the CEO and co-founder of Lisk, was part of the four-person escrow team. Lisk is also a competitor to Ethereum, on which the ICONOMI ICO was undertaken.

100 million ICN tokens were created and 85%, or 85 million, were made available during the ICO. The remaining 15% were held for the team, advisors, and for marketing campaigns.

To understand how the ICN token works, the concept of DAA needs to be explained. **DAA** stands for **Digital Asset Array**. This is a group of digital assets like Bitcoin, Ethereum, Litecoin, Waves, Lisk, and Augur. An external DAA manager creates the portfolio and sets the strategy: high risk, medium risk, low risk, or something to that effect. ICONOMI also has its own fund called **BLX (Columbus Capital Blockchain Index)** and **CCP (Columbus Capital Pinta)**.

Investors invest into these funds, which attract monthly fees similar to existing investment funds. For example, with the BLX, each investor has to pay an annual fee of 3%, which is calculated proportionally every six hours. In addition, everyone has to pay a sales fee of 0.5%. The closed-end CCP fund pays a 20% performance fee to ICONOMI. (`https://captainaltcoin.com/what-is-ICONOMI/`).

Figure 15: William Mougayar High Growth Cryptoassets Index [5]

ICONOMI then takes these fees and does an ICN buy back and burn. This, in theory, will decrease the supply and thus increase the value of the ICN token. ICONOMI's original vision was a dividend structure but this would have made it a security offering, meaning ICONOMI would have had to follow regulatory and compliance requirements in its operational jurisdiction around the world (`https://medium.com/market-caps/ICONOMI-token-usage-over-utility-ce6684db7d33`).

EOS (EOS)

From its white paper, EOS is a "new blockchain architecture designed to enable vertical and horizontal scaling of decentralized applications. This is achieved by creating an operating system-like construct upon which applications can be built. (`https://github.com/EOSIO/Documentation/blob/master/TechnicalWhitePaper.md`).

EOS claims the potential of performing millions of transactions per second and its smart contracts can be written using existing popular programming languages, avoiding the need to learn a new language like with Ethereum. EOS also designed its system with the idea of making creators of decentralized applications pay for use, instead of regular users. These are some of the reasons why many believe that EOS is the newer and improved version of Ethereum.

The key, though, is that EOS actually does not plan to be deployed as a blockchain platform of its own. It will provide the software to be leveraged by interested developers who want to develop their own blockchain solutions.

Although EOS is an Ethereum competitor, it ran a 12-month ICO on the Ethereum platform that finished on June 1, 2018, collecting a staggering 7.2 million ether or approximately $4.2 billion USD. What is interesting is that these tokens have no purpose, as stated in the EOS Token Purchase Agreement document in section 1.4:

"No Purpose. As mentioned above, the EOS Tokens do not have any rights, uses, purpose, attributes, functionalities or features, express or implied. Although EOS Tokens may be tradable, they are not an investment, currency, security, commodity, a swap on a currency, security or commodity or any other kind of financial instrument."

Some supporters believe that this is just "legal language," so EOS can steer clear of regulatory authorities, such as the US **Securities and Exchange Commission** (**SEC**), which is clamping down on ICOs, as we will discuss in *Chapter 6, Playing by the Rules.*

Bancor

Bancor is a network and a protocol. As a network, it allows anyone to convert any two tokens on the Bancor network, with no counterparty, at an automatically calculated price. As a protocol, it's a standard for ERC20 tokens, that allows smart contracts to connect to a liquidity network without needing to match buyers and sellers.

As an analogy, think of Bancor as a factory (Bancor platform) that allows you to make robots (smart contracts) that can automatically buy from or sell to anyone, at any time, any tokens that you invent. These tokens are backed by another token (reserve token) of your choice.

For example, say I invented a Toastmasters (a public speaking organization) token (TMT) and minted one million out of thin air as my supply. Members would then get one TMT for turning up, five for doing a speech, two for being the timekeeper and so on. This would be my distribution or minting model.

Currently, there are actually over 350,000 members worldwide, but imagine for the time being that Toastmasters has just started and there are only 5000 members. This is a very small market. It's difficult for a non-Toastmaster to buy a TMT token. They would have to search for or know a Toastmaster, the Toastmaster would have to be willing to sell and they would have to agree on a price. It's such an arduous process.

If the TMT was listed on an exchange, because there is a low number of participants (5,000 members) and maybe an even lower number buying and selling, this token would not be very liquid. That is, it would not be easily exchangeable and the spread (the difference between the buying and selling price) would be large (which is bad).

What I would do is choose a token that is more popular (has higher liquidity), with lots of people trading, such as bitcoin or ether, as my reserve token. So, if you wanted to buy TMT, you would use Bitcoins or ether and if you wanted to get rid of your TMT, you would get back Bitcoins or ether. The idea is that it is a lot easier and faster to go from TMT to bitcoin to USD than it is to go TMT to USD.

Bancor's ICO ended up raising $153 million USD, collecting 396,720 ether! As if that wasn't enough, the ICO did it in less than three hours.

ICOs on non-blockchain technologies

With all the commotion centered around blockchain technologies, there were some interesting non-blockchain technologies that came to light. IOTA and Hedera hashgraph are some examples.

IOTA

IOTA describes its technology as a *brand new and novel micro-transaction cryptotoken optimized for the Internet-of-Things* (http://iotatoken.io/iota.html). IOTA's approach is that instead of collecting all the transactions in a network and forming a group or a "block" of transactions, and linking them together to form a chain, all the transactions individually link to two other transactions to form this mess or tangle of transactions.

IOTA is the 9th letter of the Greek alphabet and means a small or tiny amount. As an acronym, **IOT** represents the **Internet of Things**. The A could mean anything from architecture to array or application.

Now, because IOT devices are due to explode into the billions, around low-powered sensor devices for machine-to-machine communications, IOTA intends to facilitate these transactions with a very small amount of IOTA tokens.

The token supply was initially 999,999,999 or one short of a billion tokens. The reason why it is referred to as a token is because the entire supply was distributed proportionally after the ICO, based on purchases received. For example, the idea was that if only two people invested in the ICO, by paying one bitcoin and two bitcoins respectively, then the first person would receive one third (333 million) of all IOTAs and the second person two thirds (666 million) of all IOTAs. In total there were 299 contributors.

IOTA then revised the total token supply to a whopping 2,779,530,283,277,761 which is 2.7 quadrillion tokens. This sounds like a lot, but bitcoin has 2.1 quadrillion satoshis. This is because a bitcoin can be subdivided into 18 decimal places, but the smallest unit of an IOTA is one.

The reason for the 2.7 quadrillion comes from what calculation?

$$\frac{\left(3^{33}-1\right)}{2} = 2,779,530,283,277,761$$

This is optimized for ternary computing. Ternary means that there are three states, -1, 0, and 1, instead of binary, where there are two states.

Skipping over the technical details, this is a different approach that took everyone by surprise and in November 2015, when the company launched its ICO, IOTA raised just over $500,000 USD from the community (`https://cointelegraph.com/news/iota-beta-internet-of-things`).

Hashgraph

Hashgraph, or the Hedera hashgraph platform, is a distributed ledger technology developed by Swirlds. It is a relatively new technology that claims to offer many of the same solutions as blockchain but uses a different way to send information and check transactions within the network. More formally, it is a data structure technology and consensus algorithm that claims to be faster, fairer, and more secure than blockchains.

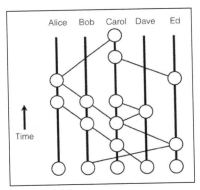

Figure 16: Visual depiction of a hashgraph

Instead of having transactions grouped together into a block and a puzzle to solve to decide the next block in the chain, information is spread to random neighbor nodes or computers constantly, in what is referred to as "gossiping." Then, agreements or decisions can be determined with a concept called "virtual voting," as described at hederahashgraph.com:

"Alice's computer does not send Bob's computer a vote over the internet, about what order the transactions were received. Instead, Bob calculates what vote Alice would have sent, based on his knowledge of what Alice knows, and when she learned it, according to the history in the hashgraph. This yields fair Byzantine agreement on a total order for all transactions, with very little communication overhead beyond the transactions themselves (https://www.hederahashgraph.com/faq#what-is-virtual-voting)."

Broadly speaking, hashgraph is another way to record transactions and agree on the state of these transactions.

[**Swirlds**: A portmanteau of the phrase "shared worlds"]

Hashgraph is the technology and Swirlds is the licensor of the underlying hashgraph technology, and has patents titled *Methods and apparatus for a distributed database within a network* (https://www.swirlds.com/ip/). Swirlds raised $3 million USD in seed funding on September 14, 2017, and as of writing has closed a $100M institutional round with a $20M accredited investor round (https://www.swirlds.com/swirlds-raises-3m-seed-round/). Hashgraph and Hedera are explained in more detail in *Chapter 12, The Future*.

The following diagram shows a landscape of how all the technologies, protocols and tokens fit together. Note that some technologies, such as bitcoin, can be both a technology, a protocol and a token, and that this is a simplified diagram.

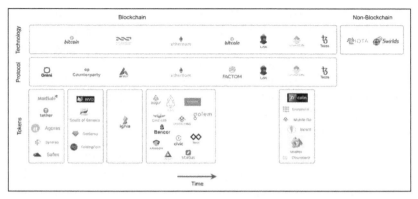

Figure 17: Distributed ledger technologies,
including the protocols and tokens they support

Summary

The blockchain and ICO landscape can be a daunting prospect to understand at first, due to the dizzying array of ICOs, but when viewed in a logical and chronological order, it should slowly start to make sense.

In this chapter, we learned that the first evolution of ICOs was when companies started building upon the existing bitcoin blockchain, such as Omni, Counterparty, and Factom. They did this to get started quickly without having to build their own blockchain. Then, alternative custom blockchains appeared, such as Nxt, Ethereum, Lisk, and Waves, each bringing their own unique advantages. Ethereum has been the stand out, though, with over 95% of ICOs performed on this platform, primarily due to first-mover advantage and the huge community support it has built up.

We have also seen the emergence of non-blockchain technologies, such as IOTA and hashgraph, that claim to be the next generation of technology, providing solutions to scalability and instant transactions, and removing the need to use enormous amounts of energy from mining. The technology is promising, but it is still very early days when compared to the 10-minute heartbeat (the 10-minute confirmation time of the bitcoin blockchain) that has been beating non-stop for almost a decade.

As all these platforms and ICO companies will continue to battle it out over the coming months and years, to provide value and build their user and supporter base, we will next look at how various companies developed the token idea and how you can start to develop yours.

References

1. https://coinmarketcap.com/currencies/omni/
2. https://coinmarketcap.com/currencies/tether/
3. https://coinsutra.com/waves-cryptocurrency/
4. https://wavesplatform.com/mining
5. https://www.iconomi.net/dashboard/

5

THE NEED
FOR A TOKEN

Blockchain and smart contract technologies have unleashed the ability to create all sorts of tokens, as highlighted in the previous chapter, including an increasing number of applications and tools to help to make the token creation process easier.

However, the most important question before we all rush out and start tokenizing the world is: what is the purpose of the token? Is it to access an application's service or product? Is it to incentivize users to grow an application or platform network? Is it, perhaps, to make an illiquid asset liquid? Is it purely to raise capital? Quite often, the answer is that a token starts out having one purpose and then changes to having a purpose that is a combination of all of the preceding points.

In this chapter, we will look at the following topics:

♦ Did these ICOs really need a token?

♦ Types of companies running ICOs

♦ Critical considerations when creating a token

There is no shortage of opinions on whether any new project in the blockchain space actually needs a token or not. On the one hand, there are critics that state that 99% of projects that create tokens don't actually need to. On the other hand, and not surprisingly, the projects themselves outline a business model that is totally dependent on a token and they explain the many uses of it. Before we look at this in more detail, let's first consider the purpose of a token.

The purpose of a token

All tokens in an ICO need to have a purpose and a function, and there are a number of models and definitions available discussing the various characteristics of tokens.

To help us to understand tokens, we can consider the money in our wallets. People work and produce goods or services, thus producing economic value. This value is exchanged for money and then the money can be spent on needs and wants, sometimes not necessarily in that order. The government controls the money supply and changes various aspects of it based on monetary and fiscal policies. The money we earn is spent within a country and if we want to spend overseas, we need to exchange it. This then creates the economy that we all participate in.

Let's now look at ICO projects where we have tokens. People work and produce value in exchange for tokens. The work can be in the form of producing content, such as blogs or videos, or the user giving their attention to an advertisement. The tokens can only be spent within the project and the ICO founders control the token supply and act like a government, where they essentially design the monetary and fiscal policies. To be spent outside the ICO project, the tokens need to be exchanged, typically for money to be spent on needs or wants. This creates the structure of an ICO token economy. It is actually a private economy because without the token, access to the ICO project's economy is not possible.

Therefore, we can compare the purpose of a token to the purpose of money, but from a slightly different perspective. From a business' perspective, the purpose of money enables it to achieve its goals: allowing new ideas, such as new platforms, systems, or applications, to be realized. From this perspective, tokens should have a similar function. The token is not the new invention: what the token enables is. With this in mind, let's see if some of these ICOs really needed a token.

Thought experiment #1 – monetizing excess digital storage

Let's create an application where users can rent out their spare hard drive space for some extra cash or, more appropriately, cryptocurrencies. Users can be a host and make storage available, and get paid, or be a renter and pay for storage.

The question is: how should we charge renters and compensate hosts? The most obvious answer is to use a cryptocurrency, such as bitcoin, not only because it is far easier but because it is more financially inclusive than fiat currency, and you don't need a bank account to send or receive bitcoins: you just need a bitcoin wallet. Imagine only five-cents-worth of storage being rented and requesting your bank to do a direct debit of five cents each day!

The challenge, though, is where to store contract information, such as the utilization of the renter or the uptime of the host, and how to ensure the reliability of the information. A regular centralized database could work, but a better option would be a distributed and decentralized database or, in other words, a blockchain (https://support.sia.tech/article/J92pGNrkTH-why-do-you-have-your-own-coin-and-blockchain).

The next question is: do we use an existing blockchain or create a new one? Let's choose to create a new one in this case. A blockchain needs its own cryptocurrency to function as an incentive mechanism in a network. This is because the native cryptocurrency of a blockchain is used to reward the transaction validator. Without this incentive, there would be no network in the first place. This cryptocurrency then becomes the native payment method for this application. In this situation, it is quite clear that this application, with its own blockchain, needs its own cryptocurrency.

The purpose of the token here is for payment between producers and consumers within this private economy. The cryptocurrency, or payment token, has enabled a new type of decentralized storage, using a trustless decentralized payment system.

This thought experiment is not entirely fictitious. Nebulous, a company established in 2014 and based in Boston, launched the **Sia** storage platform in 2015:

"Sia is a decentralized storage platform secured by blockchain technology. The Sia storage platform leverages underutilized hard drive capacity around the world to create a data storage marketplace that is more reliable and lower cost than traditional cloud storage providers." (https://sia.tech/).

Sia published its white paper in November 2014 and announced the project on bitcointalk in May 2015. Sia's own token or cryptocurrency is Siacoin and it is required to pay for storing files on the Sia network. It is also the reward that hosts receive for providing storage. This helps to align incentives across Sia's network.

The current supply of Siacoin is about 35 billion and it's important to note that there is no fixed supply. The issuance rate decreases over time and will have an inflation rate of about 2.2% in 2036. The founders have argued that, in the long run, the inflation rate will probably be lower than the Sia network growth rate minus the lost coins.

Sia built its own blockchain primarily to control its own destiny. The company did not want the risk of running the Sia application on another network and being subjected to network congestion or subjected to another party's road map. The custom blockchain has also allowed Sia to create its own smart contracts specifically for file storage.

What is interesting is that Sia has never held an ICO to fund its business. Instead, it created a second token called the Siafund and the sale of this token is how it funds its business. There are 10,000 Siafund tokens in total, of which 1,180 were sold in 2015 to help finance Sia's development team. The remainder is held by Sia's parent company Nebulous.

Sia, however, recently held another capital raise in April 2018 and sold 231 Siafunds at $7,500 each, resulting in about $1.7 million USD collected as part of its **Tokenized Security Offering (TSO)** (`https://blog.sia.tech/siafunds-tso-outcome-43bef1fed948`). Helpful statistics about Siafund can be found at `https://siastats.info/`.

Thought experiment #2 – monetizing excess processing power

Let's now turn our attention to another thought experiment, where users can be a host and provide processing power or be a renter and buy processing power. The processing power could be used to solve complex math problems or help to render graphical animation.

Again, we face the same scenario as in the first experiment, in that we need a payment system. In this example, though, instead of creating a new blockchain, let's use an existing one in the interest of simplicity and speed to market. For the sake of argument, let's choose Ethereum, which was introduced in *Chapter 2, A Bit of Coin Theory*. Now, we have a blockchain to store information on and the native currency of the blockchain, ether, to use as a payment system. Is another token really needed? It doesn't seem like it is.

Again, this thought experiment is not entirely fictitious. Golem is a global, open-source, decentralized supercomputer that anyone can access. It is made up of the combined power of users' machines, from PCs to entire data centers. Golem creates a decentralized sharing economy of computing power and supplies software developers with a flexible, reliable, and cheap source of computing power (https://golem.network/).

Golem ran an ICO in November 2016 and raised $8.6 million USD. It created one billion Golem tokens (GNT) and runs on the Ethereum network.

Golem ran a Reddit **AMA (Ask Me Anything)** on October 18, 2017, and one of the questions asked to the management team was "why is the use of the Golem network artificially gated behind the GNT token, rather than accepting ETH directly via smart contracts?" The response was as follows:

"From a purely technical point of view, you can imagine Golem without the GNT. This is not the entire picture, though, in particular this abstracts from economic rationale and incentives. Introduction of the GNT leads to network effects (e.g. interactions between projects using Golem infrastructure and thus using the GNT), as well as allows Golem to have a supportive community of users and early adopters, who are deeply interested in the platform growing. All of this would not be possible without the GNT. Also, it is obvious that the launch of the GNT made development of this project possible in the first place." (https://www.reddit.com/r/GolemProject/comments/76zddt/we_are_golem_team_ask_us_anything_we_will_answer/).

The purpose of the Golem token was to act as a form of payment, but ether could have performed this function. Golem itself admitted that, technically, it didn't need a token and the thought experiment arrived at the same conclusion. However, the arguments for the token from Golem were:

♦ The network effects
♦ It could be used as a funding mechanism

Reading between the lines, the token's purpose, first and foremost, was to allow Golem to raise funds to develop the product.

Thought experiment #3 – payment cards

Let's continue this train of thought and look at payment cards, such as TenX (previously mentioned in *Chapter 3, The Potential of ICOs*, when defining why TenX used the term "Initial Token Sale"). It raised $80 million USD in June 2017 and created a PAY token. The PAY token has two incentive schemes. First, users are rewarded in a credit-card style "cashback" program. Users earn a 0.1% reward for every purchase made, which is transferred back to the user in the form of PAY tokens, of course! Secondly, all PAY token holders will receive an incentive of 0.5% of the entire payment volume on the TenX payment platform.

However, the TenX white paper listed the main reason for the ICO, or ITS (Initial Token Sale):

"Bringing developers, marketing personnel, a legal team, designers and many other talented people on board will require additional funds. Offering an Initial Token Sale instead of a traditional venture capital round enables the community to participate in TenX's success story, rather than limiting it to a small, selected number of traditional venture capital funds." (https://www.tenx.tech/whitepaper/tenx_whitepaper_final.pdf).

From this, it is clear that the intention, or purpose, of TenX was to use the ICO purely as a funding mechanism to raise capital. The reward scheme was a secondary feature aimed at encouraging spending to earn PAY tokens, and the direct purchase of PAY tokens to effectively earn interest or dividends. The conclusion here is that payment cards do not need a token to function. Furthermore, the token itself does not carry any payment features or the ability to do anything with the token yet.

Thought experiment #4 – messaging platforms

Let's now create yet another application. This application will be a new messaging platform on the Ethereum blockchain, with the ability to:

♦ Register a username on the network

♦ Create group chats where only individuals holding a certain number of tokens can take part

♦ Pay celebrities to reply to your messages

♦ Find nearby users to buy or sell digital assets or cryptocurrencies

♦ Register decentralized applications in an app store

♦ Participate in a sticker/emoji market

♦ Vote on the direction of the messaging platform project

All of the features above could be implemented using the native ether cryptocurrency, although voting is a little challenging. It would be possible to manage the number of ether per vote, but having a custom token for voting purposes allows the ICO company more control over voting parameters, such as the price per vote, as well as the number of tokens required to vote.

Therefore, one could argue that messaging applications on Ethereum that have a voting mechanism, do require their own custom token. Status (further discussed in *Chapter 7, The Token Sales Mechanics*) and Kik Messenger are both messaging applications that created their own token (SNT and KIK) on the Ethereum platform.

Thought experiment #5 – decision-making platforms

Let's make things a bit more interesting by creating a platform where users can ask questions and receive answers. The question could be: *are multilingual people more creative?*

Using the Ethereum platform, we could ask users to send a small amount of ether to a *yes envelope* or send a small amount to the *no envelope*. This would work, but wouldn't it be better if there was an incentive mechanism for users to put their money where their mouth is, resulting in a more meaningful outcome?

An option would be to include an incentive mechanism that rewards those that predict the correct results and penalizes incorrect predictions. In this case, if someone is super confident that multilingual people are more creative, they can put more ether on the line. If the prediction turns out to be correct, they will get a return from those who predicted incorrectly.

Ether could still be used, but there would be some challenges. If the application is tightly coupled to the Ethereum platform, the application cannot create more ether or control how it is used.

For Augur, the prediction market platform introduced in the previous chapter, controlling these two aspects "was critical to the security model because a mechanism was needed for rewarding good behavior and punishing bad behavior in some situations where there is not necessarily symmetry between good actors and bad actors." (https://augur.stackexchange.com/questions/491/what-makes-rep-tokens-a-critical-component-of-augur).

Augur also has a feature where REP tokens can split into multiple versions upon a dispute. There will be one version for each possible outcome of the disputed market and token holders must then exchange their REP tokens for one of these versions. Versions of REP tokens that do not correspond to real-world outcomes will become worthless. In this design, the REP token is a utility token, and this is essential for Augur to function correctly.

Did these ICOs really need a blockchain?

We may have established whether these ICOs needed their own tokens or not, but did they need a blockchain? The ICOs that didn't need a token may or may not have required a blockchain, but there is a growing argument that suggests that although blockchain technologies are relatively new and still evolving, we could be only a handful of years away from a situation where the question will be reversed to: *why would you not build your business using the blockchain?*

There are several reasons why a blockchain is useful:

- Using a blockchain means that you don't have to build or own any databases. The blockchain concept, or system of blockchains, provides this already. Think of Ethereum connected to distributed file systems, such as the **Inter Planetary File System (IPFS)**, Storj, or Sia.

- Traditional systems generally use centralized servers, making them juicy targets for malicious attacks. Equifax, Target, and Sony may ring a bell. Instead of having a small group of centralized servers, a decentralized network makes attacks much more difficult.

- Redundancy is automatically provided. The same set of information is distributed across the world, so you don't have to worry about backups and if a handful of computers fails, the entire network is not compromised.

To make a system that is secure, resistant to failure, and redundant is hard. The blockchain network has this already and although scalability is a challenge, it's a problem in any scenario for any growing technology. To understand why you would not build your business on or using a blockchain, let's look at an analogy.

SaaS analogy

Software as a Service or **SaaS** (pronounced *sass*) is a prime example of how a new technological concept is adopted over time and how companies are predominantly designing their applications with the cloud in mind. They never used to do this!

In the mid-2000s, a huge movement was started promoting the use of software in the cloud or on the internet. Instead of buying an accounting application, such as MYOB, on a CD and installing it on a computer within a company, why not just have MYOB provide the application over the internet? This would remove the need to have a dedicated person managing that computer and all the software on it.

There were lots of arguments surrounding why this was a bad idea. For instance, the data would be stored in an unknown data center somewhere and looked after by someone else, leading to potential security issues. Another argument was that internet speeds were slow, leading to a negative user experience. The infrastructure was also immature and still needed to scale.

However, innovative companies that saw the opportunity architected their systems for the cloud, knowing that the infrastructure would improve over time, storage would become cheaper, and internet speeds would dramatically improve.

These companies then changed their pricing model, away from hundreds or thousands of dollars per year, to a few dollars per user per month and now, over 10 years later, using applications in the cloud has become normal for most consumers and businesses around the world.

In 2012, MYOB launched MYOB Essentials, which is its cloud-based accounting software product. Even Microsoft couldn't avoid the SaaS concept and created Office 365, which is its online subscription version of Microsoft Office for around $10 USD/ month for a single user.

This analogy is used to highlight that blockchain technologies will follow a similar path. Innovative individuals and companies can see the impact of blockchains and tokens, and are architecting systems and applications with these concepts in mind, believing that infrastructure challenges such as scalability will be solved. Therefore, instead of a rigid decision tree or flowchart with hard and fast rules to determine whether a blockchain is needed or not, a more open view, looking at the potential of the technology, is what these ICOs have focused on.

Types of companies running ICOs

There are two broad categories of companies running ICOs and creating their own tokens. The first and most popular category is new blockchain-based startups that plan to revolutionize the world and decentralize everything in their path. Then there are existing and established companies that want to jump on this ICO train and explore the new opportunities available. We will first explore existing companies and how they participated in the ICO craze.

Existing companies running ICOs

There are typically two categories of companies that enter the ICO space: companies that already use some sort of virtual currencies or loyalty reward systems and see crypto tokens as a natural evolution, and companies that don't but want to change their strategy to include a token of some sort. One of the most popular industries that uses virtual currencies is the gaming industry.

GameCredits (GAME)

Virtual currencies in computer games have been around for a long time but they only really took off in the early 2000s, with the introduction of games such as World of Warcraft, The Sims 2, and Second Life. These games would simulate virtual economies and marketplaces and allow players to trade all sorts of virtual goods and services. With these similarities, the industry was practically begging for a shift to actual cryptocurrencies.

In February 2014, a Gamercoin was created and announced on the bitcointalk forums (`https://bitcointalk.org/index.php?topic=481173.0`). It had a supply of 84 million coins and could be mined in a similar fashion to that of bitcoin. However, it lacked support and interest from the community, and was subsequently rebranded to GameCredits in April 2015 (`https://bitcointalk.org/index.php?topic=481173.msg10966783#msg10966783`). With a new team, new leadership, and renewed support, a company was then formed where the team consisted of several original founders of the GameCredits cryptocurrency, along with Sergey Sholom as the CEO.

Sholom co-founded Datcroft Games in 2004 and over the past 13 years, the company has developed multiple games, with more than 10 million players worldwide and over seven million registered accounts on just one game called Fragoria. Sholom combined his knowledge, experience, and background in the gaming industry with the GameCredits cryptocurrency to build real-world applications.

GameCredits, or GAME, then grew from a cryptocurrency to an ecosystem and platform, and is designed to be the basic currency of a free plug and play gaming monetization platform. In other words, the company built the whole infrastructure for gaming on top of the blockchain: a wallet, a payment and tracking system, an API, and GameHub.

GameCredits then partnered with Datcroft Games and implemented the first ever cryptocurrency mobile online gaming store. It has an in-built proprietary payment gateway, which allows gamers to use GameCredits to buy in-game content.

The next evolution was the creation of a token called MobileGo. The purpose of the MobileGo crowdsale was to help fund the marketing and branding of the GameCredits Mobile Store and the development of smart contract technology within the platform using the Ethereum blockchain (`https://gamecredits.com/wp-content/uploads/2018/03/MobileGo-Whitepaper.pdf`).

The MobileGo tokens would then be used to facilitate peer-to-peer match play and decentralized tournaments around the world. The tokens also functioned as a reward scheme for content creators and provided new opportunities for gamer-audience interaction. This was required because the original GAME coin did not have any smart contract capabilities.

GameCredits launched the MobileGo ICO on April 25, 2017, and ended up raising $53 million USD, which was the largest ICO at the time.

For GameCredits, a token was a logical choice to integrate into its offering. Its strategy was also clever. The GAME coin utility token was successful because GameCredits had a solid history and an existing community, as well as a partnership with Datcroft Games, an existing successful gaming business that provided the credibility. The MobileGo ICO then provided the additional capital to continue executing the dream. All this is something that Sholom and his team would have foreseen and capitalized on.

Kin from Kik (KIN)

Kik Messenger (known as Kik) is a free instant messenger mobile app developed by Kik Interactive in 2009 and an example of a company integrating a token into its business model. According to Crunchbase, excluding the ICO, Kik had raised a total of $120 million USD in five fundraising rounds. Prior to the ICO, the most recent fundraising round was in 2015, at a valuation of $1 billion USD.

Kik also boasts over 300 million registered users but still lags behind giants such as WhatsApp, WeChat, and Facebook Messenger. Perhaps that is why it saw a rewards token as something that could help the company and become a key differentiator.

In 2014, Kik ran a two-year experiment where users could earn points by performing valuable actions. The company observed an average of 300,000 transactions per day, reaching 2.6 million transactions a day at the experiment's peak. This experiment was invaluable for demonstrating that there was a demand for an economy around a chat-based application. Kik intended to integrate a token into its application and extend it to create VIP groups, premium user-generated content, tipping, and bot monetization.

Kik ran its ICO in September 2017 for 14 days and raised $97 million USD, creating 10 trillion KIN tokens, with around 10,000 investors. What this demonstrated was that not only was there appetite for existing companies to do an ICO, but the chance of a successful raise was increased with an existing business model and a large existing user base.

Kik, however, recently ran into technical problems with the Ethereum platform and is currently undertaking the challenging task of building its own blockchain, which will be a hybrid of Ethereum and Stellar. The good news is that the company has the funds to do this.

Brave's BAT

Brave Software is a company founded in May 2015 that raised $4.5 million USD in August 2016, in addition to the $2.5 million USD in angel funding, for its new open-source desktop and mobile browser, that blocks invasive advertisements and online trackers to provide a faster and safer web experience (https://www.wsj.com/articles/braveraises-4-5-million-to-fuel-growth-of-ad-blockingbrowser-1470060544).

At that time, Brave's aim was to change the online advertising ecosystem with faster and safer browsing, along with bitcoin micropayments and opt-in anonymous advertisements to share revenue with users and to support publishers. Brave then moved to create and support its own token (BAT) with an ICO in May 2017.

Basic Attention Token or BAT is an open-source, decentralized digital advertising platform based on Ethereum and was co-founded by Brendan Eich, the creator of JavaScript and the co-founder of Mozilla and Firefox, and by Brian Bondy.

While the BAT ICO will be remembered for raising $35 million USD in under 30 seconds, it's the backstory of what Brave is that is much more interesting. The Brave browser works in two modes. The first mode is a simple browser that has advertising blockchain technology built directly into the browser. Now, because Brave strips out many of the tracking features of adverts, it greatly speeds up page loading times. Also, because many of the data-heavy adverts are removed, less bandwidth is consumed, which is particularly relevant on mobile devices.

In the second *opt in* mode, Brave is designed to "monitor users' attention," logging what they do and which sites they visit. Brave can then build a profile with this data. Brave explains the idea:

"Ads are then anonymously matched with customer interests using local machine learning algorithms. This means less irrelevant ads."

The three components of the ecosystem are:

♦ **Advertisers**: Purchase advertising space on the platform with BAT tokens

♦ **Publishers**: Receive BAT tokens based on user attention

♦ **Users**: Rewarded with BAT tokens for their attention

The success of the BAT ICO was that it was wrapped around an existing product: the Brave browser. There was an excellent team in place, it had gone through the rigors of securing seed funding, and the ICO was a natural progression. This is another example of an existing company running an ICO very successfully.

Eastman Kodak Company – KODAKOne

The Kodak company is a story written into folklore. Founded in 1888, it commanded 90% of film sales and 85% of camera sales at its peak (*The Search for Survival: Lessons from Disruptive Technologies, Lucas, Henry C., Praeger, 2012*), only to eventually file for bankruptcy in 2012. What makes the story even more fascinating is that Steven Sasson, an electrical engineer who worked at Kodak in 1975, invented the digital camera.

Kodak is a perfect example of an existing "legacy" company, with no business model related to blockchains or tokens, jumping onto the ICO train. Kodak announced KODAKCoin on January 9, 2018 and immediately saw its share price jump three-fold.

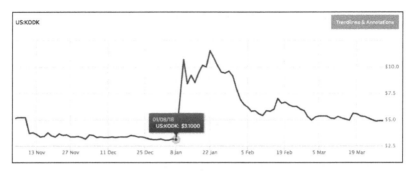

Figure 1: Kodak's share price jumps upon the announcement of KODAKCoin
(http://quotes.wsj.com/KODK/advanced-chart)

The idea of KODAKOne is to create an image rights management platform that will create an encrypted digital ledger of rights ownership for photographers, who can then license the assets from within the platform. Blockchain-based smart licensing and smart contracts will be utilized to automate the transactions and the KODAKCoin is used to receive payment and sell work.

This is basically technical jargon for a marketplace, otherwise known as a website, where photographers can sell their work and get paid in KODAKCoin. It is not entirely exciting or unique, as there are existing platforms already that allow musicians and artists to monetize their work.

The roadmap indicates that it is still early days, as the company plans to start development of the platform in the third quarter of 2018. At the end of 2018, it aims to complete the development of identity management and integration of the various proofs of concept into the platform. The anticipated **Minimum Viable Product (MVP)** launch date is penciled in for June 2019.

It is obvious that companies such as Kodak are looking to leverage blockchain technologies and ICOs to create new markets, new products, and additional revenue streams, even when there is no natural or logical fit, like with existing gaming companies or reward schemes. Companies also use the blockchain hype as an opportunity to gain some free exposure. This is not uncommon, though, because blockchain and token technology thrives on everyone experimenting, learning, and sharing.

New companies running ICOs

By far the majority of ICOs are startups created by savvy, experienced business people and internet moguls, like John McAfee and Kim Dotcom, right through to young graduates and entrepreneurs, and everyone in between. These people start companies with new and radical ideas, embracing the open, decentralized, and transparent ethos that blockchain technology promotes and include a token as part of the design process.

A blockchain-first or token-first design approach is often much simpler than trying to fit a token into an existing business model. This approach is where the application is architected in a way that focuses purely on blockchain and token constraints, instead of legacy system constraints. The advantage here is that this will promote a new way of thinking, untethered to existing systems. Humaniq is one such example.

Humaniq

Humaniq describes itself as "a new generation financial services (sic) with its own cryptocurrency, which is aimed at eradicating poverty amongst millions of people living in the emerging economies" and raised $5.1 million USD in an ICO in April 2017, where 184 million tokens were issued, with a total maximum supply of 921 million (`https://humaniq.com/`).

The platform will use the Ethereum blockchain platform for transaction auditing and will use biometric authentication to let users access its services, thus removing the need for the public and private key approach to authentication.

Humaniq makes some ambitious claims on its website:

"1 billion users in the coming years, 4 trillion potentially in user accounts and 200+ startups are planning to move to the Humaniq platform."

Figure 2: Humaniq's ambitious claims for its platform (https://humaniq.com)

Humaniq created its own tokens and made them whole numbers because it claimed that the number of satoshis in circulation is insufficient and that it wanted to avoid using fractional amounts of coins:

"Decimal fractions may be uneasy for people with little or no education." (`https://humaniq.com/pdf/humaniq_wp_english.pdf`).

A token here was logical considering what Humaniq wanted to achieve but the main challenge is not really the token model, but attempting to achieve its lofty goals of empowering a market of about two billion people who currently don't have access to banking around the world, 100% through mobile devices.

Other new companies

There are literally hundreds of other companies that fall into this category around the world that ran an ICO with mixed levels of success. Based on the CoinDesk ICO data, there were around 60 companies that raised between $1 million USD and $5 million USD in 2017 (https://www.coindesk.com/ico-tracker/). These were predominantly startups with just a website, a white paper, and a small team.

Some raised funds that they wouldn't have been able to otherwise, which is a positive, but many were very dubious ICOs without a solid business model. There is a dichotomy between creating a token to be used within an application and ecosystem, against the speculative nature of the token, and using it for trading purposes. That is why it is important to understand the purpose of the token outside of just being a fundraising model.

Critical considerations when creating a token

There are several reasons for wanting to create a token. Firstly, it is a fun exercise to demystify the technology and understand at a deeper level how tokens work. The second, more serious, reason is to participate in this token economy and provide added value to either existing or new products and services.

Whatever the reason, the first step is to understand the purpose and function of your token. The next step is to decide if an existing token can be used or if a custom token is required. The final step is then to ask if a blockchain or distributed ledger is required. Following on from the concepts of the thought experiments earlier, let's go through the steps of how a token would be created.

Step one – the purpose of the token

As highlighted earlier, tokens can fall into three main categories: payment, utility, or security. Is the token designed as a form of payment? If yes, will an existing cryptocurrency or payment token, such as bitcoin or litecoin work? Ether could be used, but the original intention of ether was to be a "crypto-fuel" for operating Ethereum, and not really a peer-to-peer payment system.

If the token is a utility token, where or how is it designed to operate in the platform or system or, in a broader sense, the private economy? What value does it bring? If the token is a security in the financial sense, the regulations it is required to abide by need to be considered.

What does the token do?

What does the token do? What does it represent? The standard general catch-all that existing ICOs provide is governance. That is, a clause that the token provides the holder rights to participate in the direction of the software application, in effect voting rights to decide what additional features should be added. Of course, most users won't really care but it's a feel-good clause. This also makes the claim that the token provides utility, therefore it is not a security. Whether this is or isn't true is another totally different question and something we will look into in the next chapter.

The token may provide revenue rights similar to shares in a company, but unlike shares, the token does not represent equity in the company, nor does the person who owns it have voting rights at a shareholders meeting. As we saw in *Chapter 4, Token Varieties*, this was ICONOMI's model until it changed it to a buy-back-and-burn model. As more compliant security tokens emerge, re-engineering around this concept will not be required.

Tokens can also provide payment rights to a network or platform. For example, to store files on the Sia or Storj network, Siacoin or Storj coins are required. This means the user must obtain the appropriate coin in order to use the product or service. Other rights also include access rights, which have a slightly wider scope than payment rights, and the right to participate in consensus algorithms, such as proof of stake.

The token could also represent "reputation" in a system, so having more tokens represent better service or represent loyalty with a reward mechanism. The options are only limited to your imagination. The next question is: will an existing token work or is a new one required?

Side note: multiple tokens

As if creating and managing a token was not challenging enough, there is a growing trend where multiple tokens are used within a system. For example, Gnosis (introduced in *Chapter 3, The Potential of ICOs*), a prediction market similar to Augur, raised $12.5 million USD in April 2017 and created a fixed supply of 10 million GNO tokens. The fees to access the platform, though, are denominated in Wisdom tokens or WIZ. To generate WIZ tokens, a set amount of GNO tokens have to be locked up in a smart contract. This is like earning interest from a bank. The smart contract will then release 30% WIZ tokens upfront and the remainder at the end of the contract.

In addition to this, the WIZ token is pegged to $1 USD, which provides a degree of price stability. Imagine if 0.01 BTC was the fee. At $100 USD for a bitcoin, the fee would be 1 cent, so at $10,000 USD per bitcoin, the fee would be $100 USD!

Havven and Maker are other examples where dual tokens have been utilized, in an attempt to achieve price stability. Stable coins and how they work can become quite a complicated topic. Here, the concepts are only briefly presented for illustration purposes.

Havven is a decentralized payment network, where users transact directly in a price-stable cryptocurrency. Its first token is called the Nomin and the supply is variable and floating, in an attempt to maintain stability at $1. The second token is called the Havven and this has a fixed supply providing collateral for the system.

Maker has a similar concept with the Dai token kept at $1. The Dai is backed by collateral, which is currently ether. For example, you send ether to what is known as a **Collateralized Debt Position** (**CDP**) smart contract. The amount of Dai created is relative to how much ether you have put into the CDP. This ratio, called the "collateralization ratio," is fixed, but can be changed over time.

If the price of ether doesn't fluctuate, it alone will ensure the Dai's stability (and the Dai token would not be required in the first place), but what happens when the price of ether varies? Should the Dai trade above $1, there is a target rate feedback mechanism to bring it back down, however, the risk is what happens when the price of ether crashes. This is what is referred to as a "black swan event."

This is where the Maker token comes in. The Maker token holder functions as a buyer of last resort and actually manages and monitors the collateral.

The concept of a stable coin and collateralized coin was actually first noted in the Omni white paper, which, if you recall, was the first ICO back in 2013.

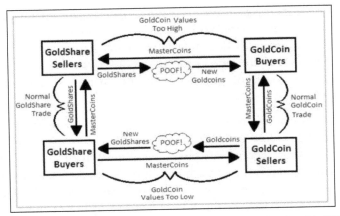

Figure 3: J.R. Willet's depiction of a stability mechanism for Omni in 2013

Step two – existing token or custom token?

In the current hype of blockchains and ICOs, it feels cool to have a token, just like it was cool to have a website in the dot-com days or it was cool to have a mobile phone back when they first came out. Nowadays, it is necessary to have a website and critical to have a mobile phone. The same will eventually ring true for tokens.

To ascertain whether a custom token is required or not, some questions to ask are:

♦ Would the system function the same or better with the native token of the platform it is built on?

♦ Would the system function the same or better with its own unique token?

♦ Does the system take advantage of the properties that the token on a distributed ledger provides, namely decentralization, immutability, and removal of a third-party intermediary?

In the crypto world, a custom token is always created for several reasons. Apart from using it as a fundraising mechanism, companies use it to decouple it from the native token, such as ether, so that if the price of ether doubles, the amount required to pay for goods or services with the custom token does not change.

A custom token provides a layer of abstraction. It decouples two systems. For instance, arcade tokens are decoupled from real coins for security reasons: a machine full of tokens isn't as attractive to thieves as a machine full of real coins. Psychologically, it increases spending because the tokens cannot be used elsewhere, so once converted, all the tokens are usually spent.

A custom token also provides control of the supply. Where applicable, more tokens can be created or destroyed based on the application. Generally, the supply is fixed at some maximum amount and the tokens are either all distributed on day one, or there is a minting process that brings tokens into the system at some rate up to the maximum amount.

Token tools

There are a number of tools and tutorials available to help to create custom tokens very quickly, which has encouraged, for better or worse, the creation of large amounts of custom tokens. In fact, the token creation becomes the easy part. It's everything else, such as building a business and/or token model and finding users, that becomes the main challenge.

Traditionally, creating tokens on the Ethereum platform would require knowledge of the Solidity programming language and tools, such as OpenZeppelin, would provide the core elements to avoid having to start from scratch. Truffle is a popular framework for testing and building smart contracts which would then be deployed on a testnet Ethereum blockchain, such as TestRPC, in conjunction with MyEtherWallet.

There is no shortage of other web-based tools, such as Token Wizard DAPP, which is a decentralized, open-source, and free-to-use tool to create tokens and crowdsale campaigns on Ethereum-based networks, with no coding skills required.

Step three – do you need a blockchain?

If your company already uses a reward scheme or points or game credits, then the decision is relatively easy. Creating a token on a blockchain makes a lot of sense because of the properties of the blockchain. Let's recap some of these properties:

- ♦ **Public verifiability**: Anyone can verify the correctness of the state of the system without the need to trust a central entity.

- ♦ **Transparency**: The data, and the process of updating it, is available, which is, in fact, a requirement for public verifiability.

- ♦ **Integrity**: Ensures that information is protected from unauthorized modifications.

- ♦ **Redundancy**: Provided inherently due to the distributed and replicated nature of the system.

All of these properties lead to a state of increased trust in the network, instead of a single party, which is the core concept of blockchains. If we look at a loyalty scheme as part of a customer retention strategy, considering a blockchain has several advantages. The first advantage is that this technology can bring efficiencies by:

- ♦ Reducing costs in system management and reporting, and the costs associated with errors or fraud.

- ♦ Reducing friction with a single, simple mobile app, that all parties can use in multiple locations.

- ♦ Increasing redemption speed, as transactions will be made in near real time. Certain loyalty schemes take weeks for the loyalty points to be credited to your account.

Other advantages include:

♦ Blockchains can provide a secure environment, by virtue of the distributed network, and can also provide other business opportunities to offer other value-added products and services to these loyal customers.

♦ A loyalty scheme can also represent a small, discrete proof of concept project, using this new technology, that has a tangible outcome, where the success can then spur further investment into blockchain-related projects.

♦ Loyalty is generic, applicable to all businesses, and simple to understand because loyalty rewards and cards are part of our everyday lives.

Even with the potential of blockchain technologies, there are voices that claim that blockchains are overhyped and misunderstood, and, more often than not, a blockchain is not required. The website DoYouNeedaBlockchain.com is based on the following flowchart from a paper titled *Do you need a blockchain?* from *Karl Wust* and *Arthur Gervais*, from the department of computer science from ETH Zurich, Switzerland (https://eprint.iacr.org/2017/375.pdf). It presents a simple decision tree to determine if a blockchain is required and if so, what type.

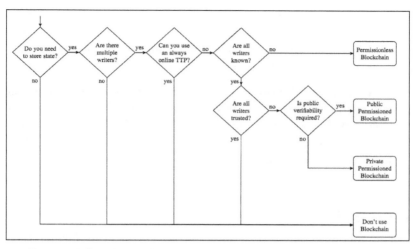

Figure 4: A flow chart to determine whether a blockchain is the appropriate
technical solution to solve a problem

Side note: public or private blockchain?

Although there are strong advocates against private blockchains,
because they go against the ethos of being open and decentralized,
the overriding purpose is to raise awareness and encourage
adoption of the technology. If private blockchains mean greater
adoption, then that should be viewed as a positive.

There is also a subtle point of difference between a private
blockchain and a permissioned blockchain. Without getting too
deep into the semantics, a permissioned blockchain has access
control put in place that requires participants to be known, vetted,
and proactively given access.

A private blockchain, however, is generally totally private to an individual or organization. In other words, it is operated by one entity. Use cases are limited and some people actually muse that a private blockchain is another word for a database.

In general, a blockchain will always be required when creating and issuing a token. Whether the business model requires a blockchain or not is another question. If the token is used as a pure fundraising mechanism, cue security tokens here, then the business can be anything but the token aspect of it is usually stored on the blockchain.

Resources

The following are some useful resources that can further help with understanding if a token is needed, the purpose or function of a token, and some of the implications of the token that you intend to create.

Coinbase

Coinbase, in collaboration with Coin Center, ConsenSys, and Union Square Ventures, has provided a 27-page document called *A securities law framework for blockchain tokens* and it is laid out in three parts (https://www.coinbase.com/legal/securities-law-framework.pdf). Part one is designed to estimate how likely a particular token is to be a security under US federal securities law. Part two sets out some best practices for ICOs. Part three is a detailed securities law analysis. There is also a proposed decision matrix included for determining how likely it is that a particular token is a security under US federal security law, where certain points are scored based on yes/no questions.

ConsenSys

ConsenSys is a venture production studio building decentralized applications and various developer and end-user tools for blockchain ecosystems, primarily focusing on Ethereum. It was founded in 2015 by Joseph Lubin, who was also co-founder of the Ethereum project.

ConsenSys consists of "hubs" that coordinate, incubate, accelerate, and spawn "spoke" ventures through development, resource sharing, acquisitions, investments, and the formation of joint ventures. These "spokes" benefit from foundational components built by ConsenSys, that enable new services and business models to be built on the blockchain. In addition to the development of internal projects and consulting work, ConsenSys is interested in the identification, development, and acquisition of talent and projects on an ongoing basis.

ConsenSys produced an interesting **Token Utility Canvas (TUC)**, which is a framework for developing technically and functionally sound tokens and business models (`https://media.consensys.net/tokenworkintroducing-the-token-utility-canvas-tuc-9a1f32979dc0`). It focuses on what it calls "consumer tokens" that are inherently "consumptive" in nature and are designed to be used or consumed in some way within an application.

Figure 5: Various ventures or "spokes" within ConsenSys
(https://new.consensys.net/labs/)

Public Trello board

There is also a publicly viewable Trello board titled "ICO – structure overview and planning," that is effectively a brain dump of things to consider when undertaking an ICO (`https:// trello.com/b/2n0i1AdV/initial-coin-offeringico- structureoverview-and-planning`). It covers concepts such as the business model, legal considerations, contents for a white paper, community development, and resourcing requirements.

Token questionnaire

The following are a list of questions to help you to get started with deciding if a blockchain is required and if so, if an associated token is required.

Do you need or want to:

◆ Increase data transparency?

◆ Remove the need to trust a single party?

◆ Provide transaction verifiability?

◆ Increase trust for your users or customers?

If you answered yes to all of the preceding points, a blockchain is a viable solution. If there are some no answers, then further analysis is required.

Recapping things to consider when creating tokens:

◆ Why do you need a token?

◆ What is the purpose of the token?

◆ What are the various ways the token can be used?

◆ What is the economic model behind the token?

◆ Do you need more than one token?

◆ How useful will the token be at $0.10, and at $1,000?

Summary

The question is not whether the world needs all these digital tokens that have proliferated on various blockchains, but what are we going to do with all these tokens? The physical world is largely represented as tokens and this shift into the digital realm is no different to the fax machine or the printing press being transformed, as technology innovates and disrupts and changes the world around us.

In this chapter, we went through some thought experiments to determine if some ICOs needed their own custom token and saw arguments both for and against. Several different companies running ICOs were examined, where the conclusion was that the more established a company was in terms of having an existing user base or a working product, the more successful the ICO was.

Finally, three main questions were highlighted around creating a token, which were to define the purpose of token, whether an existing token or custom token should be created, and if a blockchain is required as part of the solution.

The quest for a token is not so much a technical challenge as it is a business challenge, and in business, there are rules and regulations that companies need to abide by. This is important to note because in the world of ICOs, there has been very little regulation; however, this is soon about to change and we'll explore this in the next chapter.

6

PLAYING BY THE RULES

"Government's view of the economy could be summed up in a few short phrases: if it moves, tax it. If it keeps moving, regulate it. And if it stops moving, subsidize it."
(https://www.reaganlibrary.gov/sites/default/files/archives/speeches/1986/081586e.htm)

President Ronald Regan, 1986

One of the biggest challenges of playing in the ICO space is trying to understand the rules to play by. Regardless of what anyone says, we all live in a world bound by rules. We always have and always will, yet technology knows no bounds and unabatedly continuous to leap ahead, regardless of global boundaries or jurisdictions.

In the early days of ICOs, everything was experimental, but when more money poured in, and when hacks, bugs, and unscrupulous behavior started garnering worldwide media attention, the various regulatory bodies around the world started taking notice. Then, all of a sudden, the most important person in the ICO team was not the geek but the lawyer.

In this chapter, we will look at the following topics:

♦ Security tokens and the **Securities and Exchange Commission (SEC)**

♦ The global stance

♦ The SEC comes knocking

♦ Foundations and not-for-profits

♦ The evolution of white paper legality clauses

As rule makers and regulatory bodies around the world start to understand what tokens are and how they work, more clarity is being provided as to where they fit and their classification. Let's start by understanding the notion of a security token.

Security tokens and the SEC

Quite often, when security tokens are discussed, the SEC is mentioned. This is because the US Securities and Exchange Commission is an independent federal government agency responsible for protecting investors and maintaining the fair and orderly functioning of the securities markets of the largest economy in the world. So, what the SEC does matters to the rest of the world.

The goal of the Securities Act of 1933 was to remove the information discrepancies between promoters and investors. In a public distribution, the Securities Act prescribes the information investors need to make an informed investment decision, and the promoter is liable for material misstatements in the offering materials.

According to the 15 US Code § 77b (a)(1), the term **security** means *any note, stock, bond, profit-sharing agreement, investment contract, option, transferable share, or voting-trust certificate.* (https://www.law.cornell.edu/uscode/text/15/77b). This is a non-exhaustive list but serves to illustrate the point of an investment contract.

What is an investment contract?

An investment contract, for the purposes of the US Securities Act, means "a contract, transaction or scheme whereby a person invests their money in a common enterprise and is led to expect profits solely from the efforts of the promoter or a third party, it being immaterial whether the shares in the enterprise are evidenced by formal certificates or by nominal interests in the physical assets employed in the enterprise." (https://supreme. justia.com/cases/federal/us/328/293/case.html#298).

In summary, it:

♦ Is an investment of money

♦ Is in a common enterprise

♦ Has the expectation of profits

♦ Is derived solely from the efforts of others

Security tokens can be seen as an investment contract, where the main purpose of purchasing the token is the anticipation of future profits in the form of dividends, revenue share or, most commonly, price appreciation. These security tokens are essentially securities whose ownership is represented through a crypto asset that is registered on a blockchain.

This is important to understand because in the US, for example, any investment or purchase that is considered a security is subject to the Securities Act (http://legcounsel.house. gov/Comps/Securities%20Act%20Of%201933.pdf) and the Securities Exchange Act (http://legcounsel.house.gov/ Comps/Securities%20Exchange%20Act%20Of%201934.pdf), and as a result is subject to regulation and registration with the SEC.

So how does one determine what a security is? In the US, the Howey Test is employed, which was a landmark case in 1946.

The Howey Test (US-based companies)

In 1946, the Howey Company, founded by W.J. Howey, leased part of its citrus farms in Florida to finance another venture. The buyers of the land, attracted by the success of the Howey Company, invested with the expectation of profiting from its work.

Real estate contracts were offered for plots of land with citrus groves. The Howey Company offered the buyers the option of leasing the land back to it. The Howey Company would then tend to the land, harvest, and market the citrus fruits. As most of the buyers were not farmers and did not have agricultural expertise, they were happy to lease the land back to the Howey Company.

This fact suddenly made the plots of land an investment contract. The SEC moved in to block the sale and the Supreme Court, in issuing its decision, found that the Howey Company's leaseback agreement was a form of security. This was then developed into a test to allow anyone going forward to determine if certain transactions are investment contracts. If they are, they will then be subjected to securities registration requirements.

The Howey Test started a new era of defining securities by focusing on their substance, rather than their form. Simply labeling a token as a "utility" does not change the substance of a white paper. No matter how many times the word "utility" is used, it may very well still be a security under US law if it passes the Howey Test. This is why it became a common practice for the courts to review the economic realities behind an investment scheme, disregarding its name or form.

There are also others tests such as the Risk Capital Test (http://thestartuplawblog.com/token-sales-risk-capital-test/) and the Family Resemblance Test, (https://www.compliancebuilding.com/2012/05/31/is-a-note-a-security/), among others, but the Howey Test is currently the most commonly referred to.

US citizens

The reason that all of this is important is that the token issuer can be prosecuted for running a non-compliant ICO (according to the US Securities Act) if it allows US citizens to participate. The token issuer doesn't even have to reside in the US or be registered in its territories as a company. If the company is registered outside of US jurisdiction, and allows US citizens to participate in its ICO then it's automatically violating federal law.

This is why many projects often decide to avoid the sale of their tokens to US-based users. It is not that the project doesn't want US investors, it just doesn't want to deal with the headache of supplying investor background data to the government in the future.

The Monaco ICO asked if the user was a resident of, or holding a passport of, a list of countries. If the answer was yes, an apology page would appear preventing the user from continuing:

Figure 1: The Monaco ICO page citizenship enquiry

EOS provided two tick boxes asking users to confirm that they were not a citizen or a resident of the US or China. Some ICOs, particularly in the early days, did not do any further checks, but others did ask for further identification documents, such as a driving license or passport details, to be uploaded.

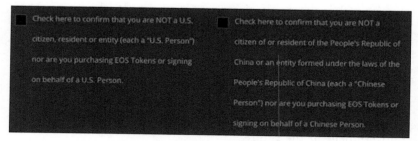

Figure 2: The EOS token sale page

Cobinhood asked users if they were a citizen of various countries that they deemed high risk in a legal sense and if so, the website redirected them to a "thank you for your interest but you cannot participate in the ICO" page. Cobinhood explained this decision:

"While most participants of any citizenship can join the ICO, unfortunately, we are unable to accept participation from citizens of the United States of America, Canada, China, and Taiwan due to existing regulations in their respective states." (https://web.archive. org/web/20180315112347/https://cobinhood.zendesk. com/hc/en-us/articles/115002484432-Are-citizens-of- certain-countries-excluded-from-participating-in-the- COBINHOOD-ICO-).

Many of the organizations conducting an ICO have been desperately trying to avoid having their tokens classified as securities. Being classified as a security automatically comes with many regulations and limitations, no matter what the country in question is, such as who can invest in these tokens and how they can be exchanged.

Secondary trading and liquidity are also greatly reduced for these kinds of tokens, as securities cannot be traded freely and are subject to many restrictions. In fact, crypto exchanges do their own due diligence to avoid listing security tokens if they are not licensed to do so. This can limit or even destroy the network effects and the use of the tokens to build a widely adopted platform or protocol. Securities laws are complex and often confusing. Terms such as "common enterprise" are imperfectly defined and different courts may apply different tests for determining whether an investment is a security or not.

In the US, and in fact in many developed countries around the world, securities are heavily regulated and selling unregistered securities can result in significant fines and prison sentences. There are also significant costs and efforts involved when complying with securities law, in order to legally accept money from investors.

AML/KYC

AML (Anti-Money Laundering) refers to policies and legislation that forces financial institutions to proactively monitor their clients in order to prevent money laundering and corruption. These laws require financial institutions to report any financial crimes they find and do everything possible to stop them.

KYC (Know Your Customer) is the process of a business identifying and verifying the identity of its clients. The main objective of this policy is to prevent money laundering, identity theft, terrorist financing, and financial frauds. Identifying contributors and complying with AML regulations is almost a necessity now for any ICO.

The most famous case of a self-imposed retrospective AML/KYC was Tezos. On June 10, 2018 the Tezos Foundation announced a KYC/AML requirement for all contributors, almost a year after its ICO:

"As the operational details for the Tezos betanet launch continue to be finalized, the Tezos Foundation would like to announce the implementation, at this time, of Know Your Customer/Anti-Money Laundering (KYC/AML) checks for contributors." (http://tezosfoundation.ch/news/tezos-foundation-announces-kyc-aml/).

The Tezos Foundation determined that this was the best way forward to avoid any future compliance complications. The Foundation reasoned that due to a maturing of the blockchain ecosystem in the 10 months since it did its ICO, KYC, and AML requirements had become standard practice, so Tezos wanted to retrospectively comply as well.

The announcement was met with some backlash online that renewed claims that Tezos was a scam, in conjunction with the infighting and the multiple delays of the platform.

SEC statements

On June 6, 2018, Jay Clayton, the Chairman of the SEC, announced that the SEC will not change securities law to cater to cryptocurrencies:

"Cryptocurrencies that replace the dollar, the euro and the yen with bitcoin, that type of currency is not a security. However, a token or a digital asset, where I give you my money and you go off and make a venture, and in return for giving you my money I say 'you can get a return' that is a security and we regulate that. We regulate the offering of that security and regulate the trading of that security." (https://www.youtube.com/watch?v=wFr1ooaVPjY).

On June 14, 2018, William Hinman, the director of the Division of Corporation Finance at the SEC, gave a speech at the Yahoo All Markets Summit: Crypto conference in San Francisco and stated that Bitcoin and Ether are not securities:

"Applying the disclosure regime of the federal securities laws to the offer and resale of Bitcoin would seem to add little value. And putting aside the fundraising that accompanied the creation of Ether, based on my understanding of the present state of Ether, the Ethereum network and its decentralized structure, current offers and sales of Ether are not securities transactions." (https://www.sec.gov/news/speech/speech-hinman-061418).

The key is that Hinman's analysis of whether something is a security or not is not set in stone. Digital assets that have utility can be sold as an investment strategy that could later be deemed to be a security. Then, as the network develops to the case where there is no longer any central enterprise being invested in, it can be deemed as not a security.

The key is around decentralization. If the network is sufficiently decentralized, the asset may not represent an investment contract because the ability to identify an issuer or promoter to make the required disclosures becomes difficult and less meaningful.

Global stance

Many regulators around the world have issued statements regarding cryptocurrencies and ICOs. The overwhelming conclusion is that while some countries, such as China and South Korea, have banned them, most are applying existing laws and are more open to having discussions with anyone looking to start a venture in this space. A few countries, such as Switzerland and Estonia, are even looking to customize ICO regulations. The following is a selected, non-exhaustive list of statements from the regulatory bodies of various countries.

Singapore (http://www.mas.gov.sg/)

In August 2017, the **Monetary Authority of Singapore (MAS)** clarified the regulatory position on the offer of digital tokens in Singapore and that they will be regulated by MAS if the digital tokens constitute products regulated under the **Securities and Futures Act (SFA)**. (http://www.mas.gov.sg/News-and-Publications/Media-Releases/2017/MAS-clarifies-regulatory-position-on-the-offer-of-digital-tokens-in-Singapore.aspx).

In November 2017, MAS then published a 13-page guide to digital token offerings providing general guidance on the application of the securities laws administered by MAS in relation to offers or issues of digital tokens in Singapore. It states, "*MAS will examine the structure and characteristics of, including the rights attached to, a digital token in determining if the digital token is a type of capital markets products under the SFA.*" (http://www.mas.gov.sg/~/media/MAS/Regulations%20and%20Financial%20Stability/Regulations%20Guidance%20and%20Licensing/Securities%20Futures%20and%20Fund%20Management/Regulations%20Guidance%20and%20Licensing/Guidelines/A%20Guide%20to%20Digital%20Token%20Offerings%20%2014%20Nov%202017.pdf).

Canada (https://www.securities-administrators.ca/)

On August 24, 2017, the **Canadian Securities Administrators (CSA)** issued a staff notice detailing what cryptocurrency exchanges and cryptocurrency investment funds are, what coin or token offerings are, and a four-prong test to determine if an investment contract exists, just like the Howey Test.

The CSA also found several factors as important considerations for whether a person or company is trading in securities for a business purpose. They are (http://www.osc.gov.on.ca/documents/en/Securities-Category4/csa_20170824_cryptocurrency-offerings.pdf):

♦ Soliciting a broad base of investors, including retail investors

♦ Using the internet, including public websites, and discussion boards, to reach a large number of potential investors

♦ Attending public events, including conferences and meetups, to actively advertise the sale of the coins/ tokens

♦ Raising a significant amount of capital from a large number of investors

The CSA does have a "Regulatory Sandbox" initiative allowing firms to register and/or obtain exemptive relief from securities law requirements, under a faster and more flexible process than through a standard application. The purpose is to test their products, services, and applications throughout the Canadian market on a time-limited basis.

China (http://www.pbc.gov.cn/)

In September 2017, the Chinese government, via a public service announcement through the People's Bank of China website, declared ICOs to be illegal in China and asked all related fundraising activities to be halted immediately (http://www.pbc.gov.cn/goutongjiaoliu/113456/113469/3374222/index.html). Shortly thereafter, cryptocurrency exchange platforms were ordered to discontinue operations. More recently, China has decided to block access to any cryptocurrency and ICO-related website for anyone within the mainland's borders.

There are rumors circulating that China will lift the ICO ban towards the end of 2018 in favor of regulated and controlled ICOs.

Switzerland (https://www.finma.ch/)

The Swiss **Financial Market Supervisory Authority (FINMA)** published market guidance in September 2017 and more recently in February 2018. Depending on the structure of an ICO, the Swiss regulator will determine, among others things, whether supervisory regulations, collective investment scheme legislation, and banking law provisions may be applicable to specific ICOs.

The key is that each case will be decided on its merits and the principle focus around the function and transferability of the tokens. Accordingly, the issuers should carefully assess regulatory status when structuring and marketing ICOs.

Hong Kong (https://www.sfc.hk/)

On September 5, 2017, the Hong Kong **Securities and Futures Commission (SFC)** provided a statement on ICOs:

"Where the digital tokens involved in an ICO fall under the definition of 'securities', dealing in or advising on the digital tokens, or managing or marketing a fund investing in such digital tokens, may constitute a 'regulated activity'. Parties engaging in a 'regulated activity' are required to be licensed by or registered with the SFC irrespective of whether the parties involved are located in Hong Kong, so long as such business activities target the Hong Kong public." (https://www.sfc.hk/web/EN/news-and-announcements/policy-statements-and-announcements/statement-on-initial-coin-offerings.html).

The general summary is that as the terms and features of ICOs may differ in each case, those engaging in ICO activities should seek legal professional advice if they are in doubt about the applicable legal and regulatory requirements.

Australia (https://asic.gov.au/)

In September 28, 2017, the **Australian Securities and Investments Commission (ASIC)** issued a guidance for ICOs with a detailed information sheet (INFO 225) that covers the legal status of ICOs, when an ICO can be an offer of a financial product, financial products that reference ICO tokens, and how prospective ICO issuers can obtain informal assistance from ASIC (https://asic.gov.au/regulatory-resources/digital-transformation/initial-coin-offerings-and-crypto-currency/).

It all boils down to whether the crypto-asset or ICO is (or is not) a financial product. The guidelines are clear on how to operate within Australia's regulatory framework, while encouraging innovation and the development of new financial business models. Ultimately, it can be seen as a positive framework for ICOs but holds them in line with the existing legislative framework in order to protect citizens against scams or fraudulent ICOs.

South Korea (http://www.fsc.go.kr/)

In late September 2017, the South Korean **Financial Services Commission (FSC)** announced that ICOs would be prohibited (http://www.fsc.go.kr/info/ntc_news_view.jsp?bbsid=BBS 0030&page=1&sch1=&sword=&r_url=&menu=7210100&no=32085). South Korea followed the Chinese model and formally introduced legislation regarding the ban. However, South Korea is preparing a policy plan for ICOs, opening the door for Korean companies to raise funds despite prior reservations. The thinking is that if the likes of Kakao (the mobile messenger operator) and Bithumb (the cryptocurrency exchange) decided to launch ICOs abroad, the blockchain sector of South Korea would lose out on multi-billion-dollar opportunities, solely due to the country's ban on domestic ICOs.

Estonia (https://www.fi.ee/)

Estonia's **Financial Supervision Authority** (**FSA**) describes a legal framework of ICOs that echoes other authorities around the world:

> *"The EFSA states that although a new technology is involved, and what is being sold is referred to as a token instead of a share or equity, a token may still qualify as a security as set forth in the Estonian legislation. Businesses should complete an analysis on whether a security is involved. Professional advice may be useful in making this determination."* (https://www.fi.ee/index.php?id=12466).

Having said this, Estonia, named "the most advanced digital society in the world" by specialist tech magazine *Wired*, has grabbed attention by offering "e-residency" to anyone from anywhere and is looking into an "estcoin" that could possibly be used within the government-backed e-residency ID program (http://www.wired.co.uk/article/digital-estonia).

In December 2017, the Estonian Ministry of Finance and the FSA worked together, resulting in the Ministry of Finance applying for funding for a project called "Opening Estonian Regulatory Framework for Innovative Technical Solutions", which is targeted at developing a favorable legal framework for crowdfunding and alternative infrastructure.

Europe (https://www.esma.europa.eu/)

On November 13, 2017, the **European Securities and Markets Authority** (**ESMA**) issued two statements on ICOs. One statement was on the risks of ICOs for investors and another on the rules applicable to firms involved in ICOs. To the firms, it was basically a reminder of their obligations under EU regulation.

The European Commission (a body that shapes the EU's overall strategy, proposes new EU laws, and policies, monitors their implementation, and manages the EU budget), recently published a 2018 Fintech Action Plan:

"In the course of 2018, the Commission will continue monitoring the developments of crypto-assets and **Initial Coin Offerings** **(ICO***) with the* **European Supervisory Authorities** **(ESAs***), the* **European Central Bank** **(ECB***), and the* **Financial Stability Board** **(FSB***) as well as other international standard setters. Based on the assessment of risks, opportunities, and the suitability of the applicable regulatory framework, the Commission will assess whether regulatory action at EU level is required."* (`https://ec.europa.eu/info/sites/info/files/180308-action-plan-fintech_en.pdf`).

United Kingdom (`https://www.fca.org.uk/`)

The **Financial Conduct Authority** (**FCA**) issued a statement in December 2017:

"Whether an ICO falls within the FCA's regulatory boundaries or not can only be decided case by case. Many ICOs will fall outside the regulated space. However, depending on how they are structured, some ICOs may involve regulated investments and firms involved in an ICO may be conducting regulated activities" (`https://www.fca.org.uk/news/statements/initial-coin-offerings`).

The takeaway here is that many ICOs fall outside the scope of existing regulations without indicating specific reasons, and the FCA seems to require a case-by-case analysis of the facts.

The FCA also provided a statement on cryptocurrency derivatives stating:

"Cryptocurrencies are not currently regulated by the FCA provided they are not part of other regulated products or services. Cryptocurrency derivatives are, however, capable of being financial instruments under the Markets in **Financial Instruments Directive II** (**MIFID II**), although we do not consider cryptocurrencies to be currencies or commodities for regulatory purposes under MIFID II. Firms conducting regulated activities in cryptocurrency derivatives must, therefore, comply with all applicable rules in the FCA's Handbook and any relevant provisions in directly applicable European Union regulations." (`https://www.fca.org.uk/news/statements/cryptocurrency-derivatives`).

New Zealand (https://fma.govt.nz/)

In May 2018, New Zealand's **Financial Market Authority** (**FMA**) outlined statements regarding ICOs and cryptocurrency services. There are four factors determining how an ICO is regulated. These are if the token is classified as a financial product, if a financial service is being provided, if the token purchaser is a retail (general public) or wholesale (experienced) investor, and if the investor is based in New Zealand or overseas.

The FMA outlines the four types of financial products: debt securities, equity securities, managed investment products, and derivatives.

The FMA is open to discussions, stating, "*Given the bespoke nature of ICOs we encourage you to approach us early in the development phase if you're considering making an offer. We can provide guidance around whether your ICO involves a financial product or a financial service, and whether fair dealing requirements are met. We expect you to refrain from seeking to raise funds while discussions with us are ongoing.* (https://fma.govt.nz/compliance/cryptocurrencies/initial-coin-offers/)."

ICOs remain a relatively new form of capitalization and every nation has generally stated that ICOs will fall into existing regulatory framework. This is of no surprise because it is the easiest form of action to apply. Let's now move on to ICOs that were contacted by the SEC and discuss the outcomes.

The SEC comes knocking

There had been much speculation about when the regulatory authorities might intervene because it was obvious that there was an increasing amount of unscrupulous behavior surfacing during the ICO craze of 2017. Sure enough, the SEC didn't disappoint.

The DAO

On 25 July 2017, the SEC released a report on The DAO in which it asserted for the first time that the sale of the DAO token constituted an illegal sale of unregistered securities. The report is incredibly well written, outlining what The DAO is, a summary of events that occurred, arguments with evidence around investment contracts and a conclusion (https://www.sec.gov/litigation/investreport/34-81207.pdf).

The **DAO (Decentralized Autonomous Organization)** was a new term used to describe a virtual organization or entity that was created with software and deployed on a distributed ledger. The DAO was created by slock.it, a German-based company that uses blockchain technology to help build an **Internet of Things (IoT)** layer to power transactions between machines and humans.

The SEC determined that slock.it created The DAO with the prime objective of operating it as a for-profit entity, where the assets obtained from the sale of the DAO token would then be used to fund projects. The holder of the DAO tokens then anticipated a share in the earnings from these projects as a return on their investment.

The ICO took place from April 30, 2016 through to May 28, 2016 and sold approximately 1.15 billion DAO tokens in exchange for approximately 12 million ether, valued at about $150 million USD at the time.

The SEC used the main points of what constitutes an investment contract and provided evidence of why The DAO was indeed an investment contract. The SEC stated that investors in The DAO invested money:

"Investors in The DAO used ETH to make their investments, and DAO Tokens were received in exchange for ETH. Such investment is the type of contribution of value that can create an investment contract under Howey."

There was a reasonable expectation of profits as well:

"Investors who purchased DAO Tokens were investing in a common enterprise and reasonably expected to earn profits through that enterprise."

The DAO's profits were derived from the managerial efforts of others:

"Investors in The DAO reasonably expected Slock.it and its co-founders, and The DAO's Curators, to provide significant managerial efforts after The DAO's launch."

The SEC concluded that The DAO was an issuer of securities but, to the relief of the creators of The DAO, decided not to bring charges in this instance but rather to caution the industry and market participants.

There was no formal reason provided on why the SEC did not bring charges but the SEC wanted to make clear that federal securities law applies to anyone who offers and sells securities in the US or to US citizens, regardless of the issuing entity being a traditional company or a decentralized autonomous organization. The first warning shots has been fired by the SEC and it was only getting started.

Harbour

Harbour (www.harbourproject.io) was a community-governed, Ethereum-based DAO for managing and holding token assets by harnessing the wisdom of the crowd. On July 26, 2017, it responded to a question on the bitcointalk forum asking, *"Does the SEC thing affect you?* with *Hi, no it doesn't affect us; we are incorporated in Canada and don't accept contributions from Americans or US-based individuals; we are completely compliant with our local jurisdiction."* (https://bitcointalk.org/index.php?topic=2041496. msg20393393#msg20393393).

Then, four days later, Harbour came out with another statement following up from its initial post:

"Over the past few days, and in concert with our legal team and advisors, we have soberly assessed the implications of the SEC's report as well as our own compliance. We have determined, in short, that there is just too much uncertainty within our current model to forge ahead without some careful assessment and perhaps revision to Harbour." (https://bitcointalk. org/index.php?topic=2041496.msg20490395#msg20490395).

Harbour canceled its planned August 1, 2017 ICO. It is still around but its blog updates and GitHub activity have dramatically decreased.

Protostarr

Protostarr was a platform to enable fans to fund their favorite content creators while maintaining partial ownership of and payment from the revenue-creating channel. The ICO raised 119.5 ether, which was about $47,000 USD at the time, but the SEC pushed Protostarr to shut down its ICO midway through on August 29, 2017 (https://etherscan.io/address/0xEa16ebd8 Cdf5A51fa0a80bFA5665146b2AB82210#internaltx).

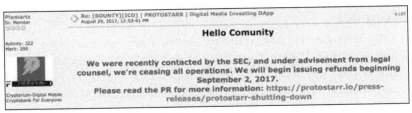

Figure 3: The community announcement of ICO closure by Protostarr
(https://bitcointalk.org/index.php?topic=2068943.msg21311353#msg21311353)

Protostarr's press release on its now defunct website said it all:

"On August 24, 2017, we were contacted by the United States Security and Exchange Commission regarding the initial coin offering of Protostarr tokens to fund the development of our Ethereum decentralized application. After consultation with multiple lawyers, we have decided to cease further operations and refund Ethereum collected in our crowdsale that began on August 13, 2017.

Like many of our supporters, we were excited to be an innovative force in the emerging space of content creation and its funding. Unfortunately, as a startup, we do not have the necessary resources to both develop our DApp and challenge the SEC's investigation regarding our ICO and its interpretation under US securities law." (https://web.archive.org/web/20170911150636/https://protostarr.io/press-releases/protostarr-shutting-down/).

Protostarr had not consulted with lawyers before launching its ICO, which eventually led to its downfall. The company started refunding investors several days later.

PlexCoin

On December 4, 2017, the SEC obtained an "emergency asset freeze" to halt an ICO called PlexCoin that raised up to $15 million USD by falsely promising a 13-fold profit in less than a month (https://www.sec.gov/news/press-release/2017-219). They were the first charges filed by the SEC's new cyber unit. Then, seven days later, the SEC were at it again.

Munchee

On December 11, 2017, the SEC issued a press release concerning the Munchee ICO, a California business that created an iPhone application for people to review restaurant meals. A cease and desist order was made public with details that the Munchee ICO started on October 31, 2017, and stopped on November 1, 2017, hours after being contacted by commission staff.

About 40 people purchased MUN tokens from Munchee. In total, they paid about 200 ether or about $60,000 USD at the time of the offering. Analysis of the SEC order provides an intriguing insight (https://www.sec.gov/litigation/admin/2017/33-10445.pdf). In particular, the SEC order highlighted the fact that Munchee described the ICO in a way that claimed MUN tokens would increase in value as a result of Munchee's efforts and stated that MUN tokens would be traded on secondary markets.

The SEC definitely did its homework and set forth the claim that the MUN tokens were securities before providing evidence as to why. The evidence included the following:

- The MUN white paper stated that Munchee had done a "Howey analysis" but did not provide any evidence of such analysis.

- Munchee told potential purchasers that they would be able to use MUN tokens to buy goods or services but no one was able to do so throughout the relevant period.

- In the Munchee white paper, on the websites, and on several other mediums, Munchee emphasized that the goal of the business was to cause the MUN token to rise in value. Munchee also said it would "burn" or reduce the supply of the MUN tokens and emphasized how potential buyers could profit from those efforts.

- Munchee intended for MUN tokens to trade on a secondary market and primed purchasers' expectation of profits with blog posts stating, *As more users get on the platform, the more valuable your MUN tokens will become.*

- In addition to blog posts, there were podcasts, public statements on Facebook, and even YouTube videos that further promoted the expectations of profit with statements like *199% GAINS on MUN token at ICO price*, and *A $1,000 investment could create a $94,000 return.*

The SEC summarized that the MUN tokens were securities because:

- They were investment contracts

- MUN token purchasers had a reasonable expectation of profits from their investment in the Munchee enterprise

♦ Investors' profits were to be derived from the significant entrepreneurial and managerial efforts of others

♦ Investors' expectations were primed by Munchee's marketing of the MUN token offering

The SEC finally concluded that *even if MUN tokens had a practical use at the time of the offering, it would not preclude the token from being a security.*

What is interesting to note is that the word *utility* was mentioned seven times in the Munchee white paper and there was a two-and-a-half-page legal disclaimer stating that it was not a security token, but this did not mean much to the SEC.

In the end, no penalties were imposed, as the SEC took into account that Munchee stopped the ICO quickly and immediately returned the proceeds, before issuing tokens and cooperating with the investigation. What this shows is that the SEC is watching ICOs and no doubt other countries around the world are watching the SEC.

We will now move away from the token aspect and focus on the company aspect. Many ICOs, especially in the early days, set up foundations in what were known as crypto-friendly jurisdictions.

Foundations

The term *foundation* in general is used to describe a distinct legal entity. The exact details depend on the jurisdiction in question, but here we take a general look at why foundations were popular with many ICOs.

In the early days, blockchain projects mostly created foundations to raise the capital needed to build the technology and make it open source and decentralized. The most famous is the Ethereum Foundation and more recently the Tezos Foundation, as mentioned earlier. This structure seemed to make sense because these international collaborators did not see themselves as a corporation. Also, a foundation seemed to have the right governance structure to keep the project alive through to completion and avoid any form of taxation, as foundations are not-for-profit entities and thus not taxable.

As a distinct legal entity, a foundation is generally established to reflect the wishes of the founder via an endowment of assets, which are managed by council members for a specific purpose and/or for the benefit of its beneficiaries.

Generally, a foundation includes the founder and a council, who sit on the board and carry out the purpose of the foundation as instructed by the charter. There are other considerations, such as members, protectors, and beneficiaries also. Unlike a company, though, foundations have no shareholders, though they may have an assembly and voting members.

In an ICO, there is usually a distinct issuer that is often referred to as a foundation, which is separate from the company that is often referred to as the operating entity. This is done primarily to separate out the legal liability, but it is also used to transfer funds to pay staff in the case where more than one operating entity in more than one country exists.

There are other advantages of a dual structure – by utilizing two entities, one can look for a suitable jurisdiction to set up, providing the lowest effective rate of taxation based on the activities of the entity.

Crypto Valley

Switzerland is often touted as an attractive place for ICOs due to favorable tax laws. Within Switzerland is a small town called Zug, named for its fishing rights, which is also a canton and home to a little under 30,000 residents. It is an affluent area, a low tax region, and a base for several multinational companies. Zug has risen in popularity due to its favorable political, economic, and technological environment. The Zug canton has been branded *Crypto Valley*, borrowing a leaf from San Francisco's *Silicon Valley*. With a growing reputation as a global cryptocurrency center, it is estimated that a quarter of the global ICO capital raised now sits in Swiss foundations.

Ethereum Switzerland GmbH, a non-profit foundation, was formed in 2014 to manage the funds raised through its ICO. Subsequently, many other non-profit foundations were formed to conduct ICOs, such as Bancor, Cardano, Shapeshift, Xapo, Lisk, and Lykke. In fact, more than 50 blockchain-based startups have settled in Zug (https://www.express.co.uk/finance/city/922260/cantonof-Zug-switzerland-bitcoin-ethereum-cryptocurrencyVitalik-Buterin).

Zug and the *Crypto Valley* seem to be powerful advocates for all things blockchain and others are catching on. Ireland is joining in on the action, with its own crypto center called *Crypto Coast*.

While Zug was hogging the limelight, other ICOs decided to structure themselves as offshore corporations in the Cayman Islands, Gibraltar, Malta, British Virgin Island, and Singapore, among others. The main motivation of this structuring was to reduce any form of taxation on the token sale.

The main takeaway from all of this is that there are many options available when performing an ICO, so the best course of action is to obtain professional advice.

LLC, Ltd, GmbH

It is not necessary to have a foundation to be successful. Having a standard company is by default the easiest and often least expensive alternative, even if certain tax advantages cannot be made the most of.

As companies try to dance around the utility versus security line, what many get lost in is the ease of raising money because often the raising is the easy part. The hard part is executing what was promised. People need to be sourced, a culture needs to be created, and a company needs to be built and run. No matter the name, the type, or the location, running a company requires regulations to be followed. Increasingly, one needs to look at how any potential conflicts of interest are handled between the token holders and the founders or shareholders.

Even in the case of bitcoin, with the most decentralized network in the world, it has seen the core group of developers create a company called Blockstream, with investment from various corporate organizations. Blockstream declared its investments:

"Blockstream is proud to be working with leading investors from Asia, Europe and North America, including alphabetically AME Cloud Ventures, AXA Strategic Ventures, Blockchain Capital, Digital Currency Group, Digital Garage, Future/Perfect Ventures, Horizons Ventures, Innovation Endeavors, Khosla Ventures, Mosaic Ventures, Real Ventures, Reid Hoffman, and Seven Seas Venture Partners" (https:// blockstream.com/about/#investors).

The evolution of white paper legality clauses

Legal clauses within white papers have certainly evolved over time, to the extent that some white papers should in fact be called an investment statement or investment prospectus. Obviously, the reason why they are not called this is because nearly all tokens claim to not be a security but a utility token.

The Omni white paper, the very first ICO to take place back in 2013, had an amusing disclaimer in *Appendix C*:

"Investing in experimental currencies is really, absurdly risky. This paper is not investment advice, and anyone predicting what will happen with experimental currencies such as those described here is indulging in the wildest sort of speculation, and that includes the speculations in the previous appendix.

Please consult your financial adviser before investing in ANY wild scheme such as this.

 Hint: They will probably tell you to RUN and not look back unless you assure them that it is money you are totally prepared to lose.

Anyone who puts their rent money or life savings into an experiment of this type is a fool, and deserves the financial ruin they will inevitably reap from this or some other risky enterprise."

Other ICOs in the early days had either very little legal disclaimers or none at all, but Ethereum very quickly changed all that. Ethereum issued a comprehensive 32-page "Terms and Conditions of the Ethereum Genesis Sale" document that very clearly outlined almost everything anyone would want to know (https://www.cryptocompare.com/media/1383735/pdfs-ter msandconditionsoftheethereumgenesissale.pdf). It started off with a number of warnings:

- WARNING: DO NOT PURCHASE ETH IF YOU ARE NOT AN EXPERT IN DEALING WITH CRYPTOGRAPHIC TOKENS AND BLOCKCHAIN-BASED SOFTWARE SYSTEMS

- WARNING: CRYPTOGRAPHIC TOKENS OF VALUE MAY EXPERIENCE EXTREME VOLATILITY IN PRICING

- WARNING: THE PURCHASE OF ETH HAS A NUMBER OF RISKS

The document then made it very clear how ether would be created and distributed, along with the growth or inflation rate. 15 risks were then listed. Examples include "Risk of Regulatory Action in One or More Jurisdictions," "Risk that the Ethereum Platform May Never be Completed or Released," and "Risk of Rapid Adoption and Increased Demand for ETH" along with the converse as well. In summary, it was a very complete standalone document.

Augur, the first ICO on Ethereum, had a 12-page purchase agreement that attempted to dot the i's and cross the t's.

BAT (Basic Attention Token) detailed its terms and conditions on its website to the equivalent of 13 pages, including 17 risk items similar to Ethereum (`https://basicattentiontoken.org/terms-and-conditions/`).

The general trend was a technical white paper and a standalone "sales terms and conditions" document or a "purchase agreement." Some ICOs started incorporating various legal clauses into their white paper. Referring back to Munchee, in its white paper it made a statement at the beginning:

"Munchee Inc. has consulted with legal counsel to assess the possible regulatory treatment by the US Securities and Exchange Commission and relevant foreign authorities in light of developing regulatory guidance."

Munchee then came to a conclusion:

"A legal analysis has been conducted to determine that, as currently designed, the sale of MUN utility tokens does not pose a significant risk of implicating foreign securities laws in jurisdictions that have addressed token sales."

Munchee then went on to predict its own fate:

"Munchee Inc.'s representations and securities assessment is not a guarantee that the SEC or any other regulatory authority will not determine the tokens to be securities subject to registration."

What tended to happen next was that some legal clauses started appearing within white papers, as well as on the ICO website. LAToken, a blockchain platform for creating and trading asset tokens that raised $19.6 million USD in its ICO in August 2017, had a whole section dedicated to *Legal Considerations.*

LAToken went on to explain what the Howey Test was in its white paper and attempted to systematically justify why LAT could not be seen as a security, and could pass the hurdles of the Howey Test. There was also a legal memo published by *White Summers Caffee & James, LLP*, LAToken's legal advisors:

"Using the Supreme Court case SEC v. W.J. Howey, we have concluded that the LAT ICO likely satisfied only two of the four prongs required for an instrument to be considered a security." (https://cdn-new.latoken.com/sale/legal-memo.pdf?_ga=2.233880344.761624833.1523063433-1311558117.1523063433).

The obvious conclusion to draw when trying to play by the rules is that it is vital to know the rules. To know the rules means finding someone who understands the rules and ideally is prepared to put their name on your white paper! The synonym for someone knowing the rules is a lawyer. The challenging aspect of all of this lies in the fact that the scope of ICOs is usually not limited to one particular country, although the trend is to limit the ICO to only targeted countries. This is generally because the global stance is constantly changing, so keeping track requires professional help.

SAFT

The **SAFT (Simple Agreement for Future Tokens)** framework was created in a joint effort by Marco Santori, a lawyer formerly at law firm Cooley LLP, and Protocol Labs as a way to perform ICOs in compliance with US securities law. Protocol Labs is a startup that was part of Y Combinator in the summer of 2014, which is a US-based company that provides seed funding for startups (https://www.ycombinator.com/companies/).

Y Combinator uses a **Simple Agreement for Future Equity (SAFE)** for its investors, so it was modified to suit a token-based framework. An excerpt from the paper titled *The SAFT Project: Toward a Compliant Token Sale Framework* states, "The SAFT is an investment contract. A SAFT transaction contemplates an initial sale of a SAFT by developers to accredited investors. The SAFT obligates investors to immediately fund the developers. In exchange, the developers use the funds to develop a genuinely functional network, with genuinely functional utility tokens, and then deliver those tokens to the investors once functional. The investors may then resell the tokens to the public, presumably for a profit, and so may the developers." (https://cdn.crowdfundinsider.com/wp-content/uploads/2018/03/SAFT-Project-Whitepaper-October-2017.pdf).

The document acknowledges that the SAFT itself is a security and must comply with the applicable securities law but dismisses the fact that the tokens may be deemed to be securities as well.

In general, a company or startup enters into an agreement with accredited investors, where the SAFT states that investors invest into the company in exchange for rights to tokens once the network is complete. There are no tokens issued at this stage, but the company does file the required forms with the relevant authorities such as the SEC in the US.

The company then uses the funds to develop the network, which could take months or even years. Once the network's basic functionality has been created, the company creates the tokens. The argument is that post-completion, utility tokens have a functional use on a software network and therefore would not be deemed as securities, even though the initial SAFT contracts would be. Therefore, purchasers can freely re-sell the utility tokens to retail investors without being deemed to have facilitated an unregistered securities offering.

The main challenge here is that SAFT agreements are being used to facilitate ICOs, but they refer to different types of assets. On the one hand, an ICO is being conducted, but what is being sold is the SAFT.

Running an ICO under the SAFT assumption carries serious risk and is viewed dimly by the SEC and many in the legal profession. Selling unregistered securities (the token and not the SAFT) is viewed as a serious violation of the law if the SEC or courts determine that the tokens are unregistered securities.

However, the first use of a SAFE was with an ICO called Filecoin, a decentralized storage network famous for raising $257 million USD in its ICO in August 2017. Filecoin was unique in that it didn't create a token and distribute it, but it promised to. Filecoin is the name of an application that uses a cryptocurrency to power a storage network. Miners earn Filecoin by providing open hard-drive space to the network, while users spend Filecoin to store their files encrypted in the decentralized network.

The company behind Filecoin is called Protocol Labs. Protocol Labs also has a number of other offerings in its suite. The **InterPlanetary File System (IPFS)** is an application that allows data to be stored in a decentralized fashion. In fact, Filecoin uses a lot of the underlying technology of IPFS. Filecoin ran its token sale on CoinList, which emerged as an independent company from collaboration between AngelList and Protocol Labs.

The total amount raised was around $257 million USD, of which $52 million USD was from an "advisors" sale from the likes of Sequoia Capital, Andreessen Horowitz, Union Square Ventures, Winklevoss Capital, and about 100 other individual high-profile Silicon Valley investors. These investors paid $0.75 USD per Filecoin. Then Filecoin opened the ICO to accredited investors and raised a further $205 million USD from over 2,100 investors at $1 USD (`https://coinlist.co/filecoin`).

The Filecoin raise was the largest ICO in 2017 and received a lot of attention, as well as scrutiny. In the legal world, a SAFT framework will not totally rule out investigation from the SEC but it certainly changed the reference point. Funds used to come from "donations" from the general public but now this is moving into the accredited and institutional investors space, which the ICO mechanism was supposed to disrupt in the first place.

Summary

When ICOs burst onto the scene, no one could have predicted how large the legal ramifications would be. For those that did, they either tried to ignore it and fly under the radar or got in fast in order to minimize retrospective effects. The challenge is that while every ICO claims utility, many business models are designed to increase utility in order to drive up demand and thus the value or price of the token. With this increase in value, many have the expectation of profits.

In this chapter, we learned what a security is in the eyes of the SEC and looked at the Howey landmark case when determining if something is an investment contract or not from a US perspective. The global regulatory stance of various countries was discussed, where, in general, other than the outright ban from China and South Korea, regulators are open to working with businesses within a framework in an attempt to not stifle innovation.

The SEC started sending signals in the latter half of 2017 and its reports into The DAO and the Munchee ICOs provide intriguing insights into the ICO world from the side of the regulators. This should not serve as a negative deterrent but as a signal to be sensible and compliant and if uncertain, to seek professional advice. The evolution of white papers then showed more and more legal clauses being included to protect the ICOs and their founders.

We will now move away from the legal aspects and will start looking at the token mechanics: the hard cap and soft cap, the presales bonus, and even the inventive modified reverse Dutch auction.

7

THE TOKEN SALES MECHANICS

Creating tokens in an ICO, as covered in *Chapter 4, Token Varieties*, was one thing, but figuring out how many to create, how much to sell, the early round bonuses, the inflation rate and everything else relating to the mechanics of the tokens was (and still is) a challenging task. All of the above had to be communicated to supporters and investors, while trying to keep things simple.

Although there was no right or wrong way to create tokens and market them, a lot of parallels can be drawn from the issuance of regular shares in a company, served with a side of economic incentives, a sprinkling of game theory, and a dust of creative marketing.

In this chapter, we will look at:

- ◆ Token supply and distribution
- ◆ Presale strategy and bonuses
- ◆ Hard cap, soft cap, and no cap
- ◆ A reverse Dutch auction
- ◆ A token mechanic blueprint

If a lawyer was important when contemplating an ICO, a **CEO** or **Chief Economic Officer** was becoming crucial when looking at structuring the inner workings of one. Of course, what really happened was that many people quickly upskilled in the basics of monetary policies, such as the model for token supply and issuance, along with fiscal policy, such as how the funds would be spent. We will first take a look at the all-important supply and distribution of an ICO.

Token supply and distribution

Looking at the number of tokens created, there was generally no rhyme or reason for the values chosen. The standard default in the early days seemed to be 100 million tokens, which was a nice round number. Others preferred a billion as a round number. The supply ranged from 2.6 million to 2.7 quadrillion:

ICO	Amount
Counterparty	2.6 million
Factom	8.8 million
Gnosis	10 million
Augur	11 million
Decent	73.3 million
Bancor	79.4 million
Firstblood	93.5 million
ICONOMI	100 million
MobileGo	100 million
Waves	100 million
Ark	125 million
TenX	205.2 million
Pillar	800 million
Humaniq	921 million
Synereo	949.3 million
Civic	1 billion

Nxt	1 billion
SingularDTV	1 billion
BAT	1.5 billion
Filecoin	2 billion
Ripple	100 billion
Kin	10 trillion
IOTA	2,780 trillion

Table 1: Examples of token supplies from various ICOs.

The reason why some of the supplies were not whole numbers was due to the sales model employed by various ICOs. For example, TenX did not select a fixed number of PAY tokens but instead chose a 200,000 ETH target and issued 350 PAY tokens for every 1 ETH. It also provided bonuses for earlier contributors, so when the calculations were done, a non-round number eventuated.

When deciding on a token supply, anything goes, but there are a few things to keep in mind. If it is set too low, your users may have to start working with fractional amounts and humans prefer to work with whole numbers. Also, consider that a proportion of tokens will be lost, which will reduce the overall supply. This can occur due to users losing private keys or tokens being sent to wrong addresses, which may make them unspendable forever.

On the other hand, creating something like 2.7 quadrillion tokens seems overly excessive. Firstly, large numbers become hard to read, say or comprehend. How many zeros does a quadrillion have again?

[A quadrillion has 15 trailing zeros.
In other words, 1,000,000,000,000,000.]

Secondly, having too large a supply tends to reduce the perceived value of the token. It is also not a good signal to the market. Scarcity is what helps to create value, not abundance, and in some cases, it is used as a marketing tool when dealing with investors.

As we can see above, several ICOs have used tokens in the billions, such as Civic (1 billion), Filecoin (2 billion) and Ripple (100 billion), which has been the upper range, if IOTA and Kin (10 trillion) are considered as outliers.

 One thing to note when choosing a supply is divisibility. Although Ripple (XRP) may have 100 billion tokens, each token is divisible to six decimal places, so 1,000,000 drops make 1 XRP. This is the equivalent of 100 cents making 1 dollar. Bitcoin, however, has 100,000,000 satoshis in 1 bitcoin. Therefore, on the surface, it may seem that there are 4761 times more XRP than BTC (100 billion divided by 21 million), but the reality is that there is only 47.6 times more.

Distribution

Token distribution started with the majority being made available to the public. This was the ideal scenario, as having the tokens held by as many avid supporters as possible was the goal. However, over time, the number dropped from the 80% mark to 70%, then 60% and then lower:

	Aug 15	Feb 16	Apr 16	Aug 16	Sep 16	Nov 16
	Augur [1]	Lisk [2]	Waves [3]	ICONOMI [4]	Synereo [5]	Golem [6]
Public*	80%	85%	85%	85%	18.5%	82%
Developers/ core team/ founders	16%	7.8%	9%	8%	10%	6%
Foundation	4%					12%

Strategic partners/ advisors		2%	4%	2%		
Early supporters		1%	1%		17.5%	
Campaigns/ bounties		4%	1%	2%	11.5%	
First-day ICO participants		0.2%				
Future team members				3%		
Future funding rounds					42.5%	

Table 2: Token distribution for ICOs from August 2015 to November 2016

* Public is the portion that is sold to buyers. The others are allocated, given, or distributed.

	Apr 17	Apr 17	May 17	Jun 17	Jun 17	Jun 17
	Gnosis [7]	MobileGo [8]	BAT [9]	Bancor [10]	Status [11]	Civic [12]
Public	5%	70%	66.6%	50%	41%	33%
Developers/ core team/ founders	95%		13.3%	10%	20%	34%
Foundation		30%		20%		
User growth/ community/ bounties			20%	20%		33%
Future stakeholders					29%	

Status genesis token holders				10%	

Table 3: Token distribution for ICOs from April 2017 to June 2017

Gnosis only made 5% of tokens available to the public, but this was due to the mechanics of its reverse Dutch auction (which will be explained later). Status distributed only 41% of tokens to the public but has since reserved 29% for future stakeholders:

	Jul 17	Aug 17	Sep 17	Sep 17
	Pillar[13]	Filecoin[14]	Kin[15]	Kyber Networks[16]
Public	72%	70%	10%	61.06%
Developers/ core team/ founders		10%	30%	19.47%
Foundation		5%	60%	
Company	10%	15%		19.47%
User growth/ community/ bounties	3%			
Future stakeholders				
Status genesis token holders				
Later funding	15%			

Table 4: Token distribution for ICOs from July 2017 to September 2017

Kin provided only 10% of tokens to the public. This was very surprising and yet it still managed to raise just under $100 million USD. Its reasoning was outlined in its white paper:

"In order to finance the Kin roadmap, Kik will conduct a token distribution event that will offer for sale one trillion units out of a 10 trillion-unit total supply of kin. The proceeds of the token distribution event will be used to fund Kik operations and to deploy the Kin Foundation. A portion of the funds raised in the token distribution will be used to execute upon the roadmap of additional feature development planned for the Kin integration into Kik." (`https://kinecosystem.org/static/files/Kin_Whitepaper_V1_English.pdf`).

Kik pre-allocated another three trillion kin to the founding members and placed the remaining six trillion kin under the control of the Kin Foundation.

EOS distribution

The EOS ICO was unique and deserves a special mention. The concept was that one billion EOS tokens were to be distributed over a period of 341 days. 200 million or 20% were distributed during the first five days, from June 26, 2017, to July 1, 2017, and an additional 700 million EOS tokens were distributed in two million blocks every 23 hours thereafter. 100 million or 10% was reserved for Block.one, an *open source software publisher specializing in high performance blockchain technologies* (`https://block.one/about/`).

Note that the vesting period of the 100 million for Block.one is 10% over 10 years. At the end of the five-day period and at the end of each 23-hour period, a fixed number of tokens were distributed proportionally amongst all the investors, based on their contributions. In other words, everyone in a specific period gets the same amount of EOS per ETH as everyone else. You only know for sure exactly how many EOS you are getting for your sent ETH once the period is over.

The EOS token purchase agreement provides a simple example (`https://eos.io/documents/block.one%20-%20 EOS%20Token%20Purchase%20Agreement%20-%20September%20 4,%202017.pdf`):

1. 20 EOS Tokens are available during a period.

2. Bob contributes 4 ETH and Alice contributes 1 ETH during the period. The period ends.

3. As a total of 5 ETH were contributed for 20 EOS Tokens during the period, 1 EOS Token will be distributed for every 0.25 ETH contributed. Therefore, Bob receives 16 EOS Tokens and Alice receives 4 EOS Tokens.

What was interesting was that all tokens from past periods were tradable and entered the public markets. This meant that there were two ways of getting EOS tokens: directly from the ICO or from previous ICO participants. It provided some interesting trading and arbitraging opportunities.

It didn't make sense to contribute to the ICO if the price was cheaper on the exchange, but it wasn't possible to know the final price until the contribution period was over. What some traders did was exercise a function within the smart contract called `buyWithLimit()`. The idea was to allow investors to specify the exact contribution period and a maximum limit of ether, but traders used this function and applied this to the current contribution period and specified the amount of ether needed to make the purchase lower than the current market rate. The trader could then claim the tokens and flip them on an exchange. The trader needed to make the transaction at the last possible moment because that was when the most amount of information was available to make the best possible decision.

Other traders took this one step further and not only contributed at the end but also sent bogus transactions to flood the Ethereum network, to push out would-be contributors. The strategy was to contribute 5 or 10 minutes before the close of the period and then send bogus transactions with abnormally high gas fees. Transactions are usually processed in order of highest fees to lowest fees, so regular EOS contributions would be temporarily squeezed out, allowing the trader to make a profit by gaming the system.

EOS ended up raising $172 million USD in the first contribution period, which took place over five days, resulting in an EOS token price of $0.86 USD ($172 million USD divided by 200 million tokens). The cheapest price was $0.48 USD at contribution period #123, which occurred on October 26, 2017. The most expensive was $19.29 USD per token at contribution period #315, which occurred on April 28, 2018.

At the conclusion of the ICO on June 1, 2018, EOS ended up collecting around 6.5 million ether, which is around $4 billion USD. EOS holds the record for not only the largest ICO raised but also the longest running:

Figure 1: The price of the EOS token at each contribution period
over 11 months (https://eosscan.io/)

The presales strategy and bonuses

In the beginning, everyone formed orderly queues and calmly sent funds to bitcoin addresses and smart contracts, but as the excitement grew, especially during the hype of 2017, tokens and cash were flying everywhere. This was primarily due to token holders doubling or tripling their investments in a very short space of time. In some cases, investors made ten times their initial investment in a matter of weeks or even days of the tokens listing on exchanges.

First, it was all about just getting the tokens. Then it became a race to buy the tokens first because bonuses were often linked to buyers in the first week or days or even the first "Power Hour." The next level was a pre-ICO, where a second smart contract would be created to handle the receipt of the funds. Then we saw private pre-ICOs before the pre-ICO. It was utter madness.

Let's start by understanding how bonuses worked.

No bonuses

Nearly all ICOs have some sort of bonus offering stage, but let's first take a look at the ones that do not. Civic is an identity verification service on the blockchain, co-founded by Vinny Lingham, who was one of the sharks on the TV show *South African Shark Tank*.

Case study – Civic

Civic's **Secure Identity Platform** (**SIP**) provides access to identity verification services that give businesses and individuals the tools to control and protect their identity. Individuals can access identity verification services by downloading the Civic App and setting up their digital identity by verifying their **personally identifiable information** (**PII**) with a trusted third party.

Additionally, Civic is spearheading the development of `Identity.com`, a decentralized identity ecosystem that will be completely open sourced, opening up access to secure, trusted identity verification services to people around the world.

The Civic App

The Civic App is designed to give users more control over when and where they share their personal data. A user's information is stored on the app, protected by biometrics and high-level encryption. Civic partners, called *Requesters*, can ask a user to provide verified personal information through custom QR codes. Once a user has unlocked the Civic App with their biometrics, the user can scan this code, review exactly which information is being requested, and choose whether to approve or deny the request.

The point here is that background and personal information verification checks may no longer need to be performed from the ground up every time that a new institution or application requires one, thus saving time and money.

The Civic token

Civic introduced a Civic token or CVC as a form of settlement and governance for participants in `Identity.com`. The user approaches a *Requester* to use a service or purchase a good. The *Requester* sends the user a list of *Validators* it accepts and the PII required. If the user has the required PII attested by a *Validator*, that is acceptable to the *Requester*, then the user selects to share that *Validator's* attestation with the *Requester*.

If the user does not already have a suitable attestation, then they will be asked to approach an acceptable *Validator* with unverified PII. Once the *Validator* is satisfied with the authenticity of the PII, it will attest to the accuracy of this information. This attestation, or digital fingerprint of the PII, is recorded onto a blockchain and the original PII is stored on the user's mobile device in an encrypted form.

The *Requester* and *Validator* mutually agree on a price for the attested PII. Once the price has been agreed, the *Requester* places CVC tokens into an escrow smart contract and the user sends the PII to the *Requester*. Once the PII attestation is received, the *Requester* inspects it and, if acceptable, provides the user with the desired service. In turn, the CVC tokens are released from the escrow smart contract and the *Validator* is paid in CVC. Therefore, *Requestors* pay for verification services with CVC, *Validators* are rewarded with CVC, and users are rewarded for sharing their information:

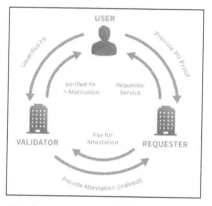

Figure 2: The interaction between users, "Validators," and "Requestors" in Civic's model (https://www.civic.com/wp-content/uploads/2018/05/Token-Behavior-Model-May-16-2018.pdf)

The use of CVCs provides several advantages over an existing token or cryptocurrency. Firstly, it shields the ecosystem from extraneous considerations, such as volatility observed in other cryptocurrencies, and secondly, it makes it possible for the community to manage incentives to better control and drive the benefits of the ecosystem.

In its June 2017 token sale, Civic created one billion tokens: 33% were allocated to be sold to the public at $0.10 each, 33% were allocated for distribution to incentivize participation in the ecosystem, and 33% were allocated to the company. There was no bonus, meaning investors couldn't get more by purchasing early. In fact, this was prevented by a queuing system, where a random number was assigned to participants regardless of the order in which they arrived:

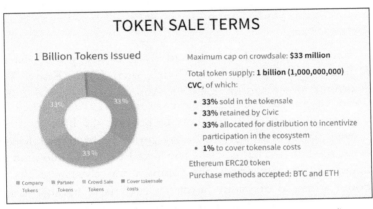

Figure 3: Civic's token sales terms (https://tokensale.civic.com/)

A bonus often helps to build momentum and attract buyers. Without a bonus structure, there is more risk that not all the tokens will be sold. To mitigate that risk and ensure that all 330 million tokens were sold, Civic held a presale for large buyers, with the provision that one-third of the tokens, or 110 million, would be available for sale during the token sale. This meant that if all 110 million tokens were purchased in the main sale, only 220 million would have been purchased in the presale. The idea here was to ensure that Civic received a much broader base of supporters to help kick-start the network. If, for some reason, Civic hadn't sold the full 110 million token allocation, then the bigger buyers would have effectively agreed to buy the difference. This meant that there were two ways that Civic's goal of ensuring all 330 million tokens were sold could be achieved. Clever!

Lingham explained Civic's strategy:

"We're creating a fixed supply of 1 billion tokens. We are pricing them at $0.10 each. We felt that we needed enough tokens to power the smart contracting system for years to come and we could go to 2 decimal places for fractional smart contract execution. 1bn felt like the right number—no crazy scientific reason here".

(https://vinnylingham.com/the-vanity-headline-is-not-the-goal-introducing-the-civic-token-sale-3675b883fb05).

Civic announced that it had over 10,000 purchases and all had to be identified via Civic's own **KYC (Know Your Customer)** process, using the Civic App (https://www.ccn.com/civic-token-sale-concludes-earlysuccessfully-with-33-million-raise/). The goal was to provide the little guys with an even playing field against the big guys. The more people using CVCs, the better. That is why Civic aimed for broad adoption and support. In its own words, the company was chasing results and adoption instead of vanity headlines, such as being able to raise tens of millions of dollars in a matter of seconds.

Civic also kept the token price simple and straightforward throughout the process, at $0.10 USD. So, in the end, there was no complicated math for token allocation based on what day or week the tokens were purchased on, and most importantly, there were no discounts, which can often attract a different kind of buyer. These buyers are often speculators who do not plan to be users of the system and tend to dump their large holdings for profit shortly after the ICO.

Cryptobeer

At the Consensus 2018 conference in May, Civic debuted the world's first anonymous age-verifying beer vending machine in partnership with Anheuser-Busch InBev, the world's largest brewer. The vending machine displayed a QR code and anyone with the Civic App, that had verified their identity, could prove to the vending machine that they were over the age of 21.

Figure 4: The Civic vending machine on display at Consensus 2018

Although this was just a proof of concept, it was a user-friendly demonstration of Civic's identity verification protocol and just one of many potential use cases for identity verification services. Based on partial-knowledge proofs, the ability to anonymously perform age verification opens up new possibilities. This process is and will continue to be free for the end users, while *Requesters* are the ones responsible for paying for identity verification.

One year after its token sale, Civic's platform includes secure login, a reusable KYC solution and ID codes, a secure relationships verification service that enables anyone to securely verify a business, advisory, or investment relationship. Civic is also rapidly expanding its partner ecosystem with over 90 so far (https://www.civic.com/solutions/partners/).

The road ahead includes enhancing security capabilities and lowering barriers to entry, such as making transactions using fiat currency an option.

Kyber Networks

Kyber Networks also had no bonus structure. What it did have was a very cumbersome registration process. There was so much demand for its token, though, that it still met its cap of 200,000 ether, resulting in $48 million USD raised in 24 hours. Users had a seven-day window to be whitelisted. Whitelisting meant signing up to Slack, Telegram, or Wechat, which meant providing an email address, along with a full name, and other personal information. The next step was that the user had a 10-day period to register by going through a KYC process. A passport or national ID had to be provided to ensure one email and one Ethereum wallet address was linked to one real-world identity and that no one could game the system and register multiple times.

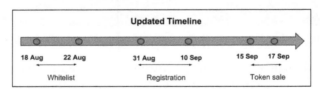

Figure 5: Kyber Networks' token purchase process
(https://blog.kyber.network/kybernetwork-public-token-sale-901b3e7f5457)

Bonuses

Civic and Kyber Networks were exceptions because ICO bonuses were so popular that they were considered the norm. A common structure was to have a *sliding scale early backer incentive mechanism* or, in plain English, an early bird discount.

MaidSafe went with a 40% bonus for those who invested in the first week, a 30% bonus in the second week, 20% in the third week, and 10% in the fourth week (`https://github.com/maidsafe/Whitepapers/blob/master/Project-Safe.md`). Lisk and MobileGo followed a similar pattern:

	MaidSafe	Lisk	MobileGo
Week 1	40%	15%	15%
Week 2	30%	10%	10%
Week 3	20%	5%	5%
Week 4	10%	No bonus	No bonus
Week 5	No bonus	NA	NA

Table 5: Comparison of early buyer incentive schemes

The incentive for providing a bonus should be of no surprise. It was designed to reward early investors with more tokens, as they were taking on more risk. However, having too large a bonus appeared to be detrimental to the ICO because it was seen as devaluing the token. A balance had to be found.

Ethereum

Ethereum had an incentive of one bitcoin buying 2,000 ether for the first 14 days and then it would drop 24 ether every day for the next 28 days. For example, on day 15, one bitcoin would only receive 1976 ether. The Ethereum team obviously had a good time playing with the numbers 1337 and 42.

> - The price of ether is initially set to a discounted price of **2000 ETH per BTC**, and will stay this way for **14 days** before linearly declining to a final rate of **1337 ETH per BTC**. The sale will last **42 days**, concluding at 23:59 Zug time September 2.

Figure 9: The Ethereum ICO token sale details using key numerical figures of 1337 and 42 (explained in Chapter 4, Token Varieties) (https://blog.ethereum.org/2014/07/22/launching-the-ether-sale/)

Waves

Bonuses then got more creative and more convoluted. Waves provided a 20% token bonus on the first day, a 10% bonus for the next 17 days, and a 5% bonus for the first half of May:

Date	Bonus
12 Apr 2017	20%
13–30 Apr 2017	10%
1–15 May 2017	5%
After 16 May 2017	No bonus

Table 6: The Waves token bonus plan
(https://blog.wavesplatform.com/waves-ico-structure-and-timeline-87db476cc586)

FirstBlood

FirstBlood is a decentralized eSports platform built on Ethereum. It effectively lets players challenge each other using the platform token as a wager or betting system. The system uses smart contracts and decentralized oracles on the Ethereum blockchain. FirstBlood gave a huge 70% bonus in the first hour, calling it the "Power Hour":

"The first hour of the crowdsale will be a Power Hour. During the Power Hour, 1 Ether will buy 170 1ST. After that, the price will change to 150:1, and then decrease every week until it reaches 100:1 in the fourth week." (https://web.archive.org/web/20170417105104/https://firstblood.io/sale/#).

Date	Bonus
Power Hour	70%
26 Sept–2 Oct 2017	50%
3–9 Oct 2017	33%
10–16 Oct 2017	17%
17–23 Oct 2017	No bonus

Table 7: The FirstBlood token bonus plan

Humaniq

Humaniq describes itself as a revolutionary blockchain-based financial services platform providing banking 4.0 services for the unbanked, utilizing mobile devices, and biometric identification systems. It provided a more granular approach to its ICO, with 50% bonus in the first two days, half of that in the following six days, and then half yet again in the next six days. It was somewhat mimicking the bitcoin reward system:

Date	Bonus
6–7 Apr 2017	49.9%
8–14 Apr 2017	25%
15–21 Apr 2017	12.5%
22–26 Apr 2017	No bonus

Table 8: The Humaniq token bonus plan

TenX

TenX provided 20% in the first 24 hours, 10% on days two and three, 5% from days four to seven, 2.5% from days eight to 14, and no bonus in the final 14 days. What TenX also did was offer two extra "goodies." Investors of more than 25 ether would receive a *highly exclusive limited edition* TenX debit card. For over 1,250 ether purchased, a founders' edition TenX platinum card would be gifted.

Date	Bonus
First 24 hours	20%
Day two and day three	10%
Day four to day seven	5%
Day eight to day 15	2.5%
Final 14 days	No bonus

Table 9: The TenX token bonus plan

TenX provided an exceptionally detailed summary analysis post ICO, which actually revealed that the bonus structure didn't mean much because the ICO was over in seven minutes (https:// blog.tenx.tech/reflecting-on-a-highly-successful-tenx-tokensale-b2705d593f1a). TenX did its presale 10 days before the actual sale and this was open to anyone willing to contribute at least 125 ETH, which was the equivalent of $40,000 USD at the time. TenX then showed the contribution address 15 minutes before the actual ICO.

Although TenX aimed for 200,000 ETH, due to price fluctuations after the conversion, it ended up with 245,000 ETH, as explained in blog.tenx.tech:

"Adding these 3 factors together increases the total ETH of slightly over the targeted 200,000 ETH to a total of 245,000 ETH. This amount may fluctuate quite heavily up or down, since roughly one third was contributed in non-ETH currencies (ERC20, BTC, LTC, DASH)." (https://blog.tenx.tech/ reflecting-on-a-highly-successful-tenx-tokensale-b2705d593f1a).

Tezos

Tezos decided to provide a bonus structure not based on time, but based on the block number on the bitcoin blockchain. There was a 20% bonus from block 0-399 and then 15%, 10%, and 5% for each subsequent 400 blocks. What this really did was introduce an extra step for everyone because since the duration of each block was about 10 minutes, the 20% bonus would last for 400 blocks multiplied by 10 minutes, giving 4,000 minutes or about 2.78 days. If Tezos was trying to test some of its users' technical knowledge, it certainly achieved that.

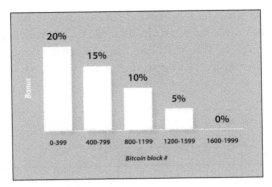

Figure 6: The Tezos token bonus plan

Synereo

Other ICOs started getting fancy by introducing different bonus layers. Synereo, a blockchain-based platform allowing direct monetization of content for content creators, had a million AMP (AMP being the token ticker symbol) bonus pool that would be proportionally distributed to all the contributors in the first 24-hour period, as explained at `blog.synereo.com`:

"For example: if Alice buys 10,000 AMPs, and the total number sold during the first day was 10,000,000 AMPs, Alice will receive an additional 10,000/10,000,000 * 1,000,000 = 1,000 AMPs."

Synereo also offered the standard sliding scale, where the earlier the contribution, the higher the bonus.

Date	Bonus
19 Sep–2 Oct 2017	~21%
3–9 Oct 2017	~10%
10–18 Oct 2017	No bonus

Table 10: The Synereo token early bird bonus plan (https://blog.synereo.com/2016/08/29/synereos-second-fundraising-campaign-coming/)

Synereo also had a further bonus based on the amount contributed denominated in bitcoins. Therefore, to obtain the maximum bonus possible, an investor would contribute 200 bitcoins within 24 hours of the ICO starting on September 19, 2017.

Amount invested	Bonus
2 BTC	3.33%
10 BTC	6%
20 BTC	9%
50 BTC	11%
100 BTC	13%
200 BTC	15%

Table 11: The Synereo token bonus plan based on amount purchased

So, what can we learn from all of this? Firstly, the bonus structures are all different. Not having a bonus structure like Civic does remove potential speculators but with no incentive mechanisms, there is a risk that there will not be enough interest. One has to be very confident to pull this off. Also, having a simple bonus structure is important. Too many dates make it confusing, as well as using block numbers instead of dates.

An incentive scheme is also designed to induce the priming effect, where having a non-empty tipping jar can start the ball rolling and give the impression that if others are doing it, I might as well do it too, similar to the follower effect. It is also designed to combat everyone waiting until the last minute because this is in fact the optimal strategy and also to create FOMO. Waiting until the last minute gives the buyer the most amount of information to make a decision, while still receiving the same amount as if there was no incentive scheme.

NEM

NEM, a blockchain platform providing the capability of creating smart assets, did a fundraiser where bitcointalk users would reserve their spot by typing I'm interested or something to that effect. After 20 pages, a small fee of 0.001 BTC or 10 NXT was charged, approximately doubling every 10 pages.

Pages	Fee
First 20 pages	Free to join
Pages 21-30	0.001 BTC or 10 NXT
Pages 31-40	0.002 BTC or 20 NXT
Pages 41-50	0.004 BTC or 40 NXT
Pages 51-60	0.008 BTC or 80 NXT
Pages 61-70	0.016 BTC or 160 NXT
Pages 71-80	0.0025 BTC or 250 NXT
Pages 80+	0.03 BTC or 300 NXT

Table 12: NEM's bonus structure was a reverse fee structure. The earlier one registered interest, the lower the entry fee.

NEM's initial concept was to distribute the tokens to around 3,000 to 4,000 supporters:

"Our current formula is number of NEM per stake spot = 4 billion/(total account stake + development stake). At the moment we are aiming for roughly 3-4000 accounts in which 5% is development stake, but it could be more, could be less depending on the fundraising." (https://bitcointalk.org/index.php?topic=422129.0).

Presales or pre-ICO and private sales

Bonuses could be considered as a presale providing greater rewards for the early adopters but this was then taken to the next level where sometimes a presale would happen a month or two before the actual ICO. In some cases, it even took place just days ahead of the ICO. When word got out that ICOs were a way to make some quick money, pre-ICOs or presales were a way to get a head start on everyone else.

Pre-ICOs sometimes came with a minimum purchase amount and the fundraising targets were often lower compared to that of the main ICO and tokens were usually sold cheaper. With private presales, they generally came with higher minimum purchase amounts than presales and they also took place much earlier. Typically, a separate smart contract was also employed to avoid mixing pre-ICO funds with the main ICO, to keep things simpler for auditing and reconciliation purposes. There was no hard or fast rule though.

OmiseGo

OmiseGo is an open payment platform and decentralized exchange based on the Ethereum platform. It had a presale requirement of a minimum contribution of $5,000 USD crypto equivalent and a maximum contribution of $100,000 USD crypto equivalent.

Simple Tokens

Simple Tokens, a platform enabling companies to create, launch, and manage their own branded digital token economy on an open and highly scalable sidechain anchored to the Ethereum blockchain, had a "private presale" with a minimum investment of $200,000 USD (https://medium.com/ostdotcom/early-access-registration-for-simple-token-sale-is-now-underway-24a84125baf3). This was effectively a private round because it then had an "Early Access" sale, which could be considered the presale and then the general or public sale.

Telegram

Another ICO that made a lot of noise was Telegram, a cloud-based instant messaging platform. Looking to raise over a billion USD, Telegram has reportedly secured $850 million USD in a "presale" from 81 accredited investors, including companies from Silicon Valley, such as Sequoia Capital and Benchmark (`https://www.sec.gov/Archives/edgar/data/1729650/000095017218000030/xslFormDX01/primary_doc.xml`). As if that was not enough, there is another Form D disclosure citing an additional $850 million USD raised from 94 investors, bringing the total to $1.7 billion USD (`https://www.sec.gov/Archives/edgar/data/1729650/000095017218000060/xslFormDX01/primary_doc.xml`).

Telegram was intending to have a public sale but since it raised too much in the presales, it did not go through with the public sale. If this is the power of having a platform of 200 million monthly active users, imagine what Facebook could do!

One of the side effects of a pre-ICO is that early investors or adopters tend to sell or "dump" the tokens as soon as they become tradable on exchanges. So, because they got the token for less than the price of the main ICO, there is almost a guarantee of short-term profits. This is more evident in ICOs that offer a steep discount, so this amount needs to be carefully selected.

Vesting periods

Vesting is a term used to mean where employees or founders of a company earn shares over time, rather than all at once. This means that instead of having immediate equity in a company, a percentage of the shares are made available or "vest" over time. Vesting protects a company from employees or founders receiving all their shares at once and then walking away from the company or project.

This can be directly translated into the ICO world, where tokens that are made available to the founders can be quite substantial. 10% of 100 million tokens represents 10 million tokens. Shared between a handful of founders, that's a cool couple of million each. Vesting can also apply to tokens granted as bonuses for ICOs.

There was no standard vesting period for ICOs, though. Filecoin had a comprehensive vesting plan where investors or supporters had a default vesting period of six months minimum if tokens were purchased in the public sale or a 12-month minimum if purchased as part of the presale. Protocol Labs and the Foundation have a six-year linear vesting period. So, because the network has yet to be created, the vesting period will commence upon network launch and not when a token is purchased. The network is estimated to be launched in the second half of 2018.

[**Cliff**: A time where a proportion of tokens will vest or become spendable.]

A vesting period of 24 months, with six-month cliffs, became very popular. This meant that if a founder received 1,000,000 tokens, 250,000 tokens would be released every six months. ICONOMI, Airclipse, and Synereo had a 30-month vesting period for their founders. Brave had a 180 day "lockup" period. Bancor founders were subjected to a three-year vesting schedule. TenX founders and employees had a four-year vesting period.

Company	Vesting period
Brave[17]	180-day lockup
OmiseGo[18]	12 months
Airclipse[19], ICONOMI[20], Status[21] and Aragon[22]	24 months with six-month cliffs for founders
Synereo[23]	30 months for founders

TenX[24]	Four years for founders and employees
Bancor[25]	Three years for founders
Filecoin[26]	Six-year linear for founders

Table 13: Sample ICO vesting periods for various ICOs

Hard cap, soft cap, and no cap

Another aspect of the token mechanics was to decide on the soft cap and the hard cap. Some even had no cap at all! These caps are effectively fundraising goals.

Uncapped ICOs

An uncapped ICO is where there is no upper limit to the amount being raised. What the company is effectively saying is that no matter what the demand is, tokens will be created to cater for it. The Ethereum ICO was uncapped and sold approximately 60 million ETH.

Ethereum

What was interesting about the Ethereum ICO was that over the 62 days that it ran for, the price of bitcoin dropped from about $618 USD to $398 USD. This is a 36% drop in value. This meant that those who invested at the very last minute, ended up paying about the same rate of $0.33/ETH as those that invested early.

This highlights two important points. Firstly, the volatile nature of the cryptocurrencies being collected in an ICO can play havoc with the expected calculations and secondly, the duration of the ICO plays a part as well. The longer the duration, the more exposure to potential volatility, in both directions of course.

Ethereum is unique in that there is no finite limit on the total supply of ether, unlike bitcoin. Bitcoin has a maximum supply of 21 million bitcoins, of which about 17.19 million are currently in existence as of August 2018 (https://blockchain. info/charts/total-bitcoins). The current supply of ether is 101,106,416 as of August 2018 (https://etherscan.io/stat/ supply). The number of ether created at its inception started at around 20% and drops in a non-linear fashion. This means that it drops approximately 4% in the first year, 3% the following year, 2% after that, and it keeps getting smaller for subsequent years (https://docs.google.com/spreadsheets/d/150B9eytmjZ642 tYD0jSdFZQHldmk7VG5Wm3KVctydpY/pubhtml).

It was assumed that eventually the annual loss and destruction of ETH would balance the rate of issuance, so that a balance or equilibrium would be reached. Ethereum, however, likes to throw the proverbial spanner into the mix and is pondering a consensus model change from the energy intensive Proof of Work to Proof of Stake, which has been given the nickname "Casper." It also has this concept of a difficulty bomb dubbed "Ice Age", which slows down the block creation process at certain times. Add to this an April Fools' 2018 joke from Ethereum co-founder Vitalik Buterin:

"In order to ensure the economic sustainability of the platform under the widest possible variety of circumstances, and in light of the fact that issuing new coins to proof of work miners is no longer an effective way of promoting an egalitarian coin distribution or any other significant policy goal, I propose that we agree on a hard cap for the total quantity of ETH. I recommend setting MAX_SUPPLY = 120,204,432, or exactly 2x the amount of ETH sold in the original ether sale." (https:// github.com/ethereum/EIPs/issues/960).

Buterin then clarified in a tweet that it was a meta-joke, but some in the community took this seriously.

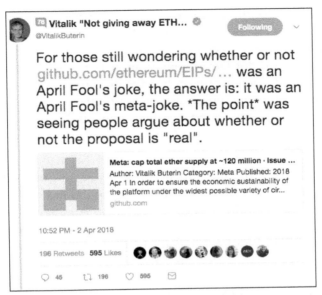

Figure 7: Buterin clarifying in a tweet that his proposal to limit the supply of ether was a meta-joke (https://twitter.com/VitalikButerin/status/980744740277661696)

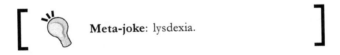

Meta-joke: lysdexia.

Tezos

Tezos took a leaf out of Ethereum's book and also had an uncapped ICO. Note that Tezos is an Ethereum competitor! The Tezos white paper gave an explanation:

"Following the example set by the Ethereum Foundation, there is no cap on the amount of contributions that will be accepted by the Foundation. This is done in order to ensure that participation is not limited only to insiders or the "fast fingered". The Tezos development team believes that an uncapped fundraiser will promote a widespread distribution of the tokens, a necessary prerequisite to launching a robust network." (https://www.tezos.com/static/papers/Tezos_Overview.pdf).

However, a counterargument could be made that Tezos did not have a specific goal in mind. There was no budget, no forecast, and no plan. Aware of this, Tezos did include a financial forecast with the heading *if the foundation is endowed with...* and provided scenarios of $6 million USD, $12 million USD, or $20 million USD. Above $20 million USD, it planned to *offer student grants for conducting projects related to the Tezos ecosystem*, and even more creatively to *negotiate with a small nation-state the recognition of Tezos as one of their official state currencies, which would immediately give Tezos favorable treatment in terms of financial regulation* (https://www.tezos.com/static/papers/Tezos_Overview.pdf). *Attempt negotiation to purchase or lease sovereign land.* (https://www.tezos.com/static/papers/Tezos_Overview.pdf).

Needless to say, with $233 million USD raised, this was significantly over the $20 million USD project, so it sounds like Tezos will be purchasing land if it ever gets through the legal issues and can access its funds!

Being uncapped also meant that the potential number of Tezos tokens in circulation is limited only by investors' willingness to participate. Scarcity is not an issue here but abundance is, along with the risk of overflooding the market with tokens when they hit exchanges, which they will.

While some entrepreneurs love the idea of having a war chest of funds and their names all over the media for being the next "largest" ICO, it can also show a lack of discipline. How many companies really need $100 million USD at the outset? With this negative perception of uncapped ICOs, capped ICOs became the de facto standard.

Capped ICOs

A capped ICO usually has two components: a soft cap and a hard cap. The decision to have a cap and have it met provides the market with confidence in the project and the team and shows that the company is not raising funds just for the sake of it.

Soft cap

A soft cap is the minimum needed for a project to proceed. This is typically determined by a project's budget and a forecast of the required funds to bring the product or service to market. The term "soft cap" is actually quite misleading because it is not actually a cap as such. A more accurate term would be a "minimum threshold" or a "minimum goal." If it isn't reached, then the project will shut down and return all the raised capital to the investors. Not all ICOs do this and some proceed with the project regardless of the capital raised. Some projects enter what some call "life support mode", where a decision is made on whether to continue, pause, or dismantle the project.

Veredictum was one such unfortunate ICO that had a soft cap of $2.5 million USD or 7,752 ETH, which it did not reach in September 2017. It then issued a blog post on how investors could reclaim their ETH.

Figure 8: Veredictum missed its soft cap and refunded ETH back to its investors

Hard cap

A hard cap is the absolute maximum an ICO will take. If reached, the ICO finishes and excess funds are returned to investors. Positive aspects about having an upper limit are that there is not an excess of investors and it creates scarcity. The investors that missed out will be eager to buy the tokens when they are made available on an exchange, for instance, and a hard cap that is reached often leads to a price increase when it is listed on exchanges. If all the investors were catered for then there is a potential for excessive selling or a "dump" when a token is listed, as investors attempt to realize short-term profits.

There is no exact science when picking a hard cap compared to a soft cap, but it does depend on the project needs. There are some general rules, though. Firstly, specify the hard cap before the launch. This figure must remain fixed to protect the token's integrity. This means that more tokens should not be created, even if it is programmatically possible to do so. Secondly, don't set a hard cap too low or else your project could be strapped for funds in the future. Thirdly, it is important to justify the amount of funds required, typically in the white paper.

The core issue with hard caps is that they tend to create an undesirable stakeholder distribution if they are reached too fast. For open-source or open-community projects, the founders will benefit from a wider distribution of ownership, with a lower average stake. Wider community-owned tokens create stronger network effects, which grow faster and are highly desirable for projects. Unfortunately, a hard cap or maximum limit naturally prevents these desirable distributions. Hard caps on popular projects create a first come, first served competition, where "whales" or large investors gobble up the majority of the supply and lock out the smaller players.

Most ICOs did not initially require identity verification or even have limits on the transaction size itself, allowing large investors to do as they pleased. In fact, those ICOs without KYC found that they could not convert their cryptocurrencies raised to fiat currency because of banking regulations. To combat the problem of not having a limit on the transaction size, maximum contribution limits were placed for each transaction. Whales then had to buy in lots of small tuna chunks! While this may be a pain, it can be easily circumvented by automating the purchase process.

Another option was to place a maximum contribution limit per transaction, plus a maximum contribution per block. For example, on the Ethereum network each block takes around 20 seconds to confirm. One could place an artificial maximum of $20,000 for every 180 blocks. 180 blocks represent one hour and therefore the contribution limit becomes $20,000 per hour. This is like a time delay for the whales, but it is still not a particularly strong deterrent.

A proportional structured ICO is an option, such as the one performed by Augur. Augur created 11 million tokens, of which 80% or 8.8 million tokens were distributed in what it saw as a fair and equitable manner. Augur called it a live action model, where the bigger the contribution, the more tokens were received proportional to everyone else. An example would be to imagine a pie with 8.8 million slices (http://augur.strikingly.com/blog/the-augur-crowdsale). That is either a really big pie or it has lots of very thin slices! If the first contributor, say Alice, paid $1 or the crypto equivalent, she would own all 8.8 million pieces. If the second person, say Bob, contributed $2, he would get twice as much as Alice. In this case, it would be 2.93 million for Alice and 5.87 million for Bob. It is basically a primary school fractions calculation.

To take the Augur model one step further, a proportional refund scheme is yet another option. Here, a maximum cap is designated where everyone contributes as much as they want. At the end, a refund is provided in proportion to how much the cap was exceeded by. For example, if the cap is $10 million USD and $20 million USD is received, then everyone gets half their contributions back. If $50 million USD was received by five people at $10 million USD, $15 million USD, $12 million USD, $8 million USD, and $5 million USD, it means that five times as much was received. Therefore 1/5th of everyone's contribution will be accepted and 4/5ths will be refunded.

OmiseGo experienced an enormous demand for its token and ended up increasing its overall hard cap from $19 million USD to $25 million USD, with its presales cap at $21 million and $4 million sold using other pre-funding platforms (https://www.omise.co/omisego-crowdfunding-structure-update).

Hidden caps and presales: Aragon

Aragon provided a presales transparency report where, interestingly, it didn't specify a minimum purchase but a maximum one. Institutional buyers were allowed to contribute the equivalent of $40,000 USD in ether, while personal buyers could contribute up to $10,000 USD in ether. For liquidity purposes, ShapeShift was also allowed to purchase an additional $20,000 USD in ether.

Aragon received contributions from six buyers during its presale, totaling 2,719 ETH, the equivalent of $170,000 USD. The buyers were CoinFund, ICONOMI, ShapeShift, Joe Urgo, Daniele Levi, and an anonymous Ethereum founding member.

The presales conditions were at a 20% discount and had a six-month vesting schedule, with a three-month cliff.

	ETH	USD
Development	1,993 ETH	$179,000 USD
Security audits	50 ETH	$4,500 USD
Legal	208 ETH	$18,700 USD
PR	107 ETH	$9,600 USD
Advertisements	134 ETH	$12,000 USD
ENS	202 ETH	$18,200 USD
Other	15 ETH	$1,350 USD
Total	2,719 ETH	$244,350 USD

Table 14: Aragon's presale allocation (https://bitcointalk.org/index.php?topic=1902482.msg19070685#msg19070685)

Aragon then employed the concept of a hidden cap in its ICO. The argument here was that an uncapped ICO would allow as many community supporters to invest as possible, but a security cap was required as a safety measure to avoid the ICO getting out of control. Therefore, a hidden cap was created, which was effectively a soft cap.

In conjunction with this, there was also a maximum hidden hard cap that was baked into the contract as a fallback mechanism. This essentially put an explicit limit on the amount raised, regardless of what happened to the hidden cap. This hidden hard cap was subsequently revealed to be 275,000 ETH, which was roughly $25 million USD.

The hidden cap was only known to the Aragon founders, Luis Cuende and Jorge Izquierdo, and was designed to incentivize small buyers. The logic here was that the whales needed to know the cap in order to be able to determine how many tokens were required to control a sizeable amount of the market. By hiding this important piece of information, a more even token distribution could be achieved.

When the ICO was about to start, the team realized that with large transaction volumes queuing up on the Ethereum network, sending a transaction signal to reveal the hidden cap was required at the start of the ICO (https://www. reddit.com/r/ethtrader/comments/6bqnhf/aragon_ico_ cap_released_275k_eth_21m/?sort=old). If they sent the signal later, the signal transaction would have been stuck in the processing queue, causing potential havoc.

Aragon produced a useful circulating supply chart that showed the various vesting periods and how they would affect the supply. The initial circulating supply was 33 million ANT, with a one-month cliff for advisors and those who participated in the presale. About five months after the ICO, on November 11, 2017, advisors' and presale tokens would fully vest. This date would also represent the first cliff for founders. Founder tokens would fully vest 18 months later.

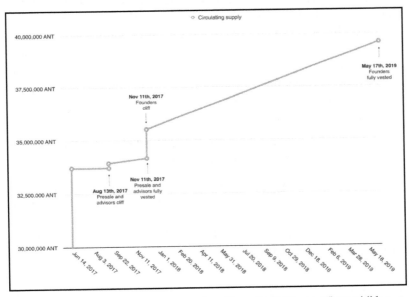

Figure 9: The Aragon circulating supply with vesting indicators (https://blog.aragon.one/the-aragon-token-sale-the-numbers-12d03c8b97d3)

The Aragon ICO ended with 2,916 transactions and 2,403 unique buyers, which Aragon believed achieved an even token distribution. While two and a half thousand contributors was a commendable amount, this paled in comparison to the likes of Status or Kyber Networks, that achieved over 20,000 contributors. Having said this, they both raised substantially more: $90 million and $48 million respectively.

Dynamic ceiling – Status

Status used the idea of a dynamic ceiling in its ICO in an effort to prevent large contributors dominating and favoring smaller contributors. A dynamic ceiling was a concept where only a maximum amount of funds would be accepted over a particular time interval. It was analogous to a series of miniature hidden hard caps.

Status set the first hard cap at 30,000 ETH, which was approximately 12M CHF (Swiss Franc) at the time (~$12 million USD). This was intentionally large and made known to incentivize large contributors. This meant that Status could make one large transaction and incur less transaction fees. Subsequent hard caps were lower, meaning that large purchases were be rejected and investors had to break them down into smaller purchases for the transactions to be accepted.

A maximum upper limit of 300,000 ETH was set as the hard ceiling or maximum contribution amount.

The Status ICO was an obvious success, raising $90 million, but the verdict is still out on the dynamic ceiling model. By Status' own admission, it doesn't see this model working in the future and to date, it hasn't been replicated elsewhere, at least not to the extent seen with Status.

Reverse Dutch auction – Gnosis

Gnosis did a very smart token sale. It did its homework and in December 2016, Chief Strategist Matt Liston released a blog titled *Introducing the Gnosis Token Launch*. This is where the concept of the Dutch auction was introduced. Keep in mind that this was five months before the actual ICO.

A Dutch auction is where a good (or service) is set at an *artificially high price where demand is known or believed to be zero.* At publicly known time intervals, the price ticks down in publicly known price values. The price continues to tick down until the first bid is received. At this point, the auction ends immediately and the bidder wins the goods at that price point. The advantage is that the buyer recognizes their fullest economic benefit from the sale because that is what they were willing to pay in the first place. It is also quick and simple to implement and understand and only one bid is required. There are not a million hands waving all over the place, for instance, like the floor of the New York Stock Exchange in the good old days! Gnosis took this concept and modified it slightly.

In February 2017, Martin Koppelmann, the CEO and co-founder of Gnosis, released a blog post titled *Why so complicated?* (https://blog.gnosis.pm/why-so-complicated-ddff533c5620). In this clever blog, he compared the impending Gnosis ICO to other past ICOs, based on several criteria.

First there was an argument made against raising funds with a fixed token supply, as in the case of Augur. Gnosis pointed out that when buyers made a purchase, the number of tokens they received in return could only decrease. This was true because after a bonus round, for example, the tokens on offer reduced. In the Gnosis-modified Dutch auction, the number of tokens a buyer received could only go up. This was because Gnosis started the auction at a ridiculously high price. Buyers then made purchases based on their own price point, until the criteria of either $12.5 million had been raised or nine million GNO tokens sold.

The last price that the GNO tokens were purchased for when the preceding criteria was met was the final price that **everyone** paid. For example, if the starting price was $30 and two people decided to contribute $100 each, the auction would still continue because the criteria would not yet have been met.

The next day it would drop to $29 and five people would contribute $500 each and this would continue until $12.5 million was reached. If the last bid just before $12.5 million was $18, for example, then this would be the price that everyone would be paying. This would mean that the two people who thought $30 was a good price would actually receive more than they anticipated because of the $18 price point. That is why Gnosis claimed that the amount the buyer received could only increase.

Gnosis also compared this to doing an ICO with an unlimited token supply, such as the case with Ethereum. Here, the buyer will not know the true value of the number of tokens held because the supply continuously increases.

In a fixed price scenario, like Civic and many others, Gnosis argued that the seller has to set the right price up front. For example, Civic decided on 33 million tokens at $0.10 USD each. Here Gnosis argued that its ICO structure allowed the market to find the best price. Gnosis was also not a fan of an early buyer bonus so didn't implement this.

This sounded great on paper, but what actually eventuated was something completely different. Gnosis sold out in 10 minutes! Due to the ICO hype and FOMO, as soon as Gnosis set that *artificially high price where demand is known or believed to be zero* of $30 USD, everyone bought what they could. This meant that the $12.5 million maximum cap was triggered and the ICO closed. At the $30 price point, only 4.17% of the allocated nine million tokens were sold (https://docs.google.com/spreadsheets/d/1vYjDa t8wLd97pEfrdkzOcHd5ZLOlYjpDSkJaTnEDe1E/edit#gid=0). The percentage of tokens sold was supposed to increase at the same rate that the price was to decrease but because the price didn't have a chance to decrease, the smallest proportion of tokens to be released was released.

This led to outrage because it seemed like out of the 10 million tokens, 90% was going to be available to the public when in reality, only 4.17% was. This gave Gnosis a valuation of $300 million (100%/4.17% x $12.5 million). There was a lot of backlash but the conclusion to this is that the market can be totally irrational. Gnosis decided to freeze the remaining 85.83% for one year. One year is not a long time so it will be interesting to see what happens to the value of the tokens that are unfrozen.

The point here is to take into consideration the hype, and the fact that markets are irrational, if a Dutch auction of this sort is contemplated. There are also improved variations of this Dutch auction that others have proposed, albeit very conveniently after the fact.

Token mechanics considerations

The following table can be used as a guideline for ideas when looking at different factors in structuring the mechanics of an ICO:

	Options	Examples/comments
Supply	◆ Pick your lucky number ◆ Proportional to funds raised ◆ Desired capital ÷ desired price	◆ 1 billion ◆ $34 million raised = 34 million tokens ◆ $50 million ÷ $0.10 USD
Price	◆ Fixed initial price ◆ Proportional	◆ $0.10 USD

Distribution	♦ Majority to supporters and true investors ♦ Incentivize core team, founders, developers, and network participants ♦ Distribute remaining as required	♦ >50% to public ♦ ~15% to developers, core team, and founders ♦ ~5% to advisors
Cap	♦ Uncapped ♦ Hard cap ♦ Soft cap ♦ Hidden cap	♦ Avoid uncapped ♦ Implement hard cap ♦ Soft cap optional ♦ Avoid hidden cap
Duration	♦ Fixed time ♦ Until cap is reached	♦ Four weeks ♦ Avoid lengthy ICOs
Presales/ bonuses	♦ Be creative but keep it simple ♦ Sliding scale for early backers	♦ Four weeks ♦ Avoid block height bonuses
Pre-ICO and private sales	♦ Recommended	♦ Get the ball rolling/ psychological "priming effect"
Vesting period	♦ Duration with cliffs ♦ No vesting period	♦ 24 months with six-month cliffs ♦ What does this signal to your supporters?

Table 15: A summary of ICO considerations

Summary

The methods of how tokens were created and sold in ICOs during 2016 and 2017 were varied, experimental, and creative. There were very few standards or patterns initially, as each ICO team experimented with the number of tokens to create, how many to distribute to their community of supporters and how many to withhold for various other purposes.

In this chapter, we learned that presale bonuses were usually a given but with insatiable demand, pre-ICOs were created, which then escalated to private sales. The rush was on to get in as early as possible, in order to essentially be able to flip or sell the tokens as soon as they hit the exchanges for a quick profit.

We learned that uncapped ICOs were frowned upon by the community, hard caps became the norm and soft caps should really be called a minimum threshold or goal. With the frantic rush in 2017 and big whales gobbling up tokens like plankton in the South China Sea, inventive ways were formed to try to decentralize token holders.

Now that we have a grasp on the mechanics of the token, let's turn our focus to the three most important aspects before the token sales can begin: the white paper, the website, and the team.

References

1. https://augur.stackexchange.com/
   questions/113/how-were-augur-ico-
   funds-and-rep-tokens-distributed?utm_
   medium=organic&utm_source=google_rich_
   qa&utm_campaign=google_rich_qa

2. https://help.lisk.io/faq/ico/how-were-the-
   initial-lsk-tokens-distributed

3. https://blog.wavesplatform.com/waves-ico-
   structure-and-timeline-87db476cc586

4. https://iconomi.zendesk.com/hc/en-us/
   articles/115002851065-ICN-token

5. https://blog.synereo.com/2015/03/18/
   crowdsale-announcement-2/

6. http://www.theicotrain.com/docs/GNTterms.pdf

7. https://www.reuters.com/article/us-
   blockchain-funding-gnosis/blockchain-
   startup-gnosis-to-freeze-tokens-after-
   strong-sale-idUSKBN17R2RD

8. https://gamecredits.com/wp-content/
   uploads/2018/03/MobileGo-Whitepaper.pdf

9. https://basicattentiontoken.org/bat-sale-
   overview-and-how-to-participate/

10. https://medium.com/@bancor/bancor-network-
    token-bnt-contribution-token-creation-terms-
    48cc85a63812

11. https://blog.status.im/status-contribution-
    period-recap-36e64d35d3e4

12. https://tokensale.civic.com/

13. https://pillarproject.io/tokens/

14. https://coinlist.co/assets/index/filecoin_index/
    Filecoin-Sale-Economics-e3f703f8cd5f644aecd7ae386
    0ce932064ce014dd60de115d67ff1e9047ffa8e.pdf

15. https://kinecosystem.org/static/files/Kin_
    Whitepaper_V1_English.pdf

16. https://blog.kyber.network/kybernetworks-token-
    sale-terms-overview-de031ce9738e

17. https://basicattentiontoken.org/faq/#distribution

18. https://cdn.omise.co/omg/crowdsaleterms.pdf

19. https://medium.com/@Airclipse/founders-vesting-
    period-b47804d0fca4

20. https://iconomi.zendesk.com/hc/en-us/
    articles/115002851065-ICN-token

21. https://status.im/whitepaper.pdf

22. https://blog.aragon.one/the-aragon-token-sale-the-
    numbers-12d03c8b97d3

23. https://blog.synereo.com/2015/03/18/crowdsale-
    announcement-2/

24. https://www.tenx.tech/whitepaper/tenx_whitepaper_
    final.pdf

25. https://medium.com/@bancor/bancor-network-
    token-bnt-contribution-token-creation-terms-
    48cc85a63812

26. https://coinlist.co/assets/index/filecoin_index/
    Filecoin-Sale-Economics-e3f703f8cd5f644aecd7ae386
    0ce932064ce014dd60de115d67ff1e9047ffa8e.pdf

8

WHITE PAPER, WEBSITE, AND TEAM

 You never get a second chance to make a good first impression.

There are lots of ingredients that go into a nicely baked ICO, but arguably the most important are the white paper, the website, and the team. The white paper has continued to evolve from a very academic-style paper, to in some cases a marketing brochure, but regardless of its form, it continues to be, for better or worse, the standard "must-have" document that all ICOs need to produce.

A white paper communicates a lot of things, but the main concept is an idea. The next step is to create a website because it is almost inconceivable in this day and age for a business or brand of any sort not to have an online presence. A website is also used to collect the funds for the ICO.

Once visitors land on an ICO's website, one of the most popular pages to browse is the "team" page or "about us." Who are the people behind this idea? Are they respected individuals in the field? Are they academics or celebrities?

In this chapter, we will take a closer look at the white paper, the website, and the team. It should be of no surprise that writing continues to be the best form of communicating detailed information at scale. Videos are great for a quick introduction or **ELI5 (Explain Like I'm 5)**, but nothing beats a well-written document.

The white paper

If you believe Wikipedia, the term "white paper" originated from the British Government, with many pointing to the Churchill white paper of 1922 as the earliest well-known example (https://en.wikipedia.org/wiki/Churchill_White_Paper). Some say that white papers developed from blue papers, but since the material was too light, they were published with a white cover instead. (http://klariti.com/white-papers/origin-of-white-papers/).

A white paper can be thought of as a persuasive essay that uses facts and logic to promote a certain product, service, or viewpoint, or an authoritative, in-depth report on a specific topic that presents a problem and provides a solution.

The actual definition varies widely from industry to industry, but in technology, a white paper usually describes a theory behind a new piece of technology.

Etymology: Although it seems that the white paper is more commonly written with a space between, as in "white paper", there is no right or wrong way. The same comparison can be made between the words "block chain" and "blockchain." In fact, in the original bitcoin white paper, the word "block" was mentioned 67 times and the word "chain" 27 times, and the closest mention of the two words together was "blocks are chained," "block in the chain," or "chain of blocks." Now, however, the word "block chain" is more widely known as "blockchain." Other similar references are "web site", now more commonly written as "website" and "e-mail" as "email."

The bitcoin white paper is the most famous white paper example, but what is fascinating is that Satoshi Nakamoto didn't call it a "white paper." On Feb 11, 2009, Satoshi called it a "design paper":

"I've developed a new open source P2P e-cash system called bitcoin. It's completely decentralized, with no central server or trusted parties, because everything is based on crypto proof instead of trust. Give it a try, or take a look at the screenshots and design paper."

Other colored papers

Although white papers are the standard, other variants of colored papers also exist.

Yellow paper

A yellow paper is a document containing research that has not yet been formally accepted or published in an academic journal. Although the original Ethereum white paper was published by Vitalik Buterin at the beginning of 2014, towards the middle of 2014 an Ethereum yellow paper was also produced by Dr. Gavin Wood, co-founder and former chief technical officer of the Ethereum project (https://ethereum.github.io/yellowpaper/paper.pdf). It is a very technical paper and is written on a dull yellow background:

ETHEREUM: A SECURE DECENTRALISED GENERALISED TRANSACTION LEDGER
PROOF-OF-CONCEPT V

DR. GAVIN WOOD
CO-FOUNDER & CTO, ETHEREUM PROJECT
GAVIN@ETHEREUM.ORG

ABSTRACT. The blockchain paradigm when coupled with cryptographically-secured transactions has demonstrated its utility through a number of projects, not least Bitcoin. Each such project can be seen as a simple application on a decentralised, but singleton, compute resource. We can call this paradigm a transactional singleton machine with shared-state.

Ethereum implements this paradigm in a generalised manner. Furthermore it provides a plurality of such resources, each with a distinct state and operating code but able to interact through a message-passing framework with others. We discuss its design, implementation issues, the opportunities it provides and the future hurdles we envisage.

Figure 1: The Ethereum yellow paper published by Dr. Gavin Wood

Grey paper

Grey papers or grey literature are normally provided by researchers and practitioners in a field outside of traditional commercial or academic publishing channels. Pillar Project published a "gray paper", for example (`https://pillarproject.io/documents/ Pillar-Gray-Paper.pdf`).

Green papers

Green papers typically set out discussions or proposals which are still at a formative stage. In fact, the Oxford English Dictionary defines a green paper as *(in the UK) a preliminary report of government proposals published to stimulate discussion.* (`https:// en.oxforddictionaries.com/definition/green_paper`).

The Melon project produced a green paper outlining its blockchain protocol for digital asset management, and Holo also created a green paper describing an ecosystem that relies on hosts to provide processing and storage for distributed applications, while earning redeemable credits (`https://github. com/melonproject/paper/blob/master/melonprotocol.pdf`):

MELON PROTOCOL: A BLOCKCHAIN PROTOCOL FOR DIGITAL ASSET MANAGEMENT
DRAFT

RETO TRINKLER AND MONA EL ISA

ABSTRACT. The Melon protocol is a blockchain protocol for digital asset management on the Ethereum platform. It enables participants to set up, manage and invest in digital asset management strategies in an open, competitive and decentralised manner.

Figure 2: The Melon project produced a green paper

Light paper

With some white papers reaching 40-to-50 pages in length, light papers started appearing, which were a more concise or sometimes simplified version, usually less than 10 pages long. KodakOne, SwarmFund, Polkadot, and many other ICOs produced light papers.

Mauve paper

Buterin created a mauve paper (https://cdn.hackaday.io/ files/10879465447136/Mauve%20Paper%20Vitalik.pdf) in 2016 that was inspired by a Dilbert (https://www.youtube. com/watch?v=bSdwqa3Y1oQ) comic, playing on the fact that when "blockchain" became a buzzword, everyone wanted one, even though many had no idea what one was. The paper covered advanced topics, such as increasing scalability, ensuring economic finality, and improving computational censorship resistance.

The original Dilbert cartoon was in reference to when SQL databases were the "in thing" in 1995 and Dilbert's boss "Pointy-haired Boss" said to Dilbert, "I think we should build an SQL database."

Dilbert replied, "What color do you want that database?"

"I think mauve has the most RAM," was the boss' reply.

A modified version was created and circulated on Twitter (https://twitter.com/jimharris/ status/950045005774692354), where the conversation was altered to the boss saying, "I think we should build a blockchain."

Dilbert replied, "What color do you want the blockchain?"

"I think mauve has the most RAM," was the response from the boss.

The joke was that it makes absolutely no sense to talk about "colors" of a blockchain or one blockchain having more RAM than another. In the cartoon, Dilbert's manager saw the term somewhere but doesn't understand what it actually means and Dilbert suspects that and asks a question to confirm that suspicion.

Regardless of the nomenclature, white papers within the scope of ICOs have certainly evolved over time.

First-generation white papers – lots of maths

White papers in the early days had certain commonalities. They were very academic in nature, had an abstract, contained complicated mathematics, and various proofs, and were generally intended for a technical audience, particularly in the fields of cryptography, distributed computing, and mathematics. This was not surprising, as consensus mechanisms involving these technical concepts were at the core of the first white papers and mathematics was required when creating a lot of these protocols.

As an example, the following equation from the original bitcoin white paper demonstrates that the probability of an attacker attempting to purchase something with bitcoin and then reversing the transaction, in what is called a "double spend attack", actually decreases exponentially over time:

$$1 - \sum_{k=0}^{z} \frac{\lambda^k e^{-\lambda}}{k!} \left(1 - \left(\frac{q}{p} \right)^{(z-k)} \right)$$

Figure 3: An example of the mathematics included in the bitcoin white paper

Nxt introduced a table of contents into its white paper, which was a novelty at the time but proved really useful.

The Ethereum white paper, while still technical in nature, spent the first 12 pages providing background and explaining the challenges of bitcoin and alternative blockchain applications, before explaining what Ethereum was. It was providing context and justified Ethereum's creation, addressing various limitations of the existing systems:

"The intent of Ethereum is to merge together and improve upon the concepts of scripting, altcoins, and on-chain meta-protocols, and allow developers to create arbitrary consensus-based applications that have the scalability, standardization, feature-completeness, ease of development, and interoperability offered by these different paradigms all at the same time."

Second-generation white papers – color

In the first half of 2016, DigixDAO, a distributed autonomous organization tokenizing gold using the Ethereum blockchain, and Waves, experimented with adding color in their white papers and removed mathematical formulas. It essentially made their white papers more user-friendly to read.

DigixDAO provided numerous colored flow charts and even included a Chinese-translated version at the end of the English version, which doubled the length of the white paper to 22 pages.

Waves introduced a full-color title page in its white paper and kept details very high level. It was only 11 pages and appeared almost too simple. Information on crowdsales, however, was provided in a separate blog post.

Third-generation white papers – project timelines

Very quickly, ICOs discovered that if they wanted to raise more capital, the information needed to be less technical and more appealing to a wider audience. What also helped was that with these ICOs launching on existing blockchains, a lot of the technical requirements were taken care of, hence making the papers less technical by nature.

In the latter half of 2016, FirstBlood started providing information, such as project timelines, funding breakdowns, and details of its team in a 26-page white paper. FirstBlood also detailed the token sale period and the token mechanics.

Synereo, though, stuck to its guns and produced a 65-page first-generation type white paper. Synereo raised $4.7 million and FirstBlood $5.5 million, so no useful correlation can be made from comparing these two white papers.

There was definitely a shift, though, as SingularDTV, Ark, and Golem maintained the color theme, and provided details of the token supply and distribution within the document.

Humaniq's white paper was a mixture of all three generations in one. It was very academic-looking, with mathematical formulas around its token distribution, a table of contents, colored diagrams, token details, and project timelines, along with a technical section on BioID and mobile transaction details on the Ethereum network. BAT's white paper also fell into this category.

Fourth-generation white papers – the executive summary

During the madness of 2017, white papers evolved very quickly. Gnosis, in one of many white papers, took things to the next level by replacing the abstract with an "executive summary" and providing a well-thought-out structure. A summary of the main headings of the Gnosis white paper are as follows:

1. Executive Summary

    1.1 Problem Overview

    1.2 Mission Statement

    1.3 Core Objectives

2. Token Mechanics

3. Platform Model

4. Gnosis Application

5. Roadmap

6. Token Auction

7. Leadership

8. Legal Considerations

9. Gnosis Architecture

Note that the Gnosis white paper has since been restructured, in the latest version dated December 22, 2017, in particular removing details on the token mechanics and auction.

Not only did white papers become more businesslike, but their length grew as well. This was greatly attributed to the legal disclaimers becoming bigger and more in-depth. MobileGo added a 10-page terms and conditions section at the end of its 32-page white paper and TenX added an 11-page disclaimer at the beginning of its 51-page white paper.

LAToken had a very clear and well-presented structure in its white paper, as follows:

1. Executive Summary
2. Value Proposition
3. Competitive Analysis
4. How It Works
5. LAT Platform
6. Key Asset Markets
7. Crypto Market Overview
8. Technology
9. Tokens
10. Legal Considerations
11. Team
12. Roadmap

Some white papers were more like marketing brochures, with fancy graphics, and they were missing a lot of key details. Monaco fell into this category, with several half-page graphics of a cup of coffee next to a laptop or a person reading a newspaper in a park. When stripped of graphics, Monaco's 32-page white paper was only 11 pages and just over 5,000 words long.

Figure 4: The Monaco white paper appeared more like a marketing brochure, with half-page meaningless graphics

As we see more and more tokens fall into the securities category, white papers will again transform and become more of an investment prospectus.

Information in a typical **Initial Public Offering (IPO)** investment prospectus includes:

1. Company Overview

    1.1 Key Management Team

    1.2 Board and Governance

2. The Market

    2.1 Industry Overview

    2.2 Marketing Strategy

3. Business Activities

    3.1 Business Plan/Model

4. Investment Overview

5. Financial Overview

6. Risks

7. Legal

The similarities are obvious. In fact, first-generation white papers are transforming and becoming known more as technical papers or research papers because the information they contain is often very detailed. This is something that Filecoin has done with its research, producing papers such as "Proof-of-Replication," "Power Fault Tolerance", and "Research Roadmap 2017", all in conjunction with its actual white paper.

IOTA has recently revamped its website and provided several academic papers to support its Tangle technology. Papers include *The Tangle*, *Equilibria in the Tangle*, and *The first glance at the simulation of the Tangle: discrete model*. The titles themselves are more than enough for the average reader to push the papers into the "too hard, I'll come back later (not really)" bucket.

White paper content considerations

Writing a white paper is not as easy as many may think. It involves explaining a novel idea to a wide-ranging audience in an easy-to-understand manner. It is also important to have a team of reviewers, quite often from different disciplines, such as legal, marketing and, of course, technical to ensure each part of the white paper is correct and accurate.

There is no standard methodology for writing a white paper, but the following presents a range of sections to include when writing one. Not every section needs to be included and the terminology can be chosen as appropriate. For example, "executive summary" has become more popular than "abstract." Some ICOs use the term "allocation", while others use "distribution" or "issuance." Some have a general "advisory board" section, whereas others split it up into more detail, such as "marketing", "technology", and "legal advisors." In essence, there is no right or wrong way:

1. Executive Summary/Abstract

2. Introduction

    2.1 About

    2.2 Vision/Mission Statement/Core Objectives

3. Value Proposition

    3.1 What Makes {*insert token name here*} Special?

4. Market Overview

    4.1 The Problem

    4.2 Our Solution

5. Business Model/Landscape

    5.1 Competitive Advantage Matrix

Website

In an ICO, something that is just as important as the white paper is the website. This is the public image of the company or startup, and there is a list of minimum requirements that a website should have.

What is this and how does it work?

The very first thing a website has to convey is the concept and although it is great to use industry jargon and technically correct words, this has to be supplemented with alternative words and analogies, to help the visitor to understand very quickly what the company, concept, or idea is.

Take, for example, Augur (`http://www.augur.net/`):

"Augur is an open-source, decentralized, peer-to-peer oracle and prediction market platform built on the Ethereum blockchain."

This is great, but what exactly is an oracle? What is a prediction market?

Other examples include Factom (`https://www.factom.com/`), ICONOMI (`https://www.iconomi.net/`), Synereo (`https://www.synereo.com/`), and Ethereum (`https://ethereum.org/`):

"A practical blockchain solution for those seeking a collaborative platform to preserve, ensure, and validate digital assets."

"The ICONOMI Digital Assets Management Platform is a new and unique technical service that allows anyone from beginners to blockchain experts to invest in and manage digital assets."

"Synereo offers blockchain-enabled Attention Economy solutions, allowing direct and platform agnostic monetization of original content posted anywhere on the net."

"Ethereum is a decentralized platform that runs smart contracts: applications that run exactly as programmed without any possibility of downtime, censorship, fraud or third-party interference."

These companies all assume that the reader knows what a dapp is, what digital assets and smart contracts are, and what is meant by an attention economy. This is one of the challenges of this nascent industry and those in the thick of it often forget that newcomers may have a different understanding of the same word or need some further context or examples to better understand it.

Augur's explanation, using an analogy, was very helpful:

> *"If you think Hillary Clinton will be elected President, the Yankees will win the World Series, or Leonardo DiCaprio will win another Oscar, then you'll buy shares in those outcomes. If you buy shares in the correct outcomes, you'll win real money profits."*

This, unfortunately, has since been removed from the Augur website as part of its refresh.

📊 **Predict the outcome of real-world events**

You make your predictions by trading virtual shares in the outcome of events happening in the real-world. If you think Hillary Clinton will be elected President, the Yankees will win the World Series, or Leonardo DiCaprio will win another Oscar, then you'll buy shares in those outcomes. If you buy shares in the correct outcomes, you'll win real money profits.

Figure 5: Augur explaining prediction markets with an example (https://web.archive.org/web/20160624021146/https://www.augur.net/)

In conjunction with examples of what the new concept is, conveying how it works is also important. Very popular are one- or two-minute videos, so new users can understand the concept very quickly at a high level, before jumping into more detail.

Token details

The "token model", a term used to define the token features and the network of stakeholders interacting with the token, should be made open and transparent on the ICO website for historical and audit purposes. Just because the ICO has finished and the tokens distributed, it shouldn't be forgotten about. Statistics on how the token sales went are often littered in bitcointalk forums, and blog posts, which makes understanding and tracking progress difficult.

The token should also be clearly explained, in particular how it is used in the application. Centrality describes how its CENNZ tokens are used and provides examples on its website:

CENNZ is a utility token that is used to connect our marketplace applications, users and provide access to Centrality software. Here are some examples of how CENNZ might be used:

- ◆ *An application can use CENNZ to purchase the modules needed to quickly build and integrate their application.*

- ◆ *An application can also use CENNZ to reward referrals of customers from another application.*

- ◆ *Applications can use CENNZ to reward customers for participation.*

- ◆ *Customers can receive CENNZ tokens from different applications to add to their token portfolio.*

Blogs

Communicating with the community is very important and blog posts are one way of doing this. Each medium has its purpose. Tweets are usually for short announcements, outages or updates on security incidents, such as the Tether tweet linking to a blog elaborating on the unfortunate $30 million stolen Tethers.

Figure 6: The Tether tweet linking to a blog post regarding the $30 million stolen Tethers (https://twitter.com/Tether_to/status/933711320586817538)

Blogs themselves are for more detailed communications with supporters and become like the heartbeat of an organization, particularly for announcements, as seen in the early days with Factom. The following shows a timeline of its blog posts, leading up to its ICO on March 31, 2015:

♦ Blog post March 9, 2015: Tether + Factom Announce Collaboration.

♦ Blog post March 10, 2015: Serica + Factom Announce Collaboration.

♦ Blog post March 11, 2015: Coinapult + Factom Announce Collaboration.

♦ Blog post March 12, 2015: Tradle + Factom Announce Collaboration.

♦ **Blog post March 17, 2015: Announcing the Factom Software Sale (that is. ICO).**

♦ Blog post March 25, 2015: Vaultoro + Factom Announce Collaboration.

♦ Blog post March 27, 2015: Rivetz + Factom Announce Collaboration.

♦ Blog post March 30, 2015: Shapeshift + Factom Announce Collaboration.

♦ **Blog post March 31, 2015: The Factoid Software Sale is Live.**

♦ Blog post April 18, 2015: Synereo + Factom Announce Collaboration.

- Blog post April 20, 2015: Infinity Algorithms + Factom Announce Collaboration.

- Blog post April 23, 2015: HealthNautica + Factom Announce Partnership.

These were very strategic posts and they also continued after the ICO. A noticeable incident was the Honduras project, which was announced in May 2015.

Blog post May 19, 2015: Honduras to Build Land Title Registry Using Bitcoin Technology.

This announcement led to much fanfare and hope, but with very little updates, and questions from the community, Factom provided an update blog on December 25, 2015, titled *A Humble Update on the Honduras Title Project*. CEO Peter Kirby made an announcement:

> *"Yes, the project has stalled. We were hoping to have a working prototype deployed by the end of the year, but as 2015 comes to a close, we'll all have to wait another year to deploy a blockchain backed land title system that is both tamper-proof and transparent."*

(https://www.factom.com/blog/a-humble-update-on-the-honduras-title-project).

There have been no updates on the Honduras project since, so it appears this project has died a slow and quiet death. Factom, though, to its credit, has been very consistent with its blogging.

In conjunction with pre-ICO blogs, a post-ICO blog summary was also popular in the early days, in line with being open and transparent. Try finding these posts nowadays! The Waves platform post-ICO blog was very detailed, with lots of fancy charts (`https://blog.wavesplatform.com/wavesplatform-ico-summary-post-ico-calendar-c37c27721cbd`).

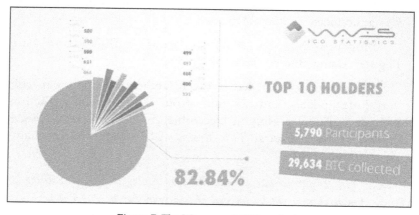

Figure 7: The Waves post-ICO analysis

Augur too provided great visual charts of its post-ICO analysis (it should also be noted that similar charts can be accessed from `etherscan.io` for any ERC20 token). Not only did Augur break down its crowdsale purchases by size, but it provided Google analytics of visitors by country, a very detailed breakdown of how much was received in each of the bonus periods and, in particular, information on late purchases that were to be refunded. Yes, this meant that some people continued to contribute after the close of the ICO.

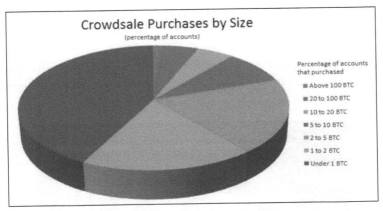

Figure 8: The Augur post-ICO analysis
(http://augur.strikingly.com/blog/the-crowdsale-what-s-new-and-what-s-next)

TenX went so far as to provide a 22-minute video blog or vlog behind the scenes of the ICO:

Figure 9: TenX added a vlog to its post-ICO analysis
(https://blog.tenx.tech/reflecting-on-a-highly-successful-tenx-tokensale-b2705d593f1a)

Pillar took this one step further and broadcasted the grand finale of its ICO to the world on YouTube. This was basically the last 40 minutes of the 60-hour ICO. Note that Pillar's ICO did not end at a specific time, but at a specific block (`https://medium.com/@pullnews/the-pillar-project-gray-paper-d252be1dc74c`).

Figure 10: YouTube broadcast of the latter part of the Pillar ICO
(https://www.youtube.com/watch?v=bd7HkK8yU_U)

Medium is a very popular platform for blogging because of the ease of use and speed of setting it up. Companies using Medium include:

- `https://blog.iota.org/`
- `https://blog.lisk.io/`
- `https://medium.com/@digix`
- `https://medium.com/iconominet`
- `https://medium.com/singulardtv`
- `https://blog.ark.io/`
- `https://blog.golemproject.net/`

- https://blog.humaniq.co/
- https://medium.com/gnosis-pm
- https://blog.status.im/
- https://blog.tenx.tech/

Once the website is up and running, with all the pertinent information, one of the pages of most interest is the "team" page.

Team

The most fascinating aspect of any ICO is of no doubt the people behind it: the leaders, the founders, and, of course, the team. It is not only standard practice to have profiles of key team members but also links to their LinkedIn profiles and Twitter accounts. For the technical members, a link to their GitHub repository adds "tech cred." In this hyper-connected world, a simple Google search not only reveals information about a person but paints a perceived picture upon which a judgment, rightly or wrongly, will be made.

In addition to this, profile pictures taken in the back garden, behind the bike sheds, or on the beach front may add character to a Facebook profile but are not suitable when looking for a professional persona.

On the flip side, some ICOs had profile pictures that not only looked exceptionally professional but were outright fake. Take the case of the Miroskii ICO, that appeared in early 2018. The Miroskii coin was developed by *experts* from China, Hong Kong, Singapore, and Japan to ease the crypto revolution in financial products.

The catch was that its graphics designer, Kevin Belanger, was actually the Hollywood actor Ryan Gosling and its advisor Joel Hermann, supposedly founder of the Mysterium Network, was actually Ben B. Rubinowitz, a lawyer from New York. Needless to say, the website has since been taken down, so it can only be accessed via `web.archive.org`.

Kevin Belanger
Experienced graphic designer with a clear focus on identities and illustration.

Joel Hermann
Founder of Mysterium Network a Decentralized Network of VPN Nodes. Huge technology fan.

Figure 11: Some of the fake members of the Miroskii ICO
(https://web.archive.org/web/20180215040651/https://miroskii.com/)

The hacker, hustler, and hipster

There is a theory in the startup world that three key types of people are required for success or an increased chance of success. The "dream team" consists of a hacker, a hustler, and a hipster, and the chances are that most successful teams have all three.

The hacker brings their technical prowess and MacGyver-like problem solving skills. The hustler has the gift of the gab and is nauseatingly charming, with a network far beyond what LinkedIn can offer. The hipster is the designer or creative genius; the one with the coolest hair and the coolest clothes.

Incidentally, William Mougayar, introduced in *Chapter 1, Once Upon a Token,* has a slightly different version in the blockchain space called the *dreamers, the drummers, and the doers.*

Most ICO will have a team resembling something of this nature and after the ICO, the team will quite often quadruple in size. Even with a modest raise, the next step will be resources and building out the team with an army of technical developers, business developers, and marketing people to get the word out.

Advisors

In the ICO world, any project that is to be taken seriously likely needs an advisory team. Typically, these are experienced professionals or experts in the industry that the ICO will address, and these advisors should provide the intellectual knowledge and support to help the ICO's management team to successfully launch the ICO, start the business, and stay ahead of compliance regulations. However, nowadays, advisors are sought after more for their networks and their reputation.

Having a popular, well-known figure as an advisor can be a marketer's dream. This is something that Buterin found out the hard way. Buterin has since officially gone on record announcing that OmiseGo and KyberNetworks are the only exceptions that he will advise on.

Figure 12: Buterin discovering that advising is largely about marketing
(https://twitter.com/VitalikButerin/status/874522987885670400)

Summary

In this chapter, we learned that just as ICOs have evolved over time, so have white papers. Traditionally technical in nature, and targeted towards a specific academic and technical audience, they have broadened in scope and language to appeal to a much wider audience. The math was removed in favor of a business and token model, easier-to-understand use cases, and friendly faces to build trust and confidence. Abstracts became executive summaries, legal sections expanded 10-fold, and white papers are now on the verge of becoming investment prospectuses.

A website is mandatory, especially since users and investors will be using it to research further on the ICO. Communicating to these users and investors using blog updates is very important also. With no updates, speculation can circulate, as in the case of Factom and the Honduras project.

It has become evident that advisors who have strong social networks are starting to change the game. Add influencers into the mix and this is bringing about a powerful concoction of social networks. In the next chapter, we will dive into looking at the deeper mindset required in order to understand why being social is important.

9

SOCIAL MEDIA AND INFLUENCERS

"You never get a second chance to make a good first impression."

— *Will Rogers*

Whether you agree or disagree, like or dislike it, use or don't use it, you cannot deny the power of social media, and the power of influencers in today's world. A growing number of people are trying to create a following, build a brand, or increase their ability to influence in an ever-growing and connected world.

The crypto and ICO world is really no different, with the focus still very much on building a community of followers, users, investors, and evangelists, who can then help to spread the word. The bigger the community, the more people there are to potentially buy the token.

In this chapter, we start a little off the beaten track by first of all considering what social media is. We then look at how ICOs use social media, before understanding the world of influencers, and who some of the key influencers are in the ICO space.

Social media, much like the world of crypto, has fundamentally changed how humans interact. To begin, let's therefore take a step back from ICOs and blockchains for a moment, to really understand what being social means.

The deeper meaning of being social

Social media, influence, and influencers are three subjects that are deeply misunderstood around the globe. Things are not what they seem and the information flowing at each of us every day, across multiple platforms, is overwhelming, confusing, unreliable, often fake, and hard to contextualize.

This affects our minds, our behavior, and our decision-making. It can also make us fearful of missing out and create a sense of personal loneliness. Does anyone really care about me or my opinion? Does my point of view have any value? What is my point of view? Do I need to have a point of view?

Let's begin, then, with the messages we receive every day. These might be via iMessage, SMS, WhatsApp, Facebook Messenger, WeChat, Line, Snapchat, or Telegram. Typically, people receive more than 100 messages per day. Do these messages have an influence on your behavior and decision-making, and can they change your mind? The answer is probably yes. Are these messages social media? The answer is probably no, but we no longer know the difference.

Are messages social (media) or not? Does social media have to be public messaging, or can it also be private messaging?

Each of us has the challenge of simply processing our daily information intake. We have to organize that information intake and, furthermore, we are bombarded with apps and websites that can supposedly increase our productivity and output. The reality is that productivity (output per human hour) has fallen every year since the introduction of the iPhone in 2007. (https://www.linkedin.com/pulse/did-original-iphone-2007-kill-productivity-todays-brad-friesen/).

Thus, we are not more productive. We are not outputting more. We are simply receiving and processing more information and information creates paralysis. Too much information creates analysis paralysis. Too much information also creates procrastination. In other words, it's easier to put off deciding than deciding. This is, of course, before we even consider our email and then our social media platforms. All in all, it is estimated that we now receive six hours of interruptions per day (`https://www.washingtonpost.com/news/inspired-life/wp/2015/06/01/interruptions-at-work-can-cost-you-up-to-6-hours-a-day-heres-how-to-avoid-them/?utm_term=.4483e7864895`).

Overwhelmed with messages and emails, the question then becomes: why bother with social media? Others ask what is social media and what is the point of social media? If the work day is taken up with private messages, emails, phone calls, and meetings, there surely isn't time for social media.

What is social media?

Social media is the art and science of brand building through community building. It's the building of a following or a fan base. It's the next generation of market analysis, corporate intelligence, and reconnaissance. It's the new culture mechanism for engaging, educating, and motivating teams of people and evolving them into a movement, a force, or a community. It's a new form of communication designed to bring about change through **Gentle, Tiny, Daily, Nudges (#GTDN)**.

One of the many misperceptions of social media is that it's about posting things, such as images, tweets, videos, and blogs. Social media is not about posting. Social media is about listening, researching, reconnaissance, understanding, uncovering, and discovering. It's about filtering information and finding the right information that you seek. Social media is about market analysis and contextualizing markets.

How has social media arisen?

Social media arose because of a desire for people to connect with one another outside of their work and outside of their general lives. What began with chat groups in the 1980s became blogs in the 1990s, became marketplaces (classified listings such as Craigslist) in the mid-1990s, became social networks in the early 2000s, and then evolved into video publishing in 2005. Once chat groups, blogs, marketplaces, social networks, and video publishing were combined, we had the emergence of social media, and this took 40 years.

Why is social media important?

Social media set the world free and set people free to be themselves. This allowed people to be who they wanted to be. It gave all of us a means for public expression and this public expression is available in multiple forms, such as in photos, in videos, and in words.

We can now express ourselves, our point of view, our values, our beliefs, our dreams, our goals, our research, our findings, our ideas, and our families and friends through social media. This is why social media is so important: it provides the ability and tools to set ourselves free.

Your brand, your voice, your face, and your profile

One point that people don't understand about social media is that this is your reputation on the line, especially if you have a high profile. You cannot say whatever you want. You cannot have a laugh unless it is a carefully managed, orchestrated, and thought-through laugh. You cannot be intimate. You cannot use sexual innuendos. You cannot bully others. Sarcasm is unwise. You cannot celebrate alcohol or meat, depending on your audience. You cannot post silly images.

This is your reputation, so be serious about it. This is about *you* and who you are. This is about what you believe in. This is about your values. Manage your social media like you do your career: *carefully.*

When it comes to public photos, "your face is your brand." Brands need to look good and so does your photo. Amateur photo: amateur brand. Unprofessional image: unprofessional person. Far away and out-of-sight face: far away and out-of-sight person. *Think.*

People look at your face in your photo for less than one tenth of one second, and that's how long you have to make an impression and a positive impact: one tenth of one second. That's the photo part. Hire a professional. Get a selection of images you like. Choose one and place that image of you (your face) on every social media platform consistently. For the average social media user who just wants to interact with their friends, it's probably not as important. If you want to use social media as a platform, however, then you have to be far more conscious of your image.

Organization

You are used to organizing, categorizing, and prioritizing your emails, your documents, and your phone calls. You have to treat your social media in the same way. After all, email is private messaging and social media is public messaging, although private messaging also plays a role. Public messaging is much harder to get right than private messaging, which is another reason many of us avoid social media: people are watching. Imagine people watching you answer your email! The horror!

Just like any personal assistant, they (the algorithms that organize data) have to understand you inside out to support you better. Software is no different, as it learns from your clicks. The more clicks it receives, the faster it learns. No clicks means no learning. No social media means no progress. Thus, with social media, listening and sharing should be your priority and not posting.

Perhaps, by not training social media algorithms to serve you better, you are actually harming yourself and your career. Why would you choose to do that based upon the excuse of "I haven't got time," or "I haven't got the skills," or "I don't understand what social media is." Get these channels and learn them. Your career is at stake.

It's not about time or skills: it's about motive. The majority of people say they "hate social media but want to look good online." Sorry, but that isn't good enough. You can't have it both ways. Either you learn it, do it, and progress, or you don't and decay. The longer you leave it, the worse the decay. It's like rotting teeth and time is an issue because algorithms (your servants) need to be trained day in and day out.

Information provides context on markets and helps with decisions you need to make, or at least consider, to move forward. Contacts are people. We need people as suppliers, we need people to hire, we need people to invest in our ideas, and we need people for clients and customers. We also need people for their networks and their contacts.

When you hire someone or work with someone, you don't just hire their skills, their knowledge, and their insights: you also hire their network of contacts. Contacts provide hundreds of relationships that you cannot tap into without their permission and their belief in you. Provided your values match, you can access their network of contacts and they can access yours. Values matter. Beliefs matter. Styles matter. Although, of course, we're all different.

The focus should always be other people's outcomes. What is it you seek? What is it you want? What is it you are aiming for? What outcomes would you like to see happen and when? What are your goals, ambitions, and dreams? This is a reminder that social media is about gathering information because social media is about informing people.

This is where influencers come in; however, we've missed something that comes first: being **Open, Random, and Supportive (ORS)**®. ORS® is a mindset, a thought process, and a form of behavior. To truly embrace the online world and live in it, with it, and through it is a huge challenge and the idea takes many years to accept, to embrace, and to adopt.

ORS®

ORS®, which I created in 2009, is the digital mindset required to build your brand and your following online. To succeed online and as part of a network, you need to be ORS® in all of your communications and your acceptance of data.

Open

Remember the old "open door policy"? Do you communicate in such a way that others will gladly engage with you or are you so academic and opinionated that others feel intimidated by you? If you are not getting interactions and no one is telling you this, and you are not getting any criticism, it may just be time to ask those closest to you, such as your partner, if you have allowed them to be honest with you in the past. If you have never allowed them to be honest with you, then that is a clear indicator that you need help.

This approach to open communication is about listening more than talking. You need to listen to understand. Look for the strengths in others and allow them to say what they need to say. You will be amazed at how quickly people become engaged when you release your need to be heard.

Random

Allow people to express themselves and remember that everyone has five primal needs: discovery, directions, disruption, distraction, and declaration. They will say what they want and need to say if you give them the platform to do this. If your leadership style does not recognize people and what they need to say, you may need to rapidly unlearn some of your bad habits.

Release your need to micromanage people: micromanagement is for products and not people. You will find that innovation lives in this randomness, and the expression and the collaboration that comes through this will amaze you.

Supportive

Your need to control things comes from processes and your beliefs about how things should be. As mentioned, you can use all your micromanagement skills on whatever it is you are producing, but support your people and you will probably find that you won't have to do so much micromanaging after all.

In this world of ORS®, you will find that people have a need to be in a community with each other and this need brings them closer. Once they are closer, they tend to regulate themselves, as no one wants to let the team down.

You will find that you have more time to do the things you wanted to do. As a leader, you need time to dream and visualize, and get a clear focus of where you are taking your team of followers.

Side note: Comparatively, to succeed offline you need to be **Closed, Selective, and Controlling (CSC)**, particularly when you are a board member of a publicly quoted company, as I have been on two occasions at QXL Ricardo PLC (London) and 9Spokes PLC (New Zealand). Offline and face-to-face, CSC is the norm and appropriate. You have to be careful what you absorb, selective about the people you connect with, and in control. Online, ORS® is the norm and appropriate, but this mindset takes years to accept and adopt.

ORS® and social media

I encourage you to be open, to be random, and to be supportive, especially when using platforms such as Twitter, LinkedIn, Facebook, Medium, WhatsApp, Telegram, Snapchat, or Instagram.

Being ORS® requires understanding, acceptance, and patience. You can get there, but it does take time. You have to swap closed for open. You have to swap selective for random. You have to swap controlling for supportive. It's a difficult journey and it's a journey on your own, and with your own mind. You will have doubts and frustrations. You will get annoyed with yourself, but work through the process. Allow ORS® into your heart and mind. Above all, take your time. Accepting new ideas, new concepts, and new approaches takes humans years.

Case study: Thomas Power

It took me from 1999 to 2009 to identify and realize that I was biologically changing through using the internet. I was migrating from a CSC mindset offline, to an ORS® mindset online.

Years later, in 2014, Penny Power (my wife) was awarded the **Order of the British Empire (OBE)** for her work on building **Ecademy**. Ecademy was the world's first social network for business. It was Ecademy that taught us ORS® (https://en.wikipedia.org/wiki/Penny_Power).

Figure 1: https://twitter.com/thomaspower

People perceive that I am posting on social media all the time. The reality is that I am listening, reading, analyzing, pondering, ruminating, considering, hunting, and connecting people with what they seek. I focus on their information needs and not my own. If they get what they want, I will get what I want: information, contacts, and deals. People seek information, contacts, and deals, particularly in business. I am a professional connector and information hunter. I read for hours and hours each day, and I try not to miss things.

In order to train the algorithms to give me more of what I want, I must share and share again because robots must be trained. As mentioned earlier, your job is to train the algorithms inside of social media to serve you best.

Twitter

Twitter is my personal favorite. I spend hours each day absorbing Twitter. TweetDeck is my favorite product and the platform I use the most. TweetDeck is the tool that allows me to be ORS® to all those around me, be they on Twitter or elsewhere.

Let's assume you have decided to spend time on a social platform and that platform is Twitter. So, what is Twitter? Twitter is an information network, a news network, a social network, and a business network. Twitter is also a perception network. Twitter is about the real you: who you are, what you believe in, and what you stand for.

Take time to consider that for a while. Look out the window, smile, doubt, question, makes notes, and then consider where else on the internet the whole of you exists. Social media is about being you, so be you and do not wear a mask.

Now, let's build a scenario on Twitter for gathering information. We know, from television, newspapers, radio, and the internet, that certain topics are popular right now:

- ◆ AI or artificial intelligence
- ◆ Blockchain
- ◆ Cryptocurrencies such as Bitcoin and Ethereum
- ◆ Cybersecurity (hackers)
- ◆ Climate change
- ◆ Nuclear weapons (North Korea)
- ◆ Food and diet

♦ Sugar and cancer

♦ Presidents Donald Trump, Vladimir Putin, Xi Jinping, and Kim Jong-un

♦ Brexit and Europe

Let's assume you wish to study one of these topics or a market such as AI, blockchain, cryptocurrency, SaaS, or social media. Where do you begin? It all starts with people's profiles and people's tweets. So, for instance, if we search "blockchain," we can see which profiles feature "blockchain" in their profile words:

`https://twitter.com/search?f=users&vertical=default&q=blockchain&src=typd`.

We can then look through these profiles and see who stands out from reading their tweets. Thus, we discover:

♦ `https://twitter.com/VinnyLingham`

♦ `https://twitter.com/SpirosMargaris`

♦ `https://twitter.com/APompliano`

♦ `https://twitter.com/cburniske`

♦ `https://twitter.com/cz_binance`

♦ `https://twitter.com/AriDavidPaul`

♦ `https://twitter.com/aantonop`

♦ `https://twitter.com/IOHK_Charles`

♦ `https://twitter.com/VitalikButerin`

♦ `https://twitter.com/KyleSamani`

♦ `https://twitter.com/TuurDemeester`

♦ `https://twitter.com/SatoshiLite`

Then, by building a Twitter list of these folks, we can research and study that market. By reading the tweets of the supposed leaders and the Twitter feed, it gives you the content you most seek based on your clicks. This is AI in action: training itself to learn from your clicks.

The more you click, the more you share. The more that is shared onward by others, the faster the AI learns to serve you better. This is corporate intelligence and market intelligence at its best. This is what board members require before making decisions. This is also what you require before making decisions: insights and connections.

So what does the future hold?

In the last few pages, I've spent time explaining what social media is and how we can use it to build a brand, a community, and a following, both for the people and companies we work for and for ourselves.

You can see how ideas and content drive conversations, and with the example of ORS®, you can see how these conversations create transactions that drive the outcomes of information, contacts, and deals, as previously mentioned.

Now we need to answer specific questions around social media: its present and its future, and how it all relates to AI, blockchains, crypto, IOCs, tokens, and tokenomics.

Where is social media going?

Social media is going to get bigger and bigger. In many ways, it's barely started. Facebook, Twitter, LinkedIn, Instagram, and Snapchat are mere embryos. These platforms will grow to be five or ten times the size and deliver five or ten times more value than they do today.

Some will become full-blown media empires such as Bloomberg. Some will become banks and financial services companies. Facebook may even become a bank (https://youtu.be/XT6b_jXsN6M). These companies have no limit. They have unlimited capacity to scale. They are very important and powerful companies and platforms. The only things standing in their way are governments, regulation, and tax. Expect more on this throughout the 2020s.

Social media in ICOs

All the ICOs to date have recognized the requirements of social media, and the need to communicate and connect with their audience. The following images are a sample of social media platforms used by various ICOs.

Figure 2: ICONOMI social media platforms: Medium, Facebook, Twitter, LinkedIn, Reddit, and Slack

Figure 3: MobileGo social media platforms: Twitter, Facebook, Google+, Slack, and Telegram

Figure 4: Humaniq social media platforms: Facebook, Twitter, Instagram, GitHub, YouTube, Slack, LinkedIn, and Telegram

Figure 5: Bancor social media platforms: Twitter, Facebook, Medium, YouTube, Steemit, LinkedIn, and Reddit

So, what should one do? How does one balance between not enough social media exposure on the one hand, versus overdoing it on the other. At the very minimum, an ICO should have a presence on the following: Twitter, LinkedIn, GitHub, a video platform, a blogging platform, an instant messenger platform, a community forum, and a channel:

- ♦ Twitter is a must. It is the voice of the ICO and the heartbeat. It tells your users that you are alive and kicking.

- ♦ LinkedIn provides the professional face of the company. The core founders and team members must have a LinkedIn profile that is legitimate and real. Transparency is key.

- ♦ In this new decentralized world, open source is very important, which is why having a GitHub repository helps to provide legitimacy for the technically inclined. GitHub is the place where all the programming source code is kept, so that anyone can view the code to check for quality and activity. A lot of activity means there are lots of developers working and improving the code, which is essential for the product or service on offer.

- ♦ A video platform is critical. It can be YouTube or Vimeo or any others. What is important is that there is a medium where information can be digested fast without having to read through pages and pages of blog posts. A one-to-two-minute summary video, followed by multiple five-to-seven-minute videos exploring various aspects of the offering, is the easiest way to know how and know now.

♦ A blog is important. Tweets have a very short life span of usually 60 seconds. Blogs, on the other hand, are like recorded mini-milestone events. This could be the launch of a new feature, a partnership announcement or a summary of how the ICO went. Many use Medium as the platform because it is very quick to set up. Having your own blogging platform such as WordPress will give you more control.

♦ Instant messaging has become very popular but takes a lot of energy and resources. It is live chats where sometimes founders, but usually key team members, can answer questions in near real time. Currently, the popular platforms are Slack and Telegram. Discord is used in some cases but has a very technical/developers feel to it.

♦ The default community forum is bitcointalk and the default community channel is Reddit. These are a must for traditional, open-source ICOs.

Facebook, Instagram, and Google+ are nice to have but not essential, as the majority of ICOs use the other channels mentioned in the preceding list. The key is to build the community so that it reaches critical mass and is self-serving. The community members end up helping other members by sharing the knowledge and answering other community questions.

In summary, successful ICOs set up Twitter, LinkedIn, a YouTube channel, a blog on Medium, Telegram, bitcointalk, and a Reddit channel and have a team dedicated to their social media strategy 24/7.

Factom

There is a danger in overdoing it, though, as can be seen with Factom, which launched with a website, blog, Google+, Twitter, Facebook, Reddit, LinkedIn, GitHub, YouTube, Vimeo, and Email.

Figure 6: Factom's initial social media platforms

What has happened since is that the blog URL has changed, so it now redirects to the homepage, the last post on Google+ was in May 2015 (`https://plus.google.com/+FactomProjectLive`), the Twitter handle has changed from @factomproject to @factom and Vimeo, with its 16 videos (`https://vimeo.com/factom`), has been superseded by YouTube. On Factom's most current website, its social networks have now been consolidated to just Facebook, Twitter, LinkedIn, YouTube, and Reddit.

Figure 7: Factom's consolidated social media platforms
(https://www.factom.com/) (July 2018)

Influencers

Influencers are experts in their chosen niches. Influencers have extraordinary power among groups of people with the same motivation, lifestyle, product, platform, focus, or purpose. Influencers are about nudges and education. Influencers are change agents who build communities. They create ideas and publish content. Influencers are a new force in marketing, who begin and lead conversations. They are a new power and reside on every social media platform now available.

Influencer power is rising and will continue to rise and become bigger than company brand power - unless, of course, the brands do the right thing and hire (retain or sponsor) them all. The latter, by the way, is highly recommended.

AAs Influencers grow their follower base, their power grows, and so do their incomes. The more followers, the more money. Income is a direct function of follower size and is typically $1 per year per follower. Thus, influencers are heavily incentivized to grow their follower base before the brands wake up to their power. This makes them incredibly creative and incredibly fast.

People are more interested in who you are than what you do

This is why you have to take time to get your content right because content is king, and your content defines you. What you share defines you. What you influence defines you. The other wonderful thing about content is what engagement it receives. If you get loads of engagement and inbound conversation, you are posting the right stuff. If not, you're not and you have to think about that.

You might think you understand a market. You might think you understand a product. You might think you understand, but if you have no inbound questions, emails, responses, and conversations, it's fair to say your content isn't working. You must come to terms with this.

Then you have to consider what you wish to say next and what you wish to share next. Measure yourself by inbound conversations and enquiries. Inbound defines your perception. No perception, no inbound. Video draws 10 times the traffic of the written word, so you must consider video.

You must also consider what's natural for you. What can you fit in? Do you have time, and do you have that much to say? Your content must fit your lifestyle and your lifestyle must fit your content. People will know if it's not natural or not you.

What's the relationship between influencers and ICOs?

The introverts among you may not like this, but if your founding team does not engage *fully* in social media, converse, and build real connections, and a substantial following, then your ICO will suffer, big time. Having the right influencers endorsing a token sale increases the hype and the size of the community.

It's just not possible to outsource everything when it comes to running an ICO. Successful projects are those that have public-facing CEOs, who engage in their community, operate transparently, and build a social following for themselves, as well as their project.

There are several great examples of this in action, such as Jason Goldberg, of **One Simple Token** (**OST**), who is on Twitter as @betashop. Goldberg has amassed an enthusiastic following of over 17,000 people on Twitter, by being truly engaged with and engaging around the tech that OST is building, and the crypto sector in general.

OST required 200 influencers, with the CEO living and breathing not just his product but the community he serves, and that generated credibility in spades. The ICO in November and December 2017 raised 46,828 ETH and this could not have been achieved without those 200 influencers (`https://twitter.com/OSTdotcom`).

This, again, is about connecting with the community around your project and giving reassurance to bigger investors. Ignore this at your peril. Now ask yourself: how important are influencers?

Influencers in the crypto community

Whether it's the Forbes billionaire rich list or a TIME most influential people list, there are those that are infatuated with lists, which has inevitably poured over to the ICO world. There are numerous lists and rankings, such as Crypto Weekly's "100 Most Influential People in Crypto" (https://cryptoweekly.co/100/) or RICHTOPIA's "100 Most Influential Blockchain People" (https://www.rise.global/top-fintech-people), and here is a sample of people from these lists ranked by Twitter followers:

Name	Twitter Handle	Tweets	Following	Followers
Vitalk Buterin	@VitalikButerin	7k	156	793k
Charlie Lee	@SatoshiLite	12.8k	380	786k
Fred Wilson	@fredwilson	16.4k	1.2k	645k
Roger Ver	@rogerkver	3k	1k	543k
Naval	@naval	17.6k	643	463k
Andreas Antonopoulos	@aantonop	21.1k	2.3k	440k
Ben Horowitz	@bhorowitz	5.2k	294	423k
Thomas Power	@thomaspower	249k	103k	340k
Erik Voorhees	@ErikVoorhees	10.4k	3k	299k
Brian Armstrong	@brian_armstrong	3.5k	528	240k
Nick Szabo	@NickSzabo4	7k	1.8k	223k
Max Keiser	@maxkeiser	73.9k	1.5k	222k
Changpeng Zhao	@cz_binance	109	29	202k
Brad Garlinghouse	@bgarlinghouse	308	423	185k
Tuur Demeester	@TuurDemeester	26.6k	1k	171k

Jameson Jopp	@lopp	21.6k	217	171k
Barry Silbert	@barrysilbert	8k	326	166k
Vinny Lingham	@VinnyLingham	17.9k	6.2k	160k
Charlie Shrem	@CharlieShrem	9k	360	153k
Adam Back	@adam3us	11.2k	349	148k
Anthony Pompliano	@Apompliano	13.7k	6k	146k

Table 1: List of the top 20 crypto heavyweights,
based on Twitter followers, as of July 2018

Granted, this is far from a fair or comprehensive list, but it does give an indication of some of the influencers within the community. Charlie Lee recognized his personal influence on the direction, or more specifically the price, of Litecoin. In December 2017, he announced on Reddit that he had sold all his Litecoin:

"In a sense, it is conflict of interest for me to hold LTC and tweet about it because I have so much influence…in the past days, I have sold and donated all my LTC. Litecoin has been very good for me financially, so I am well off enough that I no longer need to tie my financial success to Litecoin's success." (https://www.reddit.com/r/litecoin/comments/7kzw6q/litecoin_price_tweets_and_conflict_of_interest).

Lee kept only a handful of physical coins as collectibles.

YouTube influencers

As mentioned, video is a very effective way to communicate information at speed. In the current age of information overload, it is important to obtain the right information in the quickest amount of time, and this is what video allows.

YouTube influencers provide this information by analyzing, evaluating, and even recommending ICOs. The following is a non-comprehensive list of the top 20 crypto influencers on YouTube, ranked by the number of subscribers they have.

Name	Videos	Subscribers
DataDash	250	310K
Altcoin Buzz	881	209K
Doug Polk Crypto	57	201K
Boxmining	371	200K
Ivan On Tech	455	183K
Ameer Rosic	436	169K
aantonop	308	154K
Crypto Investor	112	149K
Suppoman	336	147K
Crypto Bobby	339	144K
Coin Mastery	223	132K
Crypto Coin News	439	127K
Ian Balina	430	123K
David Hay	185	123K
Crypt0	1195	116K
Crypto Daily	243	110K
Crypto Love	454	91K
The Modern Investor	607	87K
Crypto Beadles	142	80K
The Crypto Lark	592	78K

Table 2: The top 20 crypto YouTube influencers and their followers as of July 2018

Different influencers focus on different aspects of crypto. Some focus on promoting and explaining the technology, while others purely focus on evaluating and investing in ICOs. It should be of no surprise that evaluating ICOs and sharing how they made millions, and how you can do so, receives a significant amount of attention.

Ian Balina

Ian Balina is a former IBM open-source analytics sales executive and a former systems integration consultant with Deloitte. Balina rose to fame in the crypto sphere for analyzing and recommending ICOs, and for infamously being hacked and losing $2 million USD when live broadcasting on YouTube.

He started off blindly investing into various ICOs in 2017 and made slightly better returns than the stock market but knew there had to be a better way. He started to look at some of the underlying data around the ICOs. He distilled his analysis into several key indicators, including:

♦   Does the ICO have a prototype?

♦   Is there an "all-star team" or are there "all-star advisors"? (Where all-star means well-known, respectable, and reputable people in the cryptosphere.)

♦   Is there a low-to-medium hard cap?

♦   What are the token metrics? (https://www.youtube.com/watch?v=uUjqtXUbKDY)

Balina started live streaming his assessments of lots of different ICOs on YouTube, initially just out of interest. He soon found out that other people were interested in what he had to say and, in particular, his analysis of ICOs. He shared his Excel spreadsheet and also opened up his ICO investment portfolio for the world to see. With a following and an audience, Balina now had a platform to further his brand.

On April 15, 2018, Balina was reviewing ICOs on his channel as usual, when a viewer in the chat log, with the handle of "DABusiness," suddenly notified him that someone had moved tokens out of his wallet:

"Ian, did you know that somebody transferred all your tokens from your account? Hope that it's controlled movement." (https://www.youtube.com/watch?v=YpRONcOudJ8).

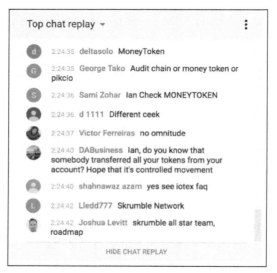

Figure 8: The moment a user notified Balina that someone had transferred tokens from his account

While Balina continued with his review, not taking any notice of the comment, the live feed eventually went down 15 minutes later. Apparently, there was a power outage but when Balina returned to continue his review, he noticed that he had been signed out of his Google Sheets account.

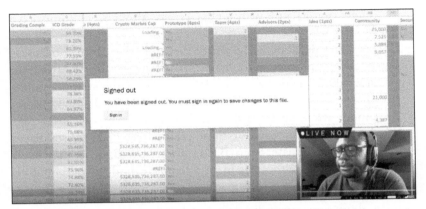

Figure 9: The moment Balina noticed he had been signed out of his Google account
(https://www.youtube.com/watch?v=AWWAyArwvxk)

According to Balina, the hacks started with his old college email address. It's listed as a recovery email address in Gmail and was apparently hacked in the past. Balina stored the passwords (private keys) he needed to access his digital assets on a cloud storage program called Evernote. Once the hacker accessed the main email, it was a simple matter of resetting the Evernote password and gaining access to millions of dollars, worth of cryptocurrency.

The wallet transactions on Etherscan show that almost all of Balina's tokens were withdrawn from his account during the livestream. This included more than 20 million Nucleus Vision, 2 million Pareto Network, 1 million Loom, 400,000 Simple Tokens, and 100,000 Power Ledger tokens, among others. (`https://etherscan.io/address/0x20f2ce82c28b726930a9b476503df7b814335642#tokentxns`).

The event is not without its critics, though, as some have questioned whether the hack was staged, as it was close to the US tax filing deadlines. The other theory is that from a business perspective, this may have been staged to get more attention. Consider the scenario where if Balina loses a large sum of money and then makes it back really quickly, he is obviously going to get a lot more attention from the media because everyone loves rags to a 'riches' stories! None of these claims have been substantiated and the latest update from Balina about the hack is that he is working with the authorities in an attempt to find the perpetrators.

There is always a risk in becoming a public figure and being open about your portfolio or token holdings in the crypto world. However, storing very important passwords using an online storage system is also a huge risk. There are definitely more secure ways, such as offline storage with two-factor authentication for instance.

Influencer ICO platforms

There are so many ICOs that attempt to tokenize the concept of influencers or celebrities that it is almost impossible to comb out the real ones with a valid business model and genuine potential, versus ones that are less genuine or, in the worst case, cleverly disguised scams. The following are random examples illustrating the creative concepts only.

TokenStars, for example, allows fans to support future stars by buying tokens:

"A rising star receives money to train, improve the skills. When successful, the star pays the platform commission from the sponsorship deals and prize money. Commission is paid in tokens, which are bought on the market." (`https://tokenstars.com/team/`).

Stars can then conduct their personal ICO on this celebrity management platform and essentially get upfront payment for exclusive communication and access to *locker-room tours, dinners, Skype chats, and merchandize.*

Global Crypto Offering Exchange (GCOX) aims to be the world's first fully licensed crypto token exchange that helps celebrities to create, list, and trade their own crypto tokens, known as Celebrity Tokens. The catch is that the **ACCLAIM** token (**ACM**) is the base currency of GCOX and is required to buy celebrity tokens or access the various celebrity features.

Influence Chain is the world's first (everything is the world's first these days!) influence value data engine based on blockchain technology. It is dedicated to building a global influencer value platform using blockchain and distributed storage technologies. It attempts to turn unquantifiable influence into quantifiable assets via tokenization and allow the monetization of an intangible asset into a digital asset via an influencer exchange. It has an influencer index to evaluate influential powers for every possible aspect of an influencer.

Kylie Jenner

Kylie Jenner is reported by Forbes to be closing in on being the world's youngest ever self-made billionaire. She is currently on about $900 million, which was amassed in less than three years (https://www.cbsnews.com/news/kylie-jenner-net-worth-forbes-20-year-old-jenner-to-become-youngest-self-made-billionaire-ever/). This empire was mainly built on social media, where Jenner has over 111 million followers on Instagram and 25 million followers on Twitter.

Kylie Cosmetics has actually done about $420 million in retail sales in just 18 months and to put this into perspective, Estée Lauder Inc was said to have reached $500 million in revenue in 10 years, while L'Oréal's Lancôme hit the mark in 2015 after 80 years (`https://wwd.com/beauty-industry-news/beauty-features/kylie-jenner-cosmetics-to-become-billion-dollar-brand-10959016/`).

Figure 10: Forbes stating that at 21, Jenner is set to be the youngest-ever self-made billionaire

What does this have to do with ICOs? Imagine what these celebrities can do if they tap into the world of tokenizing their time, their products, and their services.

Summary

In this chapter, we started out with a deep look at social media, which involved a different mindset. It's not about just sending a tweet or posting a picture on Instagram: it's reading, analyzing, pondering, ruminating, considering, and hunting for information from some of the best minds in the world. Jenner doesn't aimlessly post Instagram pictures for the sake of it. Each post has a purpose: to help her build her empire.

We then learned what social media channels are required at a minimum for an ICO and that these tweets, blogs, and chat channels allow users to keep up-to-date, and interact with the project or company members.

Finally, influencers, or experts in their chosen niches, play a crucial part in the crypto community by sharing their technical knowledge or evaluating ICOs. There are also numerous ICOs creating platforms where celebrities can create and sell their own token in return for providing their die-hard fans with a more unique experience.

With all the right social media in place and potential influencers on board, marketing is the next step, which we will explore in the next chapter.

10

MARKETING
AND THE LAUNCH

Marketing has come to play a very critical role in ICOs and as the landscape becomes more cluttered, if any ICO is to be successful, the ability to stand out from the noise is important. Your ICO marketing strategy can be the difference between success and failure. You can have the most amazing product ever, but without the right marketing campaign and strategy in place, your chances of success are greatly diminished.

In this chapter, we will look at the various marketing strategies around the four main concepts of:

♦ The state of ICO marketing

♦ The message and the tools

♦ The community

♦ The launch

While the launch may be the most exciting aspect of an ICO, a lot of work is required for many months behind the scenes to actually make an ICO successful. To start, the various aspects of an ICO campaign must be identified, understood, and planned for, and to achieve this, we must first look at the state of ICO marketing.

The state of ICO marketing

In 2017, a good digital strategy was enough to launch an ICO successfully. Even then, recent statistics from TokenData showed that 46% of the ICOs completely failed (https://blog. iqoption.com/en/token-data-about-50-of-icos-from-2017- have-failed/), and another hundred or so were classed as semi-failed because the evidence suggested abandonment: their social media was no longer active, or, and this is the key, *their community size was so small that their chance of success was highly unlikely.*

That last statement is crucial because community is a big part of any successful strategy for ICOs, but the community isn't there to fund your project: it's there to market it and give it credibility for the *real* investors.

The ideal strategy for an ICO is a two-pronged attack, with each prong depending on the other:

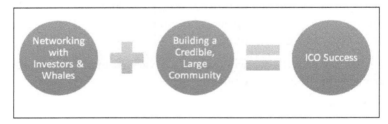

Figure 1: An ideal marketing strategy

Founders should build the trust they need by ensuring that authenticity and transparency run through all their communications from the outset. The aim of your pre-launch marketing is to increase the visibility of the project and to communicate value both to the investors, and to the product's user community, to increase the likelihood of receiving investment. Depending on the project, there are likely to be three kinds of contributors:

- **Product-driven**: They believe in the technology and benefits of your project.

- **Idealistic**: They believe blockchains and cryptos are the future, and they will back you for this reason.

- **Profit-oriented investors**: They are looking for an entry into and clear exit from your token, along with taking advantage of token liquidity.

These contributors have one thing in common: they look for signals that your project can be realized and that there is a high chance of future adoption.

Many ICOs are launched by developers who are not good at explaining, simply, what the product is, what it does, and how it will achieve an outcome. These are destined to fail, no matter how strong the idea may be in other respects. Founders need to address this challenge through the creation of a message framework, to provide real clarity on the offer. They must make it credible and easy to understand or have a dedicated marketing team to handle this. Then, they must use that framework in the creation of all content.

However, the key to all successful launches is to truly engage with the crypto community. This must be genuine, real-world engagement through global events and special, targeted content, distributed to the right channels and groups.

This is a fast-changing market, so you need to keep up-to-date. Facebook, MailChimp, Twitter, and Google (from June 2018) have either fully or partially banned the (paid) promotion of ICOs and this was the major route to engagement. The ban was to prevent misleading or deceptive ICO promotional practices; however, these bans are automated, so if you avoid the trigger words and instead focus on the story behind the launch, rather than the ICO, you can still make some use of these platforms. Of course, it helps to work with a specialist who has learned what works and what is a waste of budget.

Authenticity is everything, because there have been so many scam projects, and there is a lot of caution now in the market, and within these communities. If you are not acting and behaving rigorously and professionally at all times; if your content and the way you present it doesn't look world class; if your copy is not perfect, or if you are out there auto-translating into different languages – please don't do that – then you're not in the top five percent, and that's where you have to be. Authenticity is also important in terms of how you manage the community and how open you are about how the project is going, as all of this makes a big difference.

Don't underestimate the workload

Much of the credibility of an ICO rests on sticking to the launch date you promised, so there is no room for error. That means you cannot underestimate the workload involved, nor the expertise required.

Throughout your ICO marketing campaign, you will typically need at least seven talented people working almost full-time (certainly full-time in the final days leading up to the launch of a token sale), including:

♦ **Digital strategists**: Monitoring and deploying digital marketing on multiple platforms.

♦ **Social media marketers**: Spreading the word on social channels.

♦ **Copywriters**: For brand communication, articles, and blog posts.

♦ **Exceptional graphic designers**: Essential for being visible above the noise and establishing the visual brand of not just the business, but the ICO event.

♦ **Web developers**: For the significant integrations required across multiple channels to achieve a seamless investor experience.

- **Pay-per-click**: Ensuring that keywords are wisely and economically purchased.

- **SEO experts**: To understand the opportunity for organic ranking (SEO is a long-term strategy and won't have a significant impact in an ICO project, unless the project lead time from start to launch is six months or more. It will certainly help the project overall, though).

- **PR**: Managing the essential connections with the media and creating link value with third parties.

- **Bot developers**: To help manage the communities within Telegram as they get bigger, and leverage automations where possible.

- **Community managers**: To help build the community, typically through meetups.

This may sound daunting, but it is a false economy to skimp on these marketing activities. It is important to make sure you've got the right team around you as well: the ICO space is crowded and your ICO deserves world-class talent.

Key campaign elements and phases

No two ICOs are exactly the same, but this checklist will help you to ensure that the key elements are executed in the right order, even if you don't operate all of them.

Note, in particular, that effort upfront will yield exceptional dividends later on. The brand work, for example, will support your website build, white paper, and social activity, reducing the effort and repetition needed for the launch, when every second counts.

Build-up to brand/site launch

The following should be focused on:

- **Digital strategy**: Setting up digital channels and a content calendar (and given the nature of the crypto community, 99% of your engagement activity will be digital!).

- **Brand identity**: Visuals, tone of voice, style, spokesperson(s), and others.

- **Messaging framework**: Key messages and phrases, the elevator pitch, personas of typical targets, and others.

- **Website design and build**: The site which will act as the "HQ" for your engagement activities.

- **White paper**: The key investment document.

- **One pager**: The brief summary (this must include the what and why of the product in broad-brush terms).

- **Pitch deck**: The opportunity in highly-visual deck form. It's essential that your pitch deck and white paper are consistent in messaging and visuals.

- **Social branding**: The visual narrative. Think: after seven exposures to your social activity, it should be instantly clear, without reading, that this is a post from your ICO. This is based on a basic marketing principle that it takes seven interactions before an action takes place.

- **Initial social content**: Social content will change by necessity as you respond to the market environment, but you can produce content to follow the planned calendar and start with basic messages.

♦ **Third-party connections**: To present a seamless front to investors, you will need to align messages and technologies with a raft of partners:

- ○ Independent KYC/AML provider
- ○ Ethereum contract developers
- ○ PR
- ○ Advisory partners
- ○ Escrow provider
- ○ Audit and governance
- ○ Legal
- ○ Translations (yes, ICOs are global, so your entire marketing campaign needs to be translated and replicated)

Build-up to seed funding (private pre-sale)

In the build-up to the seed funding, it is important to ensure that there is constant and consistent messaging when considering social branding. The content should be published on all relevant platforms, as per the content plan. The Telegram community should be kick-started, as Telegram is the crypto-investor's platform of choice, along with having a forum channel growth strategy in place to develop the community into active investors.

Initial PR (through a PR partner) and **pay-per-click** (**PPC**) campaigns across all channels, should be initiated in conjunction with re-targeting tracking and analytics. It is also crucial to have a subscriber management and email marketing platform, especially in the **General Data Protection Regulation** (**GDPR**) environment. Email permissions are gold dust: they represent a key degree of commitment.

For this part, investor relations play a key role. Private pre-sale buyers are likely to be family offices, high-net-wealth individuals, and business angels. They are not easy to reach.

Build-up to the public ICO

In the build up to the public ICO, there are several key considerations. Firstly, consider the creation of videos to present a human face of the venture, highlighting the key benefits and advantages. Then, look at LinkedIn profile growth and group seeding. LinkedIn delivers remarkable credibility, so this should be leveraged to drive leads and present key players in the business. Similarly, use LinkedIn's community functionality to develop interest in relevant forums.

Use a mail platform to drip-feed emails, segmented by user types and maturity. This should be coupled with a full tracking and analytics dashboard, to understand hour-by-hour which activities are effective, and which can be punched up/down.

On the social side, social engagement should continue, either with existing materials or in response to user queries or market conditions. Write credibility-building content and interview key evangelists to provide thought leadership, and also connect with key influencers in both the crypto community and your market sector. They are more credible than you can ever be.

Finally, use affiliate marketing where appropriate and connect via affiliate schemes. Their value differs dramatically between sectors, so play carefully here. Ensure you retarget campaigns across multiple channels. Continue with the Telegram and forum channel growth. In simple terms, developing casual visitors into committed members of your community is a key objective.

Post-ICO and ongoing community development and engagement

The momentum needs to be continued post-ICO, with a partner outreach program. The credibility of your business is a function of all the participants in its development. Your partners can all play a role in promoting your name, especially if the ICO was a success. Similarly, your advisors should, in any case, be committed evangelists for your brand.

Community development and engagement is an endless activity but an important part of the process. We'll now examine some key factors across all of these activities, which deserve your prioritization.

The message and tools

Many projects struggle to get across what they're doing, and aiming to achieve, in a succinct fashion. As mentioned previously, many ICOs are executed by developers who are, by their nature, deeply technical, and so it can be very difficult for them to clearly explain the key facts at a high level. That's part of the challenge of marketing an ICO: to create a messaging framework for pitches, from which all future content can be built.

A messaging framework becomes a critical document as you go through your ICO, containing the key elements to which you will constantly return to: your elevator pitches, your straplines, your use cases, your sound-bite stories, and the features of your platform or product.

It will also help you to clearly differentiate the product from the ICO, and your product vision from the investment opportunity. It will help you to reach out to all the different audiences you want to reach, from product evangelists through to professional investors.

Quality of the brand and the presentation

Do not underestimate how big an impact the quality of the brand and the presentation has on seasoned investors in this market. In a sense, it's not surprising. Traditional investors have always been impressed by the quality of individual CEOs during investor presentations – often being swayed by their performance (or lack of it). It's also no surprise that in the remote/digital arena, the quality of brand materials carries significant value.

Now, because there is a lot of rubbish out there from second-rate ICOs and out-and-out scammers, you *have* to look world class in the way you put out your messaging, the quality of the imagery, and the presentation of your collateral. Your website must look professional, as you need to forge ahead of the less credible offerings and this is one of the key aspects that investors are looking for in ICOs.

Mind your grammar

This is absolutely critical: would you buy from a vendor who couldn't even be bothered to speak your language? Do you want to feel like you're buying from the city of London or an Azerbaijani corner shop? When you can't see into a buyer's eyes, the least you can do is present yourself professionally.

There are many poorly written ICOs online, riddled with broken English. There are also some fairly decent ICOs presented in English, but they then treat their foreign buyers as second-class citizens, by auto-translating sales materials with Google Translate.

Do not cut corners when it comes to the copy and the translation: remember, this is a competition for attention. Cutting corners here means going to all the effort of creating copy, and then abandoning its value for the sake of a little more expense. You must aim to create professional content and choose to work with, and pay for, world-class translation partners too.

Products with real users

News flash: you need a product! It's no longer acceptable to have just a white paper and expect to generate millions. Those days are long gone. You must have at least an alpha product. Ideally, you will have a beta product too and, perhaps most credibly, you need some real users. Some ICOs distinguish their offerings in different levels, in addition to alpha and beta, such as with MVP, testnet, and mainnet.

Marketing strategies for ICOs need to market the product, as much (if not more) than the token, and to incorporate the effort to attract real users.

You'll need to move away from just driving traffic to the ICO website, to picking up users for demos, and then going back out to the market with that as good news stories. As a result, the communities you grow are then also users, and so bigger advocates of the project.

It's no surprise to those of us who have been in business for a long time that you need a product and some customers to warrant investment, but it may be a surprise to those conducting an ICO as their first ever business.

Pay-per-click

As mentioned earlier, there have been quite a lot of pay-per-click bans across mainstream keyword outlets. Facebook made its stance pretty clear with a blanket ban on January 31, 2018. In its advertising policy *Section 29 Prohibited Financial Products and Services* under *Prohibited Content* it stated:

"Ads must not promote financial products and services that are frequently associated with misleading or deceptive promotional practices. Examples... New ICO! Buy tokens at a 15% discount NOW!" (https://web.facebook.com/policies/ads/prohibited_content/prohibited_financial_products_and_services).

On June 27, 2018, though, Facebook added a cryptocurrency clause to its *Restricted Content* policy:

"Ads may not promote cryptocurrency and related products and services without our prior written permission." (`https://web.facebook.com/policies/ads/restricted_content`).

On the same day, Rob Leathern, product management director at Facebook, wrote a blog post in June 2018 updating its position to relax the ban and allow some advertisements via an application process:

"In the last few months, we've looked at the best way to refine this policy — to allow some ads while also working to ensure that they're safe. So, starting June 26, we'll be updating our policy to allow ads that promote cryptocurrency and related content from pre-approved advertisers. But we'll continue to prohibit ads that promote binary options and initial coin offerings." (`https://web.facebook.com/business/news/updates-to-our-prohibited-financial-products-and-services-policy`).

It isn't a sophisticated ban: there are still ICO ads on Facebook and legitimate blockchain projects that are not doing an ICO, and not even mentioning anything to do with token sales, being banned and having their ads taken down.

It's a great shame that it's such a blanket ban and so deeply unsophisticated. Twitter is doing the same and, again, it doesn't seem that sophisticated of a ban, yet.

Google banned ICO ads from June 2018, as mentioned earlier, updating its financial services policy:

"In addition, ads for the following will no longer be allowed to serve:

♦ Binary options and synonymous products

♦ Cryptocurrencies and related content (including but not limited to initial coin offerings, cryptocurrency exchanges, cryptocurrency wallets, and cryptocurrency trading advice.)" (`https://support.google.com/adwordspolicy/answer/7648803`)

MailChimp is removing accounts that send emails to do with ICOs, which is surprising, and it makes the job of marketing an ICO extremely hard. Marketers and CEOs must find new ways around the outreach challenge.

One particularly effective way is to talk a little less about the ICO and more about the product: engaging in product marketing and attracting people to the project in that way instead. One of the ways this can be achieved is by altering the content and the focus of the pushed-out material, so that the key messaging is less a case of "token sale starting at time x," and "buy this..." and more referencing the use cases of the product and the platform, and attracting real users to alpha demos.

Alternative social media

Every sector seems to find its own place to call home and it's no surprise that something as "alternative" and countercultural as the crypto community has its own set of alternative platforms. **Steemit**, a blockchain-based blogging and social media platform, is growing by the hour and there are lots of others as well. Some will survive, some won't.

Depending on what territories you're marketing in, which will also depend on the regulations you're working to, there are plenty of other social media platforms across the globe which have not yet banned ICO talk, and which may even welcome it. Do your homework on a global level and think laterally about the places you can market.

A starter list of alternative social media platforms:

♦ Synereo.com

♦ Akasha.world

♦ Leeroy.io

♦ Vero.co

♦ Somee.social

♦ Sola.ai

♦ MeWe.comObsidianPlatform.com

Telegram

As mentioned, Telegram is a key hub of activity around most ICOs. There are legitimate ways to grow the community, but you must be careful with the way you grow your Telegram group because all sorts of people in the unregulated world of ICOs will claim to sell you Telegram members. They're not genuine members and they're not going to really help your project. In fact, they'll probably damage your credibility with any real investors who join your group, once they see a raft of spam or bots, so be extremely careful how you do it.

Although having a big Telegram community is a key factor for a lot of investors – it's certainly a factor they'll be looking at – what you must focus more on is the quality of the engagement that you're achieving. One thousand highly engaged people is always going to be better than 5,000 moderately interested people. In that respect, Telegram is no different to any special-interest community since the dawn of marketing.

Make good use of intelligent Telegram bots too, in order to remind the group of the rules, answer basic questions, and moderate content.

Email marketing

Whilst it may be getting more complex with the advent of GDPR in Europe, email marketing is still as important as it ever was to the marketing discipline – and never more so than in the marketing of an ICO.

Capturing a person's email address is one of the fastest and easiest ways to start them on their journey to investing in your ICO. However, it's what you do with the address from then on, that makes the difference.

Firstly, be compliant. To comply with GDPR in Europe, and data protection regulations around the world, you need to be clear with your subscriber about a few things:

♦ What they are signing up to

♦ How you will use their data

♦ How you will store it

♦ Who else will have access to it

♦ How they can remove themselves in the future, if they wish

Secondly, get creative. Inboxes are chaotic places: to stand out you need to use punchy and innovative messaging. You need to ensure that when your email is opened, it packs a punch both visually and message-wise in the first few seconds. Also, it needs to be optimized for mobile.

Thirdly, automate! Easy-to-use technologies now exist for building entire programs of emails, to be sent at key times from when someone joins your list. Use this to keep subscribers engaged and reminded, and to build up hype around your launches and big announcements.

The community

Earlier we mentioned the two-pronged attack. In the past, it was enough to have a loyal community around your project and to expect the funds to come from that same group. Now, that's increasingly less the case. Today, the community is there to "do your marketing for you," meaning if they are properly engaged and incentivized, then they can and will have a huge impact on your social following, and the profile of your project in the market.

Investors will look at the size of your community and following when reviewing your project. If it's very low or non-existent, they will worry about your future prospects of success. The community gives you credibility. If absolutely nothing else, it demonstrates to your investor that you have the skills and commitment to build market awareness — a key skill in selling your product and building what will eventually be your business.

ICO rating sites work on "hype scores," and your community size, social following, website traffic, and YouTube views all form part of that calculation. One popular ICO rating website has its hype score based on the following criteria:

- ◆ The number of users on the main social media pages of the project
- ◆ The number of mentions in the press
- ◆ Mentions in mainstream technology media and in prominent finance publications
- ◆ The number of search engine results
- ◆ Traffic on the main website

One crypto investor provided his personal checklist for reviewing ICOs, which was as follows:

- Social activity (numeric inputs)
- LinkedIn followers
- Subreddit followers and posts per week
- Twitter followers and tweets per week
- Telegram followers
- Alexa rank
- Google trends rank
- Development stage: white paper, mock-up, proof of concept, alpha, beta, production, and others
- GitHub (numeric inputs)

Partnerships

Partnerships can be incredibly powerful for an ICO because both their perceived and strategic value far exceed the effort required to create them — and that means less work for you!

Strategic partnerships have always been a great way to grow and scale, but in ICOs they're particularly powerful because they give reassurance to potential investors, especially if the partnerships are with people above your paygrade as a startup. So, don't underestimate the power of a really good partnership and put effort into creating a distinct partnership strategy.

One ICO from early 2018 is a company called TriForce, operating in the video game sector. Its token (FORCE) seeks to become the universal gaming currency built on the Ethereum platform.

TriForce's campaign attracted a huge partner in Latin America called Busca Todo, whose website (`levelup.com`) sees 50 million gamers visiting every month. This was, of course, a big deal for TriForce (made up of a small team from Milton Keynes, UK), which gained a gaming giant on side, with all the marketing and brand support that entails, plus access to a new community of gamers and potential investors.

This goes to show that through really good-quality visuals, branding, campaign content, PR, along with talking up the stories around users and signups, you can always punch above your weight.

Public relations

In 2018, credibility, authenticity, and authority are the key to success in almost any field, and for that you need effective PR.

There is no shortage of crypto-specific PR teams, but the vast majority are freelancers working remotely and they did not cut their teeth in the real world of traditional PR.

Few traditional PR agencies – even the financial specialists – have not risked getting involved in ICOs yet. Most are waiting for the market to become more regulated. However, traditional/ mainstream PR is going to become more important to ICO marketing than in any other space, and at any other time. This is because it is becoming increasingly hard to use other, more traditional, digital marketing methods (companies are similarly preferring to blanket ban ICO activities until the environment is more regulated – again, blame the scammers).

The recommendation is, therefore, a balanced mix of:

♦ Bitcoin PR: specialists in the sector, who are often less experienced but are connected to the crypto community, and often rapidly achieving exposure because of the hunger for content on the many crypto websites springing up

♦ More seasoned and traditional PR specialists, who will do a better job of getting your ICO, or at least the business proposition, into mainstream media

This blend is going to be key to an ICO's success in the future. Incidentally, when being interviewed by mainstream media, don't be surprised if you need to explain everything from first principles. For example, you will get questions such as "what is bitcoin all about, then?" or, even more challengingly, you may be forced to justify the wild west of ICOs, with questions such as "it's all just scams, isn't it?" That's how the press works, so be ready for it!

Networking into investor groups – without this, the ICO dies

Your ICO will likely fail unless you create a comprehensive, engaging, and motivating strategy for bringing on board larger investors, through personal approaches and introductions.

Think about a traditional IPO on a stock market: the initial credibility for the public to contribute to a sale comes from the participation of large banks – usually at a discount from the publicly available rate. The same goes for ICOs: "whale" investors and institutional interest count for a lot in credibility terms.

There has always been a mature "serious investor" network in traditional investment communities, for example, angel investor networks, venture capital organizations, and plenty in between. Not only are the same groupings springing up in the crypto community, but traditional investors are also taking an interest in crypto and ICO opportunities.

It is, therefore, essential that you nurture these connections – and in person. Many smart ICOs replicate the "Investor Tour" conducted by traditional businesses, meeting investors face-to-face in the pre-sale period.

Bitcointalk

We couldn't write a chapter on marketing an ICO and not return to **Bitcointalk**, which has been mentioned several times throughout this book. It is one of the oldest (established 2009) crypto websites on the internet. Bitcointalk is where new coins are announced.

There are a few established protocols when it comes to marketing your ICO on a forum such as bitcointalk, such as creating an official **ANN** or **Announcement Thread** for your project, which gives potential crypto investors all the information they could want.

A good ANN features a quick summary of what the token is all about. It should cover details such as the type of token you are creating, the white paper, GitHub link(s) so that code can be examined, and links to the team members to demonstrate authenticity.

As well as the ANN providing a token's elevator pitch, it has to get into the ICO details. The ANN for an ICO should cover the nuts and bolts, including how to set up a wallet, where the ICO will be hosted, the exact date of launch, which currencies will be accepted, and everything else prospective investors need to know. A good wallet is particularly important: just ask those who lost hundreds of millions of ether in the Parity hack in November 2017 (https://www.businessinsider.com.au/ethereum-price-parity-hack-bug-fork-2017-11).

Bitcointalk members are extremely knowledgeable. ANNs that aren't sound will be ripped to shreds. One key to your ANN is explaining why your product needs a new token to function. There are plenty of great blockchain products coming to market, but how many of those really need a new token to function? How many can show that blockchain adds quantifiable new value, and therefore investor opportunity?

There is no official format for an announcement, but the standard practice is to prefix the title with "[ANN]," followed by the name of the token, and then a brief description. For example:

- [ANN] FACTOM - Introducing Honesty to Record-Keeping (`https://Bitcointalk.org/index.php?topic=850070.msg9464030#msg9464030`)

- [ANN] Bancor | Protocol for Smart-tokens, solving the liquidity problem (`https://Bitcointalk.org/index.php?topic=1789222.msg17842029#msg17842029`)

- [ANN]Pillar - The Personal Data Locker - 60hr Token sale begins July 15 (`https://Bitcointalk.org/index.php?topic=1986401.msg19779596#msg19779596`)

- [ANN][ICO] SONM: Supercomputer Organized by Network Mining (`https://Bitcointalk.org/index.php?topic=1845114.msg18358362#msg18358362`)

- [ANN] [ICO 06|04|2017] Humaniq — Discover the unbanked (`https://Bitcointalk.org/index.php?topic=1711764.msg17151876#msg17151876`)

- [ANN] DECENT Announcement - Decentralizing Content Distribution (`https://Bitcointalk.org/index.php?topic=1162392.msg12245837#msg12245837`)

- [ANN][GNT] Golem Project - The world's most powerful supercomputer (`https://Bitcointalk.org/index.php?topic=1655002.msg16615613#msg16615613`)

- [ANN][XCP] Counterparty - Pioneering Peer-to-Peer Finance - Official Thread (`https://Bitcointalk.org/index.php?topic=395761.msg4271094#msg4271094`)

- ◆ [ANN][LSK] Lisk | Blockchain Application Platform for JavaScript Developers (`https://Bitcointalk.org/index.php?topic=1346646.msg13726345#msg13726345`)

- ◆ [ANN] Ethereum: Welcome to the Beginning (`https://Bitcointalk.org/index.php?topic=428589.msg4683379#msg4683379`)

- ◆ Augur - a decentralized prediction market platform (`https://Bitcointalk.org/index.php?topic=860629.msg9570567#msg9570567`)

- ◆ [ANN] MOBILEGO Crowdfund [$53 Million] - Decentralized Mobile Gaming Solutions (`https://Bitcointalk.org/index.php?topic=1792451.msg17871786#msg17871786`)

There are always exceptions, of course. Counterparty and Golem used their ticker symbols, of XCP and GNT, which can make it confusing for newcomers. Augur didn't have a prefix at all and MobileGo updated the title with the final amount raised. Ethereum had a simple tag line: *Welcome to the Beginning*.

The biggest exceptions were Filecoin and OmiseGo. They didn't even have an official Bitcointalk announcement. They didn't need to. The huge demand meant that in most cases, they were oversubscribed. Nearly all ICOs, however, did set up a Reddit channel.

Creating a Reddit channel is considered good practice as part of a successful ICO. The difference between a Bitcointalk thread and a Reddit channel is that in Bitcointalk, there is only one thread or subject and that discussion is central to that thread – the obvious being the ICO launch. In Reddit, users are encouraged to create discussions around topics of their choice, therefore Reddit contains a collection of threads or subjects.

Timing the announcements is important. Usually, they are announced anywhere from one-to-three months (if not more) ahead of the actual ICO, as part of the pre-marketing phase. Announcing after the ICO has started is definitely not a good but this is what Monaco did. It opened its ICO on May 18, 2017, but the Bitcointalk forum was created two days later on May 20, 2017 (`https://Bitcointalk.org/index.php?topic=1926269.0`). Monaco got hammered by many, who were thinking it was a scam because it popped up out of nowhere, leaving people with very little time to read and research the project.

Bounty campaigns

Bounty campaigns take their origins from the online gaming world, where rewards are offered for performing certain tasks.

When announcements are made, members usually "reserve" a language to translate the announcement. They typically get paid for this service from what's known as a **bounty**. A bounty is part of a bounty campaign, which is effectively a PR event. Various tasks, such as sending out tweets or liking Facebook pages, will be rewarded with **stakes**. These stakes are then converted to the tokens of the ICO. When the ICO starts trading, the tokens can then be converted to other tokens or to fiat, such as USD or Euro. Quite often, a percentage of the ICO tokens will be allocated to bounty programs managed by a bounty manager. In addition to translations, a typical bounty campaign usually involves the following:

- Signature and avatar campaign
- Slack campaign
- Newsletter subscribers campaign
- Facebook likes campaign

- Twitter followers campaign
- Blog post or video vlog (video blog) campaign

Designing a bounty campaign takes planning. Here is an example of Twitter campaign requirements:

- Account must be at least four months old
- Number of followers is fixed when the account is connected and doesn't change during the campaign
- Retweet news marked with *#somehashtag* from the official account within five days after its publication and not later
- Tweets not deleted until the ICO ends

Each retweet will earn the following number of stakes:

- 29 followers and less: one stake
- From 30 to 99 followers: 10 stakes
- From 100 to 249 followers: 25 stakes
- From 250 to 999 followers: 60 stakes
- From 1000 to 9999 followers: 120 stakes
- 10000 followers and more: 250 stakes

Signature campaigns

Signature campaigns are when posts on bitcointalk all have a sponsored signature, and the poster gets paid by the sponsor for every post made on the forum. There are seven ranks in bitcointalk. They are: "legendary," "hero," "senior," "full," "member," "junior," and "newbie." The higher the rank, the higher the available bounty and this is combined with posting terms, such as a minimum number of posts daily, weekly, or monthly.

Make sure to use an established bounty manager with a history on Bitcointalk, and a good following across social media and Telegram. The bounty manager is key to maintaining control, establishing the rules, and providing high-quality reporting throughout the campaign, so that you are not rewarding bots or fake accounts, and only those providing quality material are verified.

The key is motivating rewards and excellent quality control. All of this will add to your hype scores when listing (more on this in the following section) and when investors are doing their due diligence on you.

Airdrops

The most common reason for airdrops today is that airdropping (giving away for free) tokens can help expand the business opportunity to new users.

This marketing technique can help with the adoption and use of tokens, especially when they are used to incentivize potential investors and users, through activities such as signups or referrals, and joining Telegram or Twitter groups. They also serve to demonstrate to potential participants what it feels like to "own" your token.

Equally, airdrop strategies must be high value these days to grab attention, and you need to ensure that at least part of the airdrop value redemption involves contributing properly to the token sale, so that you're not just giving tokens away for nothing. So, again, airdrops are helpful to raise awareness, but you must ensure that they motivate the right sort of activity.

There are various airdrop promotional sites that will explode the reach of your airdrop, such as `airdropnotify.com` or `coinairdrops.com`, where, essentially, you provide your email address to be notified of the numerous airdrops that are constantly taking place (`https://bit.ly/2Kx9JK0`).

The launch

The ideal outcome is that your ICO begins seamlessly on the date on which it was promised. This alone is already a mark of the solidity of your outfit. In fact, ideally most of the preparations will be in place before even announcing the ICO date, to ensure the launch date does not have to be deferred. However, you should defer your ICO if you cannot check off the majority of these elements of your marketing activity:

◆ Have two-thirds of your soft cap, that was promised, before you launch: if you can achieve this with the blessing of some significant investors, who may even be prepared to offer you a testimonial, so much the better

◆ Ensure your white paper is published well in advance of your token sale and that you work hard to share it with key influencers and investors

◆ Bounty campaign running: it is essential that friend-to-friend functionality is in place

◆ Airdrop running: it is essential that the automated and instant functionality of a targeted airdrop is in place

◆ Dashboard built and tested: running blind is an unimaginable danger

◆ Investor networking well underway

◆ KYC and payment processes established and tested. Again, this is non-negotiable because nothing will open you up to customer disappointment (and possible future legal action) such as a failed KYC and payment gateway

◆ Product alpha ready and demos available: the days when an ICO could succeed with zero evidence of a working product are long gone

♦ Use case stories ready to be seeded into the press

♦ PR for the campaign launched a month before

ICO listings and ratings

Most crypto investors have their favorite ICO review/rating/ listing sites that they use to discover and study the latest and upcoming ICOs on the market. It is a critical step in your project to ensure you are exposed on as many of these as possible, as early as possible.

Some are free to list, some are paid, and some offer additional auditing services and promotional options. The key is to study the value that each will bring and decide what you are prepared to invest.

When do you list? It's important to note that, at first, the rating sites will base their score for your project on your digital footprint (as mentioned earlier, the hype score), so you need to lay some significant groundwork online before you submit your project to the listing sites. Refer back to the checklist of metrics that comprise your rating and ensure your marketing plan specifically attacks and boosts those.

It makes the task much easier when you know how lengthy or detailed the submission forms might be, so to make your life a little easier, here is a typical list of questions for which you will need to have very good answers to before you submit to an ICO rating or listing site:

♦ Your website must operate secure HTTPS

♦ Project name

♦ Token name and ticker symbol

♦ Blockchain used (Ethereum, Omni, building a new one, other)

♦ One-line description/tagline

- Logo: transparent, 256 pixels x 256 pixels square PNG image file
- Concept description: 3-10 sentences
- How the project creates value for the ecosystem and differs from competing projects, expressed with absolute clarity
- Incorporated company's country and legal formation
- Website link
- Token utility/function
- Team member names, Twitter accounts, and LinkedIn profile links
- The name of your legal counsel or law firm (not published: only used to vet projects)
- Token sale start date and time (UTC)
- Token sale end date and time (UTC)
- Main token sale (phase two) start date and time (UTC)
- Total supply of tokens for the crowdsale and team, and ideally, how they will be used
- ICO price of token
- White paper link
- Company structure (profit/non-profit)
- Blog link
- RSS feed link for automatic follower updates
- Slack invitation link
- GitHub code repository
- Bitcointalk announcement link
- Reddit link
- Twitter profile

- ◆ Facebook product page
- ◆ LinkedIn company link
- ◆ Telegram channel or chatroom link
- ◆ Discussion forum link
- ◆ YouTube introductory video link
- ◆ YouTube channel link
- ◆ Links to interviews and articles
- ◆ Smart contract address

There are numerous ICO rating and listing sites to help ICOs gain exposure, such as `icosales.com` and `tokentops.com`, so the options are vast (`https://bit.ly/2Klw9h9`).

Events

For all our talk of a digital presence, real-world engagement is also key in the ICO world. After all, it may be the only true differentiator in casual investors' eyes between your ICO and the many others out there – including fraudulent offers.

There is no (and may never be a) replacement for meeting with people face-to-face. There is no shortage of events in the blockchain and ICO space, and so the difficult task is deciding which ones to attend or sponsor, and how to evaluate the return on those investments.

Here is one way to really double down on your events strategy: decide where in the world you have the best chance of achieving significant investor traction, and focus on attending events in that region then! Globetrotting is all very well if you have an endless event and travel budget pre-ICO, but let's assume that you don't. Instead, focus on events in just a few concentrated areas that suit your overall strategy, and *really* focus on getting the absolute most out of those events.

Sponsor the event, secure a speaking engagement, and hold roundtable meetings with potential investors during the expo too. A lot of money is spent by ICOs sponsoring events, so to be a speaker at an event can cost up to $15,000 USD. For private sales, roadshows allow ICOs to connect with family offices and business angels.

Make sure you also document the entire experience, so your community can feel part of your event activities, and record, via photo/video, and speak about what happened at these events on your social media, and in your chat groups.

GDPR and marketing

We've briefly touched upon this topic already, but this time let's think about data collection (predominantly for marketing purposes) and the consumer as a couple in a relationship. They get along famously for years and things couldn't be better, until something catches the consumer's eye. There's a new mistress in town and it's making data collection's life miserable: GDPR.

Suddenly, all the consumer can talk about is GDPR. The consumer is delighted that GDPR will give them control over what they share with data collection. No longer can data collection hoard information, squirreling away facts, likes, dislikes, birthdays, and spouse names, like that flyaway comment you once made that didn't go down well and gets brought up every time there's a disagreement.

This is brilliant for the consumer. GDPR makes the consumer feel safe, listened to, and valued as an individual.

An outsider might think that things are looking bad for data collection. One might even ask: is it time for marketing-based data collection and the consumer to break up?

I hear you gasp, "No, surely not!"

Don't worry, I agree with you. Data is the lifeblood of marketing. We need data for our campaigns to work, otherwise we'd all just be shouting into the void, with no hope of our message/service/product reaching the right people. So how, as ICO marketers, can we reconcile data collection with the consumer?

Let's continue with the relationship analogy and imagine that data collection and the consumer have gone to couple therapy. Instead of seeing GDPR as the mistress (and the inherent doom that comes with it) let's think of GDPR as the therapist: it's here to improve the relationship between data collection and the consumer.

Remember, GDPR is not the enemy. GDPR is the opportunity for the consumer to tell you if the relationship has passed the point of no return, or if there's something you can do to salvage this connection.

We all know that "personalization" is the marketing buzzword at the moment. Your consumers want a personalized experience. Not only do they want this personalized experience, they both expect and demand it. Your consumers want to be listened to: they want their needs to be acknowledged, understood, and addressed.

GDPR is your chance to re-engage with your consumer and to understand what they need/want from you. You mustn't squander this opportunity to reconnect with your target audience. Some marketers worry that asking consumers for their consent to collect their data (such as from your website, your email campaigns, or your social media) may detract from the user experience. Instead, think of it this way: requesting your consumers' consent is the beginning of their user experience. In order to have a trustworthy relationship with your consumer, you need to be transparent about what you use their data for.

As an example of transparency, let's take a look at the most recent Facebook fiasco. Mark Zuckerberg appeared before Congress to answer questions about how Facebook uses its consumers' data. A poignant moment occurred, where a member of Congress asked Zuckerberg if he would like to tell the court which hotel he was staying at. Facebook's CEO said he would rather not disclose this information. Boom! There you have it: Zuckerberg would prefer not to disclose the location of his hotel and for the rest of the Congress hearing, no one randomly appeared with flashcards promoting nearby accommodation alternatives that Zuckerberg expressly did not want to see.

This is, of course, referencing former Chair of the Federal Reserve Janet Yellen's testimony in Congress in July 2017, where a person, now known as the "Bitcoin sign guy," held up a yellow "Buy Bitcoin" sign (`https://www.coindesk.com/buy-bitcoin-sign-raised-feds-janet-yellen-testifies-congress/`).

This is a prime example of data collection consent under GDPR. Zuckerberg chose not to reveal the location of his hotel: he wanted it to remain private, and denied consent for Congress to gather this data, and pitch alternative accommodation or encourage him to review/revisit his current hotel. Therefore, as marketers complying with GDPR, Congress would have to file Zuckerberg under "uninterested in receiving further information about local hotels," and remove his details from its "interested in receiving further information about local hotels," mailing list.

We must remember that the absence of the word "no" does not imply consent to data collection. In order to gain consent for data collection, we need to reconnect with our consumers and check in with them to find out what they want to hear from us.

We know that it is best practice to keep your mailing lists/ data tidy. There is no sense in hoarding data that just isn't useful to you anymore. You really don't need to keep hold of that subscriber's email address, when they haven't been active for five years. That person who signed up for updates from your website 10 years ago but has never converted: it's time to let them go.

You can think of this as both spring cleaning and a money-saving exercise. Marketing campaigns cost money and it is pointless to spend money on marketing to people who have absolutely no active interest in your product or services, but they liked a Facebook post you did back in the day.

GDPR is the chance for ICO marketers to fine-tune their relationship with their subscribers and potential participants. Yes, it could create a lot of work for some people in the short term, but this is an opportunity, not a chore.

Here are some key takeaways to review before you start to market your ICO:

♦ **Start early**: Leave at least four-to-five months before opening your pre-sale to start a digital marketing and community growth plan and strategy.

♦ **Build the right team of experts**: Don't expect to be able to outsource this to a couple of enthusiastic volunteers: that won't cut it, and it will do damage that you can't undo in the timeframe you have at hand. Hire experts and professionals who have rigor, process, testimony, and case studies behind them.

♦ Focus on quality of presentation, language, and copy throughout everything you're doing in the campaign. Don't cut any corners.

- Focus on having a product and real users, ideally before you go out asking for contributions.

- **Don't forget the basics**: This is not a surprise to experienced campaigners, but if you're brand new to business, real old-school tactics will still help you. Speaking, networking, shaking hands, picking up the phone, and attending events will all add to your general credibility and market knowledge. There's no sacrifice for events: real engagement is where you'll find some of the best connections, and it will always be that way, despite the incredible outreach of digital (even if JD Wetherspoons deleted all its accounts) (https:// www.telegraph.co.uk/business/2018/04/16/jd- wetherspoon-closes-social-media-accounts- immediate-effect/).

- What is the final message? Remember, "the community attracts the investment, but it probably doesn't provide it." Your community is a tool, not the end product.

Summary

Marketing and launching an ICO is not a task to be taken lightly. There is a tremendous amount of work that needs to be done prior, along with constant monitoring during and continuous efforts afterwards. The planning and strategy need to be more meticulous now, as the novelty of ICOs has passed and hundreds compete against each other on a monthly basis (`https://www.ccn.com/100-icos-launching-every-month-in-2018-generating-13-7-billion-pwc/`).

In this chapter, we covered some of the key campaign elements, in particular building up to seed funding and then the public ICO. We learned that the message needs to be clear, grammar needs to be spot on, and nowadays an alpha product or a proof of concept is an essential part of an ICO. Creating announcements on Bitcointalk, bounty campaigns, and airdrops will help to spread the word and grow the all-important community.

Next, we will hear from the experiences of some high-profile ICO founders.

11

VOICES OF
THE ICO WORLD

The headlines may be glamorous and lots of money may have been raised, but not many people know just how hard it is to run an ICO. And the ICO is also just the start of the journey of course: delivering on all the promises made in the white paper is actually where the "fun" begins.

In this chapter, we'll talk to some key voices in the ICO world – successful ICO founders who share their ICO experiences. We'll interview eight significant ICO founders who have been through the ICO process and are ready to share their experiences with us here. You'll hear about their thoughts on the ICO landscape, the details of their own ICOs and related work, and where they think this industry is going next. You'll hear expert views and insights from:

♦ Nick Ayton, founder of 21Million TV, Chainstarter

♦ Jonny Fry, CEO TeamBlockchain, member of the British Blockchain Association

♦ Jason Goldberg, founder and CEO of Open Simple Tokens, $20 million USD ICO

♦ Dinis Guarda, former CEO of Humaniq, $5 million USD ICO, founder Lifesdna

♦ Vinny Lingham, co-founder and CEO of Civic, $33 million USD ICO

- Aaron McDonald, CEO and co-founder of Centrality, $100 million USD ICO

- Nimo Naamani, co-founder of Horizon State, $1 million USD ICO

- Bokky PooBah, ICO Auditor

I'll introduce each ICO Expert by offering you a summary of their amazing ICO accomplishments and backgrounds, and then we'll talk to each one of them and see what they can teach us from their work with ICOs so far. At the end of the chapter, I'll wrap up and share with you my own thoughts after we've heard from all these ICO experts.

ICO expert voice – Nick Ayton, founder 21Million TV, Chainstarter

Nick Ayton is involved in many aspects of the blockchain and crypto revolution. He advises several family offices and supports their crypto investing activities. He is co-founder of a next generation token launch platform, Chainstarter, which focuses on security ICOs, a crypto exchange for listing security tokens, and Chainstarter TV, which is a new crypto gameshow concept. Nick is involved in OTC trading large amounts of BTC. He also sits on a regulated Crypto Fund in the UK as an Advisor and chairs the world's largest blockchain and investor events. Nick Ayton is known as The Sage of Shoreditch and writes for various crypto publications.

Nick is a big supporter of sustainability and social impact projects and he has stakes in several ICO projects where he's both a board member and advisor covering renewable energy, humanitarian banking, low carbon emissions, and electric vehicles.

Sean Au: Nick, what are your thoughts on the ICO landscape?

Nick Ayton: The ICO landscape has changed already. ICOs are being squeezed out of public use, and the crowd in the western world is being excluded. Investor groups are concerned, and regulators are flexing their muscles. In the last six months, we've seen the garage entrepreneurs priced out of the market as marketing and PR costs have escalated, where the average project requires $500k to get even a basic project started. Although this goes against the libertarian ethos of crypto, the ICO market remains strong because the banks are still not lending, and VCs demand too much flesh for their blood sucking stake.

We are, however, experiencing a new shift – as the concentration of global capital is seeing the crypto markets go sideways, with 80% of BTC trading going **OTC** (**Over the Counter**), which is hurting the prices. BTC futures on the other side, is starting to put those institutions in control which we dislike so much. A lot of OTC deals moving large amounts of bitcoin are not going through exchanges. The buyers are investment banks, government pension schemes, and small states, which is reflected in the BTC price (or not). These institutions are stockpiling (HODL), which will move the price ticker away from the public, the small person, and create additional volatility; but at the moment, this opens the door again.

Institutions like governments think they can control bitcoin – but they are wrong. The EU and other regulators are about to squeeze harder, pushing all tokens towards a definition of a security, which is something I predicted in early 2017 and many ICOs now come under prospectus laws.

Notwithstanding **Collective Investment Scheme (CIS)** Rules and other securities, nor the payments and crowdfunding regulations, it is logical that a struggling set of regulators will look to push the entire crypto world through existing law. To date, such institutions have little understanding of how to define new laws. Some, like FINMA in Switzerland, define three types of token: a security or asset backed (delivering a financial entitlement), a payment token, and a utility token (for access to a product or a service of a Dapp). However, in less than three years (it could be 18 months) I predict that ICOs in their current form won't exist, because investor backlashes are pressuring regulators to take action – and they are indeed taking action.

However, this ultimately will not deter a new crypto capital market infrastructure from being established. ICO platforms like mine (Chainstarter) are engineered around a crypto exchange where we will soon list or create tokens from within a primary market. Tokens will be launched within markets, delivering immediate liquidity, and they will be for accredited investors only. Then again, 80% of capital flowing into ICOs is now through private placements.

Sean Au: What will happen, then, to existing capital markets?

Nick Ayton: The current range of financial products, mortgages, pensions, and insurances are failed products. They are designed for the organizations that sell them, to pay commissions and fees to the layers of useless people that sell and support them. These old products are nothing more than scams that are aimed at taking money from hard-working people, and they leave those people with very little at retirement.

Crypto capital markets will create a new class of financial products that deliver *for* the people. New classes of tokens are emerging, for example, using tokens as Municipal Bonds to fund public infrastructure. We recently designed a new generation of tokens that have three different roles: convertible note, a yield bearing instrument, and equity status. Although these tokens won't be purchased through public coin offerings, they will be highly liquid from day one and issued through exchanges.

Much of capital raising is about investment, and we are sponsoring some important investor events, dragging entrepreneurs with us and putting them in front of investors the old-fashioned way, for pitching. Crypto investing is becoming somewhat conventional.

Many entrepreneurs need coaching as to how to pitch their proposition. I spend a great deal of time re-shaping their proposition and re-engineering their token structure for dual investor and platform tokens that aid the passing of value as a product or service. Cascading income and revenue models in a token structure can require a few days to get right. This is the essence of any ICO.

Sean Au: What are your thoughts on SAFT agreements?

Nick Ayton: SAFT agreements are confusing the audience and these days they are not that helpful, based on the old SAFE agreements which focus on utility. A new generation of token sale agreements handle convertible notes and loan notes in private placement, which entitles the owner to gain access to a token. SAFT agreements struggle if the conversion isn't done in weeks.

The relationship between the investor token and the platform (utility token) can exist as long as the tokens linked to products or services are stable and pegged to fiat, reducing volatility and platform inflationary effect. Utility tokens cannot float in this model. Volatility exists with fixed supply, which is the point of bitcoin, but most people fail to understand this – as opposed to M0 and M1 money supplies, which are in the hands of criminal central banks.

Therefore, we have security tokens designed around a new type of security token agreement, which gives investors some recourse, delivers governance and some assurances, and allows the token as an instrument to be defined on the investor balance sheet as yield bearing. **Rate of Return (ROR)** can vary and thus we put into the smart contract the exit input for IPO or trade sale. Then we have the ethical balance sheet.

Sean Au: What are your thoughts on ICO advisors?

Nick Ayton: Beware of the ICO advisor, and the so-called Blockchain expert. It seems that everyone is an ICO advisor, although few have done an ICO themselves. This is already hurting the ICO market, because the advice they are handing out for a fee is mostly wrong. They have no concept of crypto economics, let alone tokenomics, and we have spent time undoing the damage done.

These apparent advisors push forward with tokens and propositions that simply don't work for anyone. The token's utility is confused, trying to be several things at once, which makes the ICO worthless to any buyer. Ninety-nine percent of these so-called ICO advisors have no clue how to sit the main proposition tech stack on to a blockchain, let alone anything about the limitations of the underlying tech itself. I have clients that have spent a lot on the guidance from advisors, people who have jumped on the crypto and blockchain bandwagon. Then we get a call and its often too late: they have spent their money and we are out of time.

This market is increasingly about credibility. Have the people you are talking to getting advice from actually done the job before – or are they like everyone else just jumping on the bandwagon? Are they advising you on things they don't fully understand? Can they demonstrate knowledge and experience? This is why many of us in the community have to create standards and squeeze out the scammers, the fake advisors, who talk about crypto and blockchain – but have no clue. It is these people who are making it hard for regular people to use crypto, and it is these people who are making regulators nervous.

When you're engineering propositions with crypto and blockchains, it can be complex, and the gaps between the right path and wrong path are narrow. Some of these top blockchain lists and influencers are filled with people who have no clue: they just have a large social media following or community. Rather than help with PR and marketing, they stray into blockchain and tokenomics and do a lot of damage. The most powerful people in blockchain are usually not on *any* list, while many scammers actually trade off these lists and dupe projects into hiring them as an advisor.

Then we have ICO rating services, which refuse to let anyone know who they are and do not declare their management team or how their assessment services work. For instance, ICO Bench. Who are they? How does their algorithm work? Who programmed it? What is their revenue model? Is it aimed at just rating people at face value? There are so many unanswered questions.

Sean Au: Can blockchain scale?

Nick Ayton: Some of our clients already have 10M to 20M people using their product, app, or service, and there are others again who will scale to 100M users quickly. Houston, we have a problem! blockchains cannot scale to anywhere near this kind of performance.

Then there are scaling problems around **Distributed Ledger Technologies (DLT)**, which focus on the transaction, but they will struggle to cover a business model reliant on a token structure. Another problem at scale for blockchain is PoS, where there is the possibility of collusion, and the people with the largest amount of resources win.

However, I do like the Lightning Network and how it works – where the proposition involves lots of updates as value is created, moved, and exchanged. We are engineering value as code to ultimately be fungible, and to be an enabler for the platform to deliver great services to customers... but we can't forget that we're also here to deliver for all stakeholders. Failure to consider *all* the stakeholders is a mistake that so many people continue to make. Many engineer the solution for one community or just for the platform functions, with users and investors left wondering.

Sean Au: What bout new Crypto Capital Markets?

Nick Ayton: At Chainstarter, we are building a new capital markets infrastructure. Our ICO platform only handles securities. Our crypto exchange only handles security tokens and we are close to agreeing a deal with a jurisdiction.

Chainstarter technology is complete and tested, unlike other new exchanges such as Polymath or TenX, where they are still building and testing, and boy do we need them in the tent with us. Although they are also using an ICO process to raise capital, we have the technology and just need the regulations.

Chainstarter will trade the top 20 security tokens (and have several others that we will make a market for) on day one for primary and secondary markets, and it will make markets for tokenizing new assets. We already have a Custody, FX, and OTC trading business to handle crypto, and we may try for a banking license (crypto bank), which would help us create a full-service capital markets set of services.

The required tech must exist, although not necessarily engineered to a blockchain yet. The user apps or interface (fat protocol layer) must be largely available, to the extent we have worked the token structure into the Dapps model. All new projects will need to port to a new blockchain, as Ethereum and bitcoin derivatives don't scale, as we await blockchain 2.0.

ICO expert voice – Jonathan Fry, CEO TeamBlockchain, and member of the British Blockchain Association

Jonny Fry is a blockchain, Crypto economics, ICO, and funds specialist, and has helped a number of firms that have raised capital using Tokenomics. He is also CEO of TeamBlockchain, which is a UK-based international influencer network.

TeamBlockchain works with a range of service providers such as lawyers, accountants, exchanges, custody, and insurance providers, plus a wide range of both private and public companies. TeamBlockchain offer thought leadership, incisive analysis, and strategy helping to commercialize ideas into reality.

Jonny has over 25 years' experience as CEO of an asset management business which he floated in London with over £1 Billion under management. His focus has been on the dynamics of financial innovation, advising on ICOs, Tokenomics, and Crypto funds. He is a regular speaker on these topics.

Jonny has extensive knowledge and experience of the financial services sector, looking after private clients, and institution's assets, managing funds in the UK and globally. He has been CEO and on the board of a variety of regulated and unregulated companies in the UK and internationally, in a number of different industries.

Sean Au: Jonny, what trends do you see for blockchains, and public companies doing ICOs?

Jonny Fry: No one foresaw the rise in bitcoin going from one cent to $20,000 USD. That was compounded by Ripple appreciating in value in 2017 over 35,000%, up from about half a cent to a peak of $3.50 USD last year. A lot of this was driven by fear and greed – and off the back of that, we are seeing blockchain technology being embraced by almost every sector in society.

So blockchain is becoming more mainstream. For example, in May 2017, when conferences were held on blockchain, you'd be lucky to get a dozen people turn up. In May 2018 alone, I've either spoken or been on a panel for many organizations, including large asset management companies, compliance, and consulting firms, quoted companies in North America, and several global legal firms. The attendees at these events were somewhere between 60 and 130 at each event. These are not retail investors.

For retail investors, there was *Blockchain Expo*, which had over 20,000 people register for its blockchain conference in London in April 2018 and over 10,000 people actually turned up. The London Crypto Currency Show had over 2,500 attendees. What we are seeing is that the retail investors are wanting to find the next Ripple or Bitcoin. The professional investors, though, are interested in taking these concepts to quoted (publicly listed) companies or mutual funds.

On the flip side, we are seeing a dearth of IPOs because the cost of doing an IPO is substantial. It's not just the cost of the lawyers, accountants, and brokers, but also the personal cost. For example, the CEO of Barclays was personally fined $1.5 million USD for trying to unmask a whistleblower. The personal liability of being a director on a quoted company is substantial. If you can find a way of raising money where on the surface it means no equity dilution, and no added debt, why wouldn't you?

The institutional market is saying okay, these things can be used to raise money, but they can also be used to solve a few other problems. One of them is how do I get your attention as a potential buyer of my product? With people estimated to be exposed to over 10,000 adverts a day, this is becoming a greater challenge to get and retain our attention, especially as we become more and more exposed to the digital economy. How do I keep you as a client? How do I turn the mentality of my company from that of a hunter that is always looking for new clients, into a farmer where I look after what I've got?

Sean Au: And haven't we seen a recent increase in loyalty programs?

Jonny Fry: Yes, we've seen a phenomenal rise in loyalty programs – such as airline programs – because if you are spending in a digital environment, you want to reward your customers digitally as well.

As an example, let's take a marketing executive who has been given a budget to spend on a flying loyalty scheme. The more you fly with the airline, the more points you get. The trouble is that this can potentially create a massive intangible liability on the balance sheet for the airline, which won't impress the finance director. This is because the more successful the marketing is, the worse it is for the balance sheet of the company. It's a double whammy – by financing the marketing and then getting whacked with intangible liability in the future, because people don't necessarily cash it in now... but do so in the future. This is like every country in the world having issued un-franked stamps at the post office, and at some time all those stamps you bought at Christmas are instead used during the year.

With a token, what a company can do is set up a loyalty token as a *separate entity* and offer perks or travel upgrades to customers. The company can even have joint ventures with restaurants, hotels or car hire firms, and that liability is held in a separate token company.

Now, taking a step back, say that we both work for BMW with a **P/E (price to earnings ratio)** of 10, and let's also say the marketing costs are $1 million USD a year. Now if we took the marketing department out of BMW and put it into say, a CarCoin company, then the value of BMW as a company would, in theory, increase by $10 million USD. BMW and CarCoin are separate companies, perhaps with a common director, but CarCoin has a primary focus and the responsibility of submitting a marketing plan to the board of BMW. That marketing plan would have to be approved, and then CarCoin would need to do what it planned to do. In other words, CarCoin can't start marketing Ford cars.

However, if CarCoin were successful, it may be able to create some IP and specialist skills, which in time may allow it to provide the ability to white label and subsequently market to other car companies down the track because it is now a marketing entity that really understands the car market, and isn't involved in the production issues, or supply chain challenges and so on. Its sole purpose is marketing. Who knows – CarCoin could one day acquire BMW!

Next, I would like to consider potential conflicts of interest between the token holders and shareholders of an ICO. Let's assume an ICO is acquired at some time in the future by Amazon, happy days for the shareholders but what happens to the token holders? What happens if Amazon doesn't want the token holders because Amazon has its own tokens? In essence, the token holders have no equity and therefore no rights.

I raise this question because companies need to consider how to manage the potential conflicts of interest between shareholders and token holders. On one hand, there are the shareholders, who are usually the founders; and on the other hand, there are the token holders, whose capital has been used to finance the company. Not many people have addressed this, but you can be assured that the lawyers are looking at this conundrum.

Sean Au: When a token is bought in an ICO, are there any rights associated?

Jonny Fry: There are usually no rights associated, especially if the token is a utility token, which is what most tokens claim to be so far. This is because when token holders are given rights, it potentially turns that token into a security. The catch is, the majority of the tokens that have been issued are securities anyway. So, one of the problems that regulators are having is that they look at these things and say: it looks like duck, it swims like a duck, it flies like a duck, why are you saying it's an ostrich? So, there is a lack of honesty and a huge amount of nonsense, which is one of the big things the regulators are struggling with.

Once you get publicly listed companies involved, they can't afford to have the potential liability of misrepresenting what they are doing. Therefore, I think that we'll see many global brands getting involved with cryptocurrencies, but they will issue them as a security token, which is currently the stance that the SEC in the USA seem to be taking. Interestingly, one company that claims to have been responsible for over 15% of ICOs, in 2017, are saying that their current focus is on "security tokens".

Sean Au: Going forward, do you see a huge regulatory lockdown happening?

Jonny Fry: I do, but I also think we will see tokens being used to tackle different challenges, such as digitizing loyalty programs and giving away tokens via Airdrops.

A great example is the large e-commerce and media company Rakuten, which owns Viber and is known as the Amazon of Japan. Rakuten has announced a blockchain-based cryptocurrency loyalty token that could be worth over $9 billion USD.

Also, in Japan, we recently saw Line, a social messaging platform, carry out an Airdrop to its 200 million customers – in effect giving away tokens and then having them listed. Clients of Line can therefore be incentivized to use the platform, by being given tokens that can be sold on an exchange or used to get additional service on the Line platform.

We're likely to see a number of new stablecoins being issued. Stablecoins are cryptocurrencies that are backed by Fiat Currencies, which will allow cheaper and faster payments to take place. IBM have announced they are doing a stablecoin backed by the US Dollar. We now also have a Yencoin, which is another stablecoin.

There are other things to consider as well. Say an ICO raises $100 million USD, then where are the tokens physically held and who has access to them? The safe custody of the asset is a challenge. If we look at a custodian, this is an entity that can verify that you own something. Isn't that what blockchain does? So why are we trying to centralize and digitize a custodian using a decentralized technology? Potentially, this means that token holders are trusting that an individual will be honest and ethical. Usually, companies can insure against these types of risks but currently the majority of underwriters will not insure companies funded by cryptocurrencies.

Also, the merger and acquisition world for tokens hasn't even started. There could be a situation, from the preceding example above, where CarCoin becomes more valuable than the BMW company itself and CarCoin could potentially perform an acquisition and buy BMW. Indeed, how long will it be before we start seeing coin companies bidding for traditionally financed companies? This makes for a very interesting future.

ICO expert voice – Jason Goldberg, founder and CEO of Open Simple Token, $20M ICO

Jason Goldberg is the Founder and CEO of Open Simple Token and a board member of the OpenST Foundation. He is a veteran internet entrepreneur with an 18-year history of scaling products to millions of users. Since 2016, Jason's passion has been to drive mainstream consumer adoption of blockchain technologies. (http://www.ost.com).

Sean Au: What is Open Simple Token?

Jason Goldberg: **Open Simple Token (OST)** is a set of tools that allows anyone to create a blockchain-powered economy on open scalable sidechains. OST provides numerous features, such as enabling token design and providing analytics, administrations, and APIs.

Sean Au: What lead you down the crypto rabbit hole?

Jason Goldberg: I was familiar with bitcoin by around 2010 and I was looking at a number of things and even seeing if Fab, a previous company I'd founded, would accept bitcoin but it wasn't quite ready at the time. Then, in 2016, we were building an app called Pepo, where the vision was a decentralized community marketplace for user-generated reviews, tips, and recommendations.

The idea was that we wanted to create a fair and open market for advice when it comes to where to go, what to see and where to eat. So, we started studying token economics, looking at the models as well as the technologies, with an intention to roll out a cryptocurrency.

We looked at the existing technology, and the "ah ha" moment was around April of 2017. We'd done a lot of user experience design and we realized that we would have had to build so much technology for this one app that it would take years to get it production-ready. That was the business idea right there! We realized that we should build it for everyone to use. At that moment, when I was making the rounds talking about Pepo in conjunction with Simple Token, everyone was saying: go and do Simple Tokens!

What we realized was that a lot of projects in the early stages are at the protocol level, which is where they should be. After this, there is the middleware layer, providing integration points, APIs, SDKs, and recipes to integrate into existing business applications. Then we have the **SaaS** (**Software as a Service**) layer where SaaS tools are used to deploy and manage the blockchain implementation and the crypto tokens. This is where Simple Token sits. It's a big build, and we've got a great team behind us, and great partners, and it's all coming together well.

Sean Au: Did you wish you thought of Simple Tokens earlier?

Jason Goldberg: Not really. I think the timing is right to build this now because even Ethereum itself is an alpha product, so we are building an alpha product on an alpha product. These are early days. Imagine building the internet technology pre-1994. We're still in the early days of infrastructure and it's the equivalent of building the Netscape Enterprise Server.

Sean Au: Can you share your experiences during the ICO of Open Simple Tokens?

Jason Goldberg: The ICO period for OST was the hardest 70-80 days of my entire career. We had a team of about 30 of us full-time preparing for the ICO and on product development to first prove the protocol. We then open sourced it on GitHub and did an integration to Pepo to demonstrate that the utility had been established, before we actually did the ICO. Then there was a team of about eight of us for the actual token sale, and that was all about the community, marketing, and driving awareness of the token sale.

We built this funnel all about education, connection, and purchase. We really focused on the project and what we were trying to build, avoiding the hype to just buy the token. It was more that, if you believe in this project, then learn about it, and once you've learnt about it, come and connect with us.

We were active on Telegram twenty-four hours a day to answer questions and we know that people who learned about Simple Tokens and connected with us ended up buying it, and it was intense.

Timing is important as well, and at the beginning, timing wasn't on our side. When we launched our ICO, the crypto market was really in a downturn. At the end of October and early November 2017, the Ethereum price was around $300 USD so it was a bit of a struggle to get people to take their ETH and turn it into something else. Then we fell into an upturn in the market, which was good and bad. The good news was that suddenly everyone got more excited, but the bad news was that the people who bought in the first couple of days didn't get such a good deal, so there were lots of nuances.

Our approach was not to raise tons of money. Our target was that if we raised $7.5 million USD in our token sale, then that was enough to kickstart the project — so we didn't go out trying to raise $30 million USD or $40 million USD. We ended up achieving 189% of our target, which was a great success from that standpoint.

OST is a utility token – and creating value for the token in the market is an essential function of the protocol. The way it works is that companies mint their own tokens on open, scalable utility side chains backed by the value of OST.

Sean Au: There are currently 142 applicants for the beta application, building interesting projects, so how does it work?

Jason Goldberg: So, the first phase was around stake and mint, which was staking OST and then minting your own tokens, and it was opened up for anyone to participate. This was really part of the stress test of the system. 1,600 branded tokens were created, running over 21 million transactions, which gave us a sense of volumes and speed and the optimization we needed to do. This was called alpha 1.

The second phase, alpha 2, was to get developers to use some of the APIs we were building, and to get feedback from our users as well. Any development team could apply, and the criteria was for them to submit a project to us. They then had to do a proof of concept integration of OST into an app or website that they could realistically build in 6-8 weeks, and that they could demonstrate ran 1000+ transactions. We received around 250 applicants and from that we choose 142 projects.

The main criterion was that there was a viable chance of being completed instead of having an ambitious project that would take maybe five years to complete. Of those 142 projects, 85 of them met the first "gate" where they had to submit their progress at the halfway point. What this allows us to do is learn from real-world integration. The idea is to keep doing this with alpha 3, alpha 4, 5, and so on. This is like agile on steroids with continuous feedback.

Sean Au: What is your vision for Simple Tokens, where do you see tokens five years from now?

Jason Goldberg: With Open Simple Tokens, we believe that we're building a decentralized application for a decentralized internet – and so the starting point for us has been enabling companies to mint their own tokens without having to have their own blockchain developers, and without having to worry about scalability issues. That is what we are solving in OST.

In the next stage, that we call *Mosaic,* we're offering economic finality of transactions on the side chains on public Ethereum. What this means is that you can have completely trustless transactions at high volume and high throughput, at internet scale.

Our next step of the vision is then token exchange across any blockchain, not just Ethereum. So that anyone who is holding any token can exchange that for any type of token or asset, and in a fully scalable trustless environment. It could be on Stellar, Bitcoin, ECO, Neo, or the US dollar, it doesn't matter. At first, this is like, "transact with your economy;" then it's like, "transact across any OST economy;" and then it will be "transact across the Ethereum economy," and then "transact across the world." This is an entirely inter-operable transacting environment, and it is scalable.

Beyond that, our vision for OST is to enable machines, through AI, to do smart transactions based on observed behavior, so that there's no need for humans to execute these transfers. It's a big vision and something we're planning to work on for a long time, and we plan to be leaders in this field.

ICO expert voice – Dinis Guarda, former CEO of Humaniq, $5M ICO, founder Lifesdna

Dinis Guarda is an author, serial entrepreneur, advisor, and experienced CEO. He creates and helps to build ventures focused on global growth, 360 digital strategies, sustainable innovation, blockchain, Fintech, AI, and new emerging business models such as ICOs and tokenomics.

Dinis is the founder/CEO of Ztudium/Lifesdna, one AI P2P, blockchain, search engine, and PaaS in consumer wellness healthcare and life sciences, with a global team of experts and universities.

Some of the companies Dinis has created or has been involved in have reached USD billions in valuation. Dinis has advised and was responsible for some top financial organizations, 100 cryptocurrencies worldwide, and Fortune 500 companies.

Dinis has been working with the likes of UN/UNITAR, UNESCO, European Space Agency, Philips, Saxo Bank, Mastercard, Barclays to name a few. He has advised governments and regulators all over the world. Dinis holds a BA from Lisbon University, a Master's from London South Bank University, and is attending a Blockchain Strategy Program at Oxford Said Business School.

Sean Au: How did you first get involved in Humaniq?

Dinis Guarda: Humaniq was actually just the result of working a lot with the Ethereum community in London years earlier, and with blockchain technologies. Humaniq is not just about tokenomics and ICOs but the wider concept of blockchain technology as a revolutionary disruptor.

Having put together lots of thoughts on a paper around the idea of the blockchain as an ideological, decentralized, and distributed technology that can power the digital economy worldwide; and having worked with lots of experts in the space, the founders of Humaniq approached me with an opportunity to take it to the next level, around governance, among other things.

Sean Au: When did you first come across tokens, and what are you focusing on now?

Dinis Guarda: Humaniq was the first big token project but being involved in and around the DAO with the likes of Stephen Tual and other members of the team was a great experience and allowed me to rethink a lot of things.

I'm currently focusing on several areas: LifeSci, Glance, and Ztudium. LifeSci is about putting health care on the blockchain. Glance is a mobile payment solution. Ztudium is a technology specialist providing digital transformation, AI, blockchain, and crypto consultancy for the information age. There are a large number of other ICOs that I do also contribute towards with varying levels of involvement.

Sean Au: What have you learned from doing all these ICOs?

Dinis Guarda: It really boils down to three main questions:

♦ What problem are you solving?

♦ Who are the people involved?

♦ What is the business model?

Blockchain technology can only be useful if it can be used to solve real-world problems. Following from this is the team behind the scenes trying to bring the solutions to life. The final point is that all of this requires a sustainable business model because there are legal and compliance considerations that cannot be ignored.

It is also very important to have clear written governance, particularly around the people and the technology – and also around the people and the ICO. ICOs should not be regulated, but there is a definite need to create rules and guidelines.

Sean Au: What are your general thoughts on ICOs?

Dinis Guarda: The ICO business model can power a new economy, not only from an innovation aspect but also from looking at the risks behind it, particularly as someone who has created a bank before. We are in a twilight zone where there is only really a small percentage of people who are in the know – and then there's the rest of the world, who are wondering what on earth is going on.

Then there is the speculative part, which is quite scary, such as trying to use tokens as stocks to inflate the price, working with governance, and, of course, the ever-lingering issue around tax.

This new funding mechanism is no doubt very innovative, but then there are all the questions such as the challenges of creating a decentralized world economy when the majority of the world is centralized, and what kind of regulatory framework do we put on this?

Another fundamental challenge are the three general profiles in the industry. The second and third of these profiles can be a particularly dangerous mix when combined:

♦ Technologists

♦ Speculators, looking to make a quick buck

♦ Cypherpunks, who that think they can change the world economy, even if they have to destroy the current systems in the process

The ICO process is also becoming very mechanical, so that anyone can do it – but a lot of thinking has to be done around regulation, business models, and governance. The biggest systemic risks are around the long-term speculators. I've been approached, in the past, by top executives who are very successful in their own right but still want to make a quick buck through an ICO, and I find that very concerning, especially when there was no focus on the technology, and the problem being solved was mediocre at best.

There are three key historical moments for us:

♦ The great depression of 1929

♦ The 2000 dotcom boom and bust

♦ The financial crisis of 2007

After the dotcom boom we got the huge innovations that the internet brought, particularly with the digital economy. The same can be said now with blockchains – around identity projects and creating new business models using blockchain technologies. But we need to be realistic, and we need to keep our feet on the ground. Tokens are becoming mainstream. When Humaniq did its ICO the price of bitcoin was $1200 USD. Now it is significantly higher. We might say that 50 million people are trading bitcoins but what happens when 100 million or more come in and try to buy tokens?

Sean Au: What is your view on centralization versus decentralization?

Dinis Guarda: There is a great book called *The Starfish and the Spider: The Unstoppable Power of Leaderless Organizations* by *Ori Brafman* and *Rod A. Beckstrom*, where he compares two interesting concepts. A star fish has a decentralized neural structure, which permits regeneration, whereas if a spider's leg is cut off, it dies. Centralization reflects 90% of the world's society, religion, and governments, and it is reflected in nature as well.

Sean Au: Are ICOs decentralized or centralized?

Dinis Guarda: ICOs need to be both centralized and decentralized. There needs to be a clear management team, and the founders need to be responsible and liable, unless it's a **DAO** (**Distributed Autonomous Organization**) but then a DAO is not an ICO. Regulatory framework and governance also need to be in place.

Sean Au: Is LifeSci centralized, decentralized, or half and half?

Dinis Guarda: At the moment, as global data becomes the biggest asset of society, with health data and AI we can have a *Blade Runner* type scenario. Blockchains can be used to decentralize the data, but this has to be done by stages – because in many instances, we don't even have the tech yet. The fundamental solution of the health data will be decentralized. The management team will be centralized, because they will be the ones responsible and held accountable. At the end of the day, it's the people that drive everything.

ICO expert voice – Vinny Lingham, co-founder and CEO of Civic, $33M ICO

Vinny Lingham is a serial entrepreneur and Co-Founder and CEO at Civic. He is also a general partner at Multicoin Capital, a venture-style fund that invests in liquid crypto-assets, co-founder, and limited partner at Newtown Partners, a blockchain investment and advisory services company, and a board member of the Bitcoin Foundation.

Vinny previously founded numerous companies such as the digital gift card platform, Gyft, which was acquired by First Data Corporation in 2014, Yola, and incuBeta. He is also a shark on the popular TV show Shark Tank South Africa.

Civic conducted a "token sale" in June 2017 and successfully raised $33 million USD. Civic's visionary blockchain identity-verification technology allows consumers to authorize the use of their identities in real time, and the mission is to provide every person on Earth with a digital identity that they can use to interact privately and securely with the world.

Sean Au: What is Civic?

Vinny Lingham: Civic is a **Secure Identity Platform** (**SIP**) that enables people to take control and protect their identity. Users essentially download the Civic app and verify their identity to become a Civic user. The app stores the user's data securely with a biometric lock. The app then enables users to share and manage their verified identity data. Basically, you're putting your data on your device.

Sean Au: To confirm, there are "requestors" who present a QR code and as a user, I scan it?

Vinny Lingham: Yes, and the data also stays on your device and once we validate it, you can scan a QR code and confirm who you are. Validators will attest to the requestor that the data is correct, and we use something called "zero knowledge proof" as well so that we can move away from physical forms of identity like passports, and instead towards digital signatures to confirm identity.

Sean Au: How did you come up with the idea of identity on the blockchain?

Vinny Lingham: Generally, the biggest problem with payments is not being able to know who is on the other side of the transaction, and so if you can solve that then you could also solve other problems such as voting. In fact, one of the reasons why I like this space is because blockchains can be used for voting and when doing this on your mobile device, you need to have a good identity layer. So, there are lots of opportunities to expand the scope of Civic.

Sean Au: What was the Civic ICO like for you?

Vinny Lingham: I was there at four in the morning! It was the most stressful and most difficult thing I've done in my life, and I just sold a company a few years ago for comparison!

Sean Au: What made it so challenging?

Vinny Lingham: It was all the unknowns of the ICO process. At the time, the requirements around the registration, and the legal aspects, were not clearly defined – and so staying out of jail was a high priority! We had a couple of partners to help with the ICO, but we did it all in-house.

Sean Au: Would Civic work without a Civic token?

Vinny Lingham: Not without a significant loss in privacy. Currently the Civic token is an ERC20 token on the Ethereum network with a smart contract behind it, but the volatility around this arrangement is concerning, and there are a lot of compliance issues that need to be dealt with. In essence, it didn't work in the way we envisioned it.

Sean Au: Who are the competitors in the identity space?

Vinny Lingham: There seems to be a lot of competitors in the identity space, such as uPort, Blockstack, IBM Trusted Identity. If I ask anyone to name three competitors, they'll never name the same three but generally Civic will be there.

We are quite advanced in terms of tech, progress, and development – and so everyone else is fighting for the number two spot. No one knows all these other platforms out there and I can't even keep up with them because there are too many. We have first mover advantage, we have the biggest user base as far as I know, and we have a live implementation, so the Civic tokens are being used and everyone else is trying to play catch up. I think the first mover advantage is very strong and the question is: how do they compete with Civic?

Sean Au: Looking into the future, do you think there will be one global identity token or potentially one per country or per state?

Vinny Lingham: I think it will be very similar to the payment network, where you have the likes of Visa, Mastercard, Amex, Discover, JCB, and a handful of others but it's a very short list. You'll have the big one like Visa, and then Mastercard second, and so on. Civic is well placed at the top and it's ours to lose. Also, our target market is not focusing on countries, and they move a lot slower, so we are just focusing on building great consumer products and making sure that consumers like what they see.

Sean Au: Do you buy into the new tokenized economy where everything is being tokenized?

Vinny Lingham: I think the world can handle a couple of hundred tokens, market share wise. I think we're past that now, so I'm a little concerned how big the token market will get, because it's not practical. No normal person, or trader, will hold 200 tokens in their pocket – so they'll consolidate, or they will just die. I mean, 95% of these tokens won't survive or won't reach critical mass.

Sean Au: How far away is Civic from critical mass and what's in the pipeline for Civic?

Vinny Lingham: Definitely a couple of years away, as we're still in the early stage. We're launching ID Code very soon. It's in private beta right now and that is the next product in the suite. Hilo is using the ID code now. ID Code enables anyone to securely verify a business, advisory, or investment relationship – or any relationships.

Sean Au: Where is Civic heading into the future in terms of applications?

Vinny Lingham: There are lots of future applications, including vending machines and voting, and we're looking at access controls in hotels. I think the number of places you can use Civic is unlimited because identity is an issue in so many situations.

For the beer vending machine that we displayed at Consensys, we worked with a third party who built the software. The machine would present a QR code and the user could prove that they were over 21 in order to purchase the beer. It was definitely a big hit having a demonstrable product and it was a partnership with Budweiser as well.

ICO expert voice – Aaron McDonald, CEO and co-founder of Centrality, $100M ICO

Aaron McDonald is the CEO and co-founder of Centrality, based in Auckland, which is a venture studio that partners with leading innovators in key industries to create a marketplace of applications. These applications allow consumers to manage everyday tasks and experiences using peer-to-peer transactions, all via one login and using blockchain-enabled infrastructure. Centrality raised $100 million USD in its ICO with over 8000 registered buyers in January 2018. (https://www.centrality.ai/).

Sean Au: What is Centrality?

Aaron McDonald: Centrality is a platform that lets people build applications, and together build an ecosystem that helps everyone work together better. It's analogous to App Store, where each application helps other to grow.

The pressure is getting harder and harder for startups to succeed because the key is data, and who has the data? Not you, but to get the data, you have to scale; but to scale, you need data; which is a chicken and egg scenario. Centrality is looking to help overcome these hurdles for startups by providing the right ingredients to help them to scale.

Sean Au: How did you first started getting interested in Bitcoin?

Aaron McDonald: In 2016, while coming to the end of working at a startup, and figuring out what to do next, blockchains were something that came up and a group of us were looking at how we could create the next startup together. We looked at ideas and tried to figure out the chances of success of these ideas. There were so many hurdles to overcome for startups, so the problem statement became: how do you make *any* startup scale?

That concept was then flipped around to: how can an environment be created where startups have a greater chance of success, by removing or reducing the hurdles or barriers to success? Then, one of the partners at MME in Zurich suggested that blockchains had to be part of the concept, which was really the starting point to giving this thing a crack – to take the power of decentralization and smart contracts to enable applications to trust each other, and for users to contribute their data without it being used inappropriately.

I have always been a technology person and the real inspiration was that conversation in Zurich, combined with the thinking of how startups can successfully scale. This was the chance to allow innovators, or the small guys, to have a crack on the big guys.

Sean Au: How did the name Centrality, and CENNZ token, come about?

Aaron McDonald: The name Centrality was born around June 2016 and while a lot of people think of the contradiction with decentralization, the name actually comes from mathematics, where centralities are the nexuses of graphs in a network. This is similar to apps evolving in the Centrality ecosystem, where they would come together and connect for certain purposes. For example, a food ordering app could connect with a transport app to deliver food. Underlying all of this would be some intelligence that would drive everything, hence AI in the name in www.centrality.ai.

Originally, the token was going to be called Centra, but literally days away from minting the tokens from the smart contract, there was an ICO promoting a Centra coin. It was issuing a prepaid debit card of some sort, so a new name was required! This was actually a blessing in disguise, because the founders of Centra Tech have recently been charged by the Securities Exchange Commission in the US with running a fraudulent ICO.

The jumping between the apps in the marketplace was akin to jumping between movie scenes, so it was called "scene jumping" or just "scenes." Then someone said can we just call it "cennz," which is how the name of the token came about.

Sean Au: What was the ICO journey like?

Aaron McDonald: It was started as a non-traditional model compared to most ICOs. It was self-funded early on with core investors, and Centrality built technologies and proof points. Hypotheses were created and tested with a bunch of companies, and we went beyond the thinking into what the implementation would look like, and forwards into proving that it could be done.

We first considered doing the ICO when we proved that the technical hurdles could be overcome. There were several funding options, but we thought that, to be truly decentralized, the funding should be decentralized and the way the ecosystem delivered value should be decentralized as well.

Sean Au: How does the CENNZ token work?

Aaron McDonald: There are a few uses of the CENNZ token. First of all, for app developers to build applications in the Centrality app store, the developers need to be connected to the app store network. In order to do that, a developer has to run a node on the Centrality blockchain called CENNZ net, and stake tokens. Developers then own a stake in the app store. The CENNZ tokens can also be used as a voting and a reward mechanism. Lastly, for each application in the app store that develops tokens, a portion will be airdropped to people who own CENNZ.

There is also a second token called is a "spending token," which is similar to gas in Ethereum. The idea behind keeping them separate is to keep the transactions cheap and reliable. Some apps will have their own token, especially when it is integral to the app, such as Silo, a messaging application and platform, but not all the apps in the marketplace will require their own token.

Sean Au: How did the Centrality ICO go?

Aaron McDonald: Just to follow on from the non-traditional approach of actually building a company before doing an ICO, a non-traditional ICO was run. It was actually a Token Generating Event because, at the time, Centrality was one of the few doing this in a highly compliant way, working with governments to make sure it was legal, building technology to make sure investors were compliant and protected and building the decentralized sales process. It was done through Blockhaus, which is a separate independent company that Centrality supports from a technology perspective.

There was a lot going on, coming up to the ICO, but because the sale was over in six minutes, there wasn't a lot of time sitting there and watching the screen. With all the chatter in the community, meetups, conferences, and the feedback, we had an idea that it was going to be successful, but we did not anticipate how successful it would be. In fact, just before going live there was so much demand on the servers that some started to crash; more capacity had to be provisioned prior to turning on the tap.

There was a lot of work, and not everyone saw the twelve months before, which were spent proving concepts and building a community, which was an important part of the process. During the ICO moment, there was almost a sense of disbelief because after having worked so hard for this goal, going from nights where at 2am in the morning I was figuring out how to extend my credit card to pay the staff, to having the resources to make the dream real, it was a crazy time.

The room was ecstatic one moment and then shocked, so there were all of the emotions that you could possibly experience, all happening in one half hour period.

Sean Au: Would you do another ICO again?

Aaron McDonald: Yes, we actually have done another ICO since then. Blockhaus is doing this all the time, with Centrality supporting the process. A number of applications in the Centrality marketplace are also doing their own ICO, so around eight main or pre-sales have been done this year, and combined, they have raised close to $330 million USD between them, leveraging the tools that Centrality built for their ICO.

Sean Au: Where do you see blockchains and tokens five years from now?

Aaron McDonald: There's still a long way to go. The uptake of technology amongst the mass consumer is pretty slow. For example, with internet banking, there's probably a generation of people who still don't use internet banking and humans take time, even if the technology is there, to adapt. Centrality's focus is on mass market consumer adoption, with apps that anyone can use every day, in their lives, and breaking down some technology hurdles around key management. But in five years from now we would definitely expect to start seeing mainstream adoption.

ICOs over that five-year time frame will inevitably see more consumer protection. Having run ICOs in five jurisdictions, and having conversations with governments in eight jurisdictions, they are really positive about building this new tokenized economy. We can see the benefits of a tokenized economy with more transparency, and more participation with economic models, and breaking down some monopolies. At the same time, governments want to make sure that scams aren't being run, and if they are, that they're prosecuted. We'll see more regulations coming in, which is a positive thing, and we'll see securitization become much more prevalent.

ICO expert voice – Nimo Naamani, co-founder of Horizon State, $1M ICO

Nimo Naamani is the Co-Founder of Horizon State, which is a secure community engagement and voting platform delivering trust through blockchain technologies. Nimo was formerly Chief Technology Officer at iPayroll and is an entrepreneur and software developer with 20 years of experience building products. Horizon State raised over $1 million USD from hundreds of supporters from around the globe in October 2017 (https://horizonstate.com/).

Sean Au: What were you doing before getting into the crypto space?

Nimo Naamani: Coming from Israel and having spent a few years working in software in the Israeli Army, I moved to New Zealand and worked at Datacom. After almost six years as Chief Technology Officer of a company called iPayroll, I was shoulder-tapped to be part of Horizon State, which was a great opportunity.

Sean Au: What was your personal journey that led you to blockchains and cryptocurrencies?

Nimo Naamani: To be honest, it was a missed opportunity. Back in 2014-15, a good friend invited me to lunch and said, "We have to do it! We have to set up a company that does Ethereum, blockchains, and smart contracts. I don't know what we are going to do but when stuff starts happening, we'll be there at the forefront."

I said to my friend that it was a great idea, but I didn't do anything about it. My friend now doesn't have to work anymore, but that was when my interest did start to pick up and then it was around the beginning of 2017 when the rabbit hole journey really begun for me.

Sean Au: How did Horizon State start?

Nimo Naamani: Horizon State began with MiVote, which is a neo-political democratic movement that started in Melbourne, Australia. The idea of MiVote is to get people to vote on everything that matters in one's life. So, instead of voting once every three years for a representative in parliament, who will then choose what to do on your behalf, you get to vote, on the MiVote website, about every major decision that happens in your community, your city, or your country gets put on a vote on the MiVote website. Everybody gets to participate.

We ran the MiVote system for them in February 2017 but after a few months, the potential became quite obvious, so we decided to split and create a commercial entity around the voting product using the blockchain. That commercial entity was Horizon State, which ran an ICO with an MVP that was already in use.

Sean Au: How did the ICO go?

Nimo Naamani: If I had to run a presentation, I would call it "how not to run an ICO" because there were external pressures that meant it had to happen in October 2017 to align with events that were happening with MiVote. A lot of time and energy was put into the whitepaper, particularly reviewing it with other people, but the main takeaway I would share is simply not to run an ICO yourself. There are people around who specialize in that and it's their job. Use them!

In terms of marketing, the Horizon State platform is targeted towards businesses – because it's the city councils, commercial organizations, or countries that will be using our system. For this reason, our marketing was targeted towards not only people who were going to buy tokens, but also towards governments and businesses.

The other point we learned was not to pre-mint the tokens. Exactly 40% of the tokens were created ahead of time for Horizon State, and 60% for the public. The supply was one billion but being pre-minted meant that 400 million were created on day one – which was bad, because when investors bought the tokens, they could see that there were 400 million already in existence. Looking back, it would have been better to create the 400 million tokens at the end.

We did the ICO ourselves, deployed the contract, made it public on the website and watched the transactions come in. About halfway through the ICO, the soft cap had been met and after a slight adjustment in our message, a few YouTube influencers approached us to make a deal to promote the ICO. This resulted in the last few days raising almost as much as the entire ICO duration up to that point. Unfortunately, there were contributions after the ICO ended as well, but they couldn't be accepted because the contract was killed.

A **Content Management System** (**CMS**) was not used at all because of the security risks. The Horizon State website was file-based on Amazon S3, secured with two-factor authentication and locked down like Fort Knox. Retrospective analysis showed thousands of requests going to /wp-admin, which is the default login page for the WordPress CMS. On the day the ICO was run, only static files were being served to the user.

Sean Au: What is the business model of Horizon State?

Nimo Naamani: Horizon State is B2B (business to business), which makes it a little unique. For example, if Horizon State approaches a government of a country, that country is not likely to buy tokens from an exchange and use it to vote. Horizon State provides a quote of the cost to run a vote, for example, $5 million USD, and if accepted, then the government pays $5 million USD to Horizon State, which will then purchase the tokens on their behalf, at whatever the current spot price is.

The neat thing about this is that if one HST is $1, five million HST are created to vote. If voter turnout is low and only three million HST tokens are used, then the balance can be used for another vote, or sold back to the exchange. This is in contrast to the same sex marriage vote, which cost Australian tax payers $122 million USD regardless of the turnout.

The number of tokens purchased from the $5 million USD is irrelevant, because when each person votes, the tokens used will be in proportion to the amount purchased, and the tokens can also be divisible to 18 decimal places, so there are actually more than people realize.

The MiVote voting application was already using the blockchain, but Horizon State revamped it to include the ability to use tokens as the key driver. An important point here is that the tokens do not go to the voters, because this could lead to the selling or buying of votes.

A decision was made early on to not deal with voter identity, which is a good thing. This avoids the situation where Horizon State may know the identity and the vote cast. Horizon State uses a plugin authentication model and receives a list of eligible voters via a hash, which is like a unique identifier. Horizon State performs a second hash and it is this second hash that is put on the blockchain to protect voter identity. If the original hash was placed on the blockchain, the government or local council providing the hash would be able to determine who cast what vote.

Sean Au: What is the business model?

Nimo Naamani: For each voting "project," 80% of the tokens are burned. The figure of 5% go to various charities that Horizon State supports, and 5% go to public infrastructure projects that Horizon State is working with. The last 5% goes back to Horizon State.

Sean Au: What is the point of creating a Horizon State token?

Nimo Naamani: It could be said, for a lot of ICOs, why not use ether instead of creating one's own token? With MiVote, it was discovered that when using ether, the cost couldn't be controlled, and so the token provides a layer to isolate the customer from price volatility. This is important because governments need to know the exact costs of a project.

Sean Au: If Horizon State is burning tokens, will new ones be created?

Nimo Naamani: New tokens are not created. If all goes well, we will run out of tokens. Currently, there are approximately 48 million tokens, which are the 31 million tokens in circulation and the 17 million tokens held by Horizon State.

One thing Horizon State is looking at is obtaining community feedback on where the 5% of charity tokens should go. For example, if 10,000 tokens can be sold for $50,000 USD, that can build a handful of schools in Rwanda, so why not?

Sean Au: What is the on horizon for Horizon State?

Nimo Naamani: There are three basic products. The first one is voting on the blockchain with tokens, the second is community engagement, leading to the third, which is the product of client engagement with commercial organization – or in other words, helping organizations to know what their customers think. These are some of the exciting things in the pipeline for Horizon State.

ICO expert voice – Bokky PooBah, ICO auditor

Bokky PooBah is an actuary and quantitative software developer with over 28 years of industry experience. Bokky has been working with clients from bank and corporate treasuries, investment managers, government entities, exchanges, and financial soft vendors in Australia, New Zealand, Asia, the UK, and Europe.

Bokky's ICO audits include FunFair, Dao.casino, Status Network Tokens, Santiment, InvestFeed, Aigang, Stox Token, Veredictum, RocketPool, LookRev, Cindicator, ChonoLogic, Gimli, SnipCoin, Aion, Privatix, indaHash, Gizer, Bluzelle, LveEdu, Simple Token, Devery, GazeCoin, Sirin Labs, and Shipchain.

Bokky is active on `Ethereum.StackExchange.com`, `github.com`, and `reddit.com/r/Ethereum`. Bokky is now working to bring decentralized, trustless exchanges (`www.cryptoderivatives.market`) and traditional fiat financial instruments, to the Ethereum trusted and decentralized blockchain platform. Bokky also runs BokkyPooBah's Ethereum Workshop in Sydney (`www.meetup.com/BokkyPooBahs-Ethereum-Workshop`).

Sean Au: What made you interested in bitcoin and blockchains?

Bokky PooBah: I'd been working in banking and finance, writing software for financial market applications, risk management, and creating systems. In about March or April 2015, I went to a talk with a colleague about a trust platform that bitcoin has called blockchains. I'd heard about bitcoin previously, but with a trusted platform that you can actually make programs on and actually get to do something, that sounded much more interesting. So, I did some research and found out that you couldn't do *that* much with bitcoin, but in July 2016, the Ethereum network went live and I started looking into that and, once again, that looked pretty interesting, so I pursued it further.

I discovered too many unanswered questions, so a few months later I set up a miner to see what would happen, and that led to even more questions. You learn more, but then more questions appear. So, I started answering Stack Exchange questions and I treated it as a learning exercise in looking at the source code, digging around, finding the answer, and writing it up. I learned a lot in that process.

My involvement in the Ethereum community was just before the DAO hack. Prior to the DAO hack, I was writing scripts to pull out the data. Then, when the DAO hack happened, I used those techniques to work out what the refunds were. I then helped to reconcile what the numbers should have been, and I got in touch with the people in the Ethereum community through that process. It's been pretty satisfying.

Sean Au: How did you get into the ICO audit space?

Bokky PooBah: In 2016, I got in touch with a group at DevCon 2, and through them one of the guys wanted to write an ICO contract. So, they started putting one together and I helped them to audit that ICO contract. I started doing these for free just out of interest. Then, after doing a few of these for colleagues, other people caught on that I could check their stuff making sure there was no leak. Once you put a smart contract on the Ethereum platform, you want to make sure it's water tight. That is one of the fastest ways to learn smart contracts. I started with some boring smart contracts working with ether, which gives you the discipline to make sure no one can steal ether from it.

I've participated in a small handful of ICOs but saw a desire to hold on to ether versus putting it into ICOs because of the relative growth. One of the ICOs I participated in went down to 20% of its worth in ether and it's still hovering around that mark one year later. So, I now focus on "crowdsales" projects, helping the Ethereum community to reduce the number of scams or bugs. So that's why I do the audits.

Sean Au: Where do you see tokens in five years?

Bokky PooBah: I think there is going to be a situation where there are so many tokens and so many decentralized exchanges that we get a cloud of these tokens and decentralized exchanges. Then, there will be a service that says there is a SeanToken and there will be a market somewhere for SeanTokens to be exchanged for something and, if I'm holding some BokkyPooBah tokens, there will be a market somewhere to exchange them for something as well. A service will then just go through and connect our exchange.

So, for example, say there are 10 SeanTokens and for the amount of volume required, this service comes back with a price that is approximate enough, and it goes through a whole set of links in the transactions to give you the liquidity to sell your tokens. Currently, the decentralized exchanges are one token to another, but it's going to be more fluid in the near future.

We've currently got the internet, and we've got the Internet of Blockchains; well, there's also going to be an Internet of Tokens, and an Internet of Decentralized Exchanges. These will all culminate into what will be *the cloud*.

Sean Au: Have you looked into the mechanics of how a two-or-more token system works?

Bokky PooBah: MakerDAO has several tokens that interact with each other with equations via smart contracts. They have spent a long time working on them because they are complex beasts. On the programming side, I'm trying to verify the relationships between the components, and to make sure that there are no bugs – but on the market side, there could be situations in the future where it is profitable to short a position and make money. This is possible with derivative contracts, which will eventually come with the Dai stable token.

Sean Au: Why did you choose to work on the Ethereum platform?

Bokky PooBah: It comes down to the fact that I like the people and their attitude as well. The first thing you want to do is create the tech that will allow developers to create complex programs to represent value, and not focus just on the price of the token. A lot of the other tokens have people trying to increase the price because it makes them wealthier. With Ethereum, a lot of the developers in the space have the attitude of improving the system and creating a rich environment to get stuff done with.

Sean Au: Is there any use of a utility token going from 10 cents to $1000?

Bokky PooBah: Systems will be built with adjustment mechanisms – so right now, today, if you want to pay with one unit of computing resource and it costs one token at $1, then if that token price increases by 10 times, the system should adjust downwards to only require 0.1 tokens. A lot of it is supply and demand.

Sean Au: Talking about supply and demand, are ICO token supply values pulled out of thin air?

Bokky PooBah: Yes, but then they are just units because you can just adjust it by decimal places. I think there was a plan originally when they were trying to work out the number of decimal places for ether, which is 18, that it could cover the usage across the universe.

Sean Au: You are relentless in running these local workshops, so what are you currently working on?

Bokky PooBah: So yes, we are up to workshop number 54. We have just started to try and build a project at the start of May 2018, which is called the Babysitters Club. My kids, when they were younger, were part of a babysitting arrangement where you enter the group and get some credit points. You use these points to pay someone to babysit your child, and you can earn points by babysitting someone else's child.

The Club had a ledger, which was a register or book, and this rotated around the members each month. This is a classic blockchain use case. I'm trying to bring it to life so that there is a reliable system that doesn't crash and burn if the operator decides to stop the service and erase the data. We are at a stage now where we want to start building in the workshop.

Summary

We heard loud and clear in this chapter, from eight astonishing and successful ICO experts, how undertaking an ICO is a challenging task. There are only a small group of people that can claim to have truly gone through this process. We gained from these genuine ICO experts, many new perspectives into what goes on behind the scene of an ICO.

We learned many times how these founders first got into the bitcoin and crypto space, what their projects are about, and how their ICO went. One common theme we saw across these founders was that many were experimenting through the whole process: there were no standards to follow.

We saw how many of these founders believe in the future of tokens and the potential that Tokenomics holds. Some of them have been back through the ICO process since, and many of them continue to invest in the changing shape of the token economy.

Regulation continues to be a huge topic for most of these experts, and there are many views on the best way forwards around regulation. We saw that a decentralized economy is a step in the right direction towards building a decentralized web. And I think we saw that all of these experts continue to look forwards for new opportunities in the future in the field of tokenomics and beyond.

Speaking of the future, the next and final chapter explores the future of technologies driving tokenomics, and we'll take a good look at where we could be heading with cryptocurrencies, blockchains, and the token economy.

12

THE FUTURE

"The best way to predict the future is to study the past,
or prognosticate"

— *Robert Kiyosaki*

With all the excitement generated in 2017 from the ability to raise large sums of money more easily, quickly, and in a way never seen before, and as new ideas surface and technology marches forward, the question now on everyone's lips is: where to from here? The key to answering this question is not with random guesses but with careful observation, combined with an understanding of how we got here and why.

We conclude our journey by coming full circle and back to where we started with bitcoin, the technology that opened up this whole new world. We will then look at where tokens will take us in the future, before taking a more holistic view of the crypto phenomenon.

This chapter can be summarized as follows:

♦ There is only one bitcoin

♦ The Internet of Tokens

♦ Future technologies

We got to where we are today with bitcoin and many people often forget this very important point. It was bitcoin that started this revolution that has already changed the world as we know it forever. Bitcoin shone a light on many concepts, such as decentralization, personal data sovereignty, and privacy, and the true meaning of a trustless economy, that were previously only discussed in cypherpunk forums and technical conferences. So, what made bitcoin so special?

There is only one Bitcoin

There may be over 20,000 forks, or people who have copied the bitcoin source code in GitHub to study, learn, and experiment from, and there may be over 30 variations of bitcoin, such as Bitcoin God, Bitcoin Top, Bitcoin Oil, Bitcoin Ore, Bitcoin Candy, and even Bitcoin Pizza (what is it with resources and food?) but there will only ever be one bitcoin (`https://github.com/ bitcoin/bitcoin`).

Bitcoin, as we all currently know it, is the cryptocurrency with the largest market share, the highest price, and the longest chain, at this current point in time at least. Bitcoin's market share, however, dropped from around 85% in February 2017 to around 30% 12 months later, but this was always going to happen. In fact, bitcoin started out with 100% market share because it was the only cryptocurrency in existence for the first two years and the only way was down, considering all the altcoins that appeared and now the ever-growing number of tokens that are constantly being created.

Bitcoin certainly has the highest value by a country mile, currently bouncing between $6,500 USD and $7,500 USD, with Bitcoin Cash in a distant second at around $700 USD at the time of writing, but what does all this have to do with ICOs? The new token economy will require an international standard *reserve* currency, much like how gold was the international standard for a long time and currently the United States Dollar is the standard fiat currency. Bitcoin is and will be the international standard and there are several reasons why.

Firstly, unlike Ethereum, where Vitalik Buterin is revered everywhere he goes, and Litecoin, where a tweet from Charlie Lee would send prices skyrocketing or crashing, bitcoin is the only cryptocurrency that has no leader. Control of bitcoin is delicately balanced between the developers, who hold custodial rights to the code, the miners who secure the network, and arguably the most important stakeholders— the users like you and I who choose to believe, trust, and participate in this almost surreal, hallucinatory, and abstract concept that we call money. This is the triangle of power.

Secondly, because bitcoin has no leader, it is the most decentralized of all cryptocurrencies. Some argue that it is highly centralized because only a handful of Chinese miners control most of the network, but this is short-sighted. The triangle of power ensures that if bitcoin mining becomes too centralized, users will flee, adoption will stagnate, and the price will drop. This is detrimental to miners, as they receive their income in bitcoins. It is actually in the interest of miners to self-regulate to ensure the success of bitcoin, due to the significant amount of capital that has been invested.

The bitcoin software developers are formally called Bitcoin Core to distinguish them from the other bitcoin flavors or copycats. The official website is https:// bitcoincore.org

In fact, in June 2014, a popular mining pool called Ghash.io managed to exceed 51% of the network (https://techcrunch. com/2014/07/16/popular-bitcoin-mining-pool-promises- to-restrict-its-compute-power-to-prevent-feared-51- fiasco/). This led the community to self-organize and Ghash. io to release a statement promising that it would not exceed 40% of the network hash rate. Ghash.io, however, eventually closed in October 2016.

If the bitcoin core software developers make a change that is against the will of the community, users and miners can fork the software and create their own ecosystem. This is exactly what Bitcoin Cash did, based on the much-publicized *Great Bitcoin Scaling Debate* (https://en.bitcoin.it/wiki/Block_size_ limit_controversy).

The debate was where there was a difference of opinion on how to scale bitcoin. One group proposed a quick solution of increasing the block size to enable more transactions, while the second group preferred to keep the block size the same but work on what is termed a "second layer technology," providing a more longer-term solution but one that would be slower to implement.

The third and final point is that the majority of exchanges around the world generally list bitcoin with the greatest number of trading pairs. Poloniex, for example, has 66 bitcoin trading pairs and only 12 ether trading pairs. Binance lists both bitcoin and ether with over 100 trading pairs. Cryptopia has just under 600 bitcoin trading pairs.

This means that in order to buy smaller unknown cryptocurrencies, bitcoin must be purchased first and then traded. This is what will continue to make bitcoin the global reserve cryptocurrency.

The reason why this is an important point is that as more and more tokens are created by centralized companies, with a management team that has to be trusted and with a controlled supply that could be manipulated, there has to be a safe haven.

The killer app

Everyone is looking for the killer app in the cryptocurrency space; the one app that changes everything. Is it programmable money or smart contracts, or maybe inter-changeable AI-driven smart tokens? However, what if the killer app has already been invented? What if it has been under our noses ever since 2009? What if the killer app is called bitcoin?

Money has not undergone a major technological revolution in several decades. Complicated financial instruments may be constantly invented, with seemingly new services and products, but this is all within the existing financial infrastructure that we know, are familiar with, and essentially have no choice but to be part of. What bitcoin has done is brought us full circle back to the days of direct commerce. It is an exchange of goods or services between you and I, with the help of great mathematics in the form of cryptography. Fax machines, VHS and cassette tapes, and the 35 mm film are just some examples of how technology has progressed. Money or currency is no different.

Bitcoin will continue to innovate and improve, but it doesn't need to have all the bells and whistles all the other blockchains widely advertise. As mentioned above, it has unique properties that no other blockchain has. Bitcoin just has to be the best at what it does. It is a new form of money with the highest degree of trust. Tokens, on the other hand, will have to continue to innovate and integrate with each other. In other words, they must become smart tokens in this decentralized token economy.

The Internet of Tokens

On the surface, ICOs can be thought of as an innovative way to raise capital or create tokens in exchange for money, but it is so much deeper than this. These tokens have unique properties, such as being open, transparent, and decentralized, not to mention being programmable! These tokens need to have a purpose or a function. The economics of the token model, the potential interaction between tokens, and the regulatory impact all culminate into this token entanglement that will help to redefine the future of tokens.

ICOs

As tokens flourish, ICOs will also flourish, but just not in the same form as the craze of 2017. ICOs will be more measured as regulations set in. Expectations will be reset, such that a website, a white paper and an idea do not blindly raise $50 million USD. If this happens, the raise will be much lower and be under more scrutiny. Investors are now savvier and more knowledgeable.

As a form of raising capital, an ICO is very powerful and spurs innovation. Being able to raise millions of dollars from a white paper, with a proof of concept and a sound business model, from thousands of supporters around the world, is the way of the future as the world grows smaller and our interconnectivity grows larger.

These supporters who see, align with and believe your vision, and are keen to use your product, can also help to beta test your product and provide instantaneous feedback via online channels, such as Slack or Telegram, to the product team. All of a sudden, everything becomes a lot more fluid. This is where innovation thrives.

Compare this to the traditional models of funding, with a handful of private investors or venture capitalists, and then an **Initial Public Offering (IPO)**, which is the *normal* way to substantially increase the investor base. Private investors require connections to enter the venture capital world. IPOs carry enormous overheads, so as an entrepreneur, the advantages of ICOs are obvious and clear.

On the other hand, more traditional companies will use their existing business model and existing user base to raise more funds. Examples include Telegram, with its 200 million user base. Just wait until Facebook creates a **FaceBookCoin (FBC)**, **FaceBookToken (FBT)**, **FaceCoin (FC)** or maybe a social network token. Apple, Google and Amazon are sure to follow suit.

A prime example is where a company has already gone through several rounds of traditional funding: series A, B, and maybe more. Instead of giving away more equity in further rounds of a capital raise, an ICO can be used instead. In fact, ICOs are transforming and becoming **Security Coin Offerings (SCO)** or **Security Token Offerings (STO)**.

Tokenization of securities and real-world assets

The argument against a utility token is: what is the underlying value? With a security token, the answer is obvious: it is the underlying asset. Therefore, the tokenization, or the digitization, of securities that provide access to more liquidity online, that everyone can access, is a powerful concept. This can be seen as an evolution, not a revolution, because it is taking what is standard practice and moving it one step along the evolutionary chain of technology.

In the traditional exchange world, traditional public equities and assets are usually only listed on one exchange. In contrast, in the crypto exchange world, tokens are listed on as many crypto exchanges as they can be. As more and more security assets get digitized, crypto exchanges will soon start to specialize based on access to a special liquidity pool or maybe special trades.

Traditional exchanges are also entering the fray, such as an announcement in early August 2018 that **Intercontinental Exchange (ICE)**, the owner of the **New York Stock Exchange (NYSE)**, is partnering with Microsoft to build a platform to serve as a *ecosystem for digital assets*, including bitcoin. Starbucks and **Boston Consulting Group (BCG)**, amongst others, are listed as partners. The new company will be known as Bakkt and intends on leveraging Microsoft's solutions. The integrated platform will enable consumers and institutions to buy, sell, store, and spend digital assets on the seamless global network (https://www.bakkt.com/index).

Taking this concept further, regulators may even mandate that all securities digitize. In this new world, a lot of the processes can be automated and tracked with a much higher degree of efficiency. The protocol can then restrict users performing a non-compliant trade, saving regulators time, money, and resources.

Building on this concept, when something is tokenized, you can typically access or bring together a larger number of investors. This is akin to email, where the technology has allowed us to more efficiently communicate with a larger number of people. Therefore, taking real estate as an example, it is traditionally challenging to get a more diversified investor base from around the world, but with a token representing the real estate asset, whole new opportunities open up. Several examples include Atlant, Real Property Token, Property Coin, Swiss Real Coin, and BrickBlock.

Then, this real-world stable asset can be combined with the crypto economy to back or help to stabilize volatile assets. For example, stable coins traditionally use one form of cryptocurrency to back another or act as collateral. Bitcoin or ether is typically used as this collateral. By collateralizing with real estate instead, this would increase trust in the stable coin and unleash further potential for commerce, trading, and the creation of further markets.

The key takeaway is that most security tokens are based on some underlying asset and there are existing regulations on how to regulate these assets. Therefore, the regulation of the token representation of the asset is then relatively straightforward.

Non-fungible tokens (NFT)

Token discussions have centered around fungible tokens because bitcoin started with the concept of money. Everyone was thinking in terms of fungibility or the ability of a good, or asset, to be readily and easily interchanged with other individual goods, or assets, of the same type. However, as alluded to in *Chapter 2, A Bit of Coin Theory*, colored coins were one of the first attempts to tie unique properties to a digital asset back in 2013.

While the concept struggled to gain attention, and thus adoption, due to the ICO craze, CryptoKitties, through the ERC-721 standard, is revitalising the concept in an attempt to fulfil the initial promise of colored coins. That is, tying unique properties, and in certain cases real-world assets, to crypto assets.

> *"ERC-721 is a free, open standard that describes how to build non-fungible or unique tokens on the Ethereum blockchain. While most tokens are fungible (every token is the same as every other token), ERC-721 tokens are all unique. Think of them like rare, one-of-a-kind collectables."*
>
> — erc721.org

The most obvious example of NFT are digital collectables, but there are other possible applications, such as something that is earned to prove some sort of status. For example, upon receiving a certain number of tokens, a holder receives special recognition by way of a secondary unique token that has a higher value than regular tokens.

NFT could also represent identities on the web, with attached transaction histories, content, and reputation. Imagine open-source Facebook profiles—for fictional or real identities, or for digital devices with digital intelligence. Other experiments with NFT include an equivalent of Robot Wars on the blockchain, where the parts used to build the robots are individual NFT parts. This can be thought of as CryptoKitties 2.0.

This then will lead to new marketplaces being created, as NFT are traded in a slightly different way than traditional crypto assets (as every token is different, think about how baseball cards were traded on the school fields during recess). These marketplaces will see an emergence of trading platforms dedicated to them because providing liquidity is very important in a market.

Token volumes, saturation, and communication

The number of tokens being created on a daily basis is constantly increasing. Some will be original, but the majority will be copycats. Some will be utility tokens, while others will be security tokens. What this means is that sooner or later, there will be an over population or *token saturation* and many will not make it to the other side. The surviving tokens will need to learn to talk and communicate with other tokens. This is something we are seeing with cryptocurrencies.

Take, for example, when you travel abroad and swipe your credit card, and get your cup of coffee. You don't need to know how the Visa network works, but you know that you'll have a bank statement upon your arrival home, to which you may gasp at the true cost of that cup of coffee. Visa Bitcoin debit cards work in a similar way. Bitcoin can be converted to a handful of major currencies, such as USD, EURO, or GBP, to be used on the Visa network.

Let's extend this concept to where it doesn't matter what cryptocurrency you have, be it bitcoin, ether, or litecoin, because a swipe of the card will get you that cup of coffee. In the background, some smart algorithm will figure out the best crypto to use based on the current exchange rate, the time of day, and perhaps even the fastest settlement network, and work it all out for you.

This somewhat messes with the decentralized concept of cryptocurrencies, if laid on top of an existing centralized infrastructure, such as the Visa platform, but baby steps are the name of the game. Take this concept a final step further and imagine a world where everything is tokenized. Why not? After all, it is very simple to create a token to represent anything.

In this tokenized world, tokens could also be earned in multiple ways and not just bought directly from exchanges. Cross-token or inter-token rewards will eventuate, and although tokens may all say they only work within one particular ecosystem or application, what happens when two token companies merge or there is an acquisition? Remember the various white papers that stated a fixed supply and that no more would be created ever? The reality is that of course more tokens can be created within a token economy and if the story is persuasive enough as to why more are needed, we will start to see this happening.

The Internet of Things

The Internet of Things refers to the billions of devices and sensors around the world that are now connected to the internet, collecting, storing, and sharing data. Refrigerators talking to supermarkets, self-driving cars receiving traffic update reports, or clothing with health monitoring sensors are examples. Combine this concept with the proliferation of tokens and we get a beautiful mechanism for transferring value between the Internet of Things via the Internet of Tokens.

How does a refrigerator pay the supermarket to have a drone deliver a loaf of bread? How does the traffic report service charge for the data feed? How can we monetize our health data and be rewarded with lower health insurance premiums for exercising more regularly?

Devices on the internet will start to transact by grabbing the required type and number of tokens automatically, and start to make decisions seamlessly. Automated bots, agents, and even **artificial intelligence** (**AI**) will start buying, selling, borrowing, loaning, and swapping numerous tokens simultaneously. As things appear to get more complex, they will also get simpler because the complexity will be hidden from the human eye.

These smart tokens will run complex algorithms and calculations, and appear smart by making the best decision available in the least amount of time. Tokens will then become a language just like money; a language expressing value, used to communicate, and to create social bonds.

Tokens in a virtual world

The world is changing fast and each year, events such as CES, F8, and Google I/O attempt to wow audiences by giving us a sneak peek into the future. Facebook recently unveiled a new consumer-grade virtual-reality headset called the Oculus Go. It is definitely a step up from slotting your mobile device into a cardboard-framed headset. This provides an improved experience when playing FIFA World Cup or Counter Strike.

As this technology improves and more and more people discover the possibilities of not only playing games but working with technology, by meeting clients or attending conferences from their living room sofa, we will eventually end up living in this virtual world by spending more time in it than out of it. Cryptocurrencies and tokens are the perfect fit in this scenario. A quote from the movie *Ready Player One* can be adapted:

> *"People will flock to virtual reality for all the things*
> *they can do, but they'll stay for all the things they can be."*

As climate change continues to throw planet Earth into hotter summers and colder winters, and movie scenes from *2012* or *The Day After Tomorrow* inch closer to reality, it becomes obvious why Elon Musk, Richard Branson and others push forward with devising plans to conquer the final frontier, and why mere mortals will want to board the space rocket to Mars. Gold will be worthless as weight will be a premium. Bitcoin, however, or even a MuskCoin or a BransonToken could be the golden ticket. No chocolate candy bar wrapper needed here!

Being at the cutting edge can be risky. There have been scams since the beginning of time and they are prevalent in any industry. Physical coins had ridges to combat *coin clipping* because prior to the 18th century, coins were made of precious metal, such as silver, and people would shave the edges of a coin due to its intrinsic value beyond its stated denomination. Laws and regulations are designed to protect the general public and this will not change in the foreseeable future in this new decentralized token economy.

The panacea of a fully decentralized and autonomous virtual-reality-based token economy may still be a way off, but so was the thought of having the computing power of NASA's first lunar mission in your pocket in the form of a mobile phone.

Technology

The crypto economic revolution is not going away. The idea that we can have a digital consensus network, without trusted third parties, is too powerful, so the concept of a giant, scalable, distributed grid of the internet is the real internet that many of us were hoping for.

There is a constant battle between the centralized and the decentralized world. Some ICO companies are looking to bank the unbanked, by providing services to an estimated 2.5 billion unbanked adults around the world (https://www.weforum. org/agenda/2016/05/2-billion-people-worldwide-are-unbanked-heres-how-to-change-this). Other ICO companies, such as OmiseGO, are looking to unbank the banks, but it is not all black and white. There are degrees of decentralization.

On the one end of the spectrum there is bitcoin, which, as previously mentioned, is decentralized to the degree where there is no leader. The trade-off here is that making decisions becomes difficult and slow, as demonstrated in the *Great Bitcoin Scaling Debate* highlighted earlier. On the other end of the spectrum, we have centralized governments and centralized financial institutions with rules that everyone needs to play by.

Decentralization

We are arguing for the re-decentralization of the web because we are living in an era with **Google, Apple, Facebook, and Amazon (GAFA)**, and competing with these data monopolies is not possible by offering a better service.

Blockchains are open public data stores and GAFA will not be able to open up a data set, so this will be the next wave of technological disruption. To allow new, emergent players in, the only way is to either change the game or change the rules, and this is the best chance we have.

Decentralized exchanges

The first step of the creation of a fully decentralized economy has been achieved with the invention of bitcoin and all the other cryptocurrencies. The second step is the creation of decentralized exchanges, which is well underway with the likes of BarterDex, bitShares, OasisDex, 0x, and many others.

Currently, the majority of exchanges in the world are centralized and there is a popular saying in the crypto world from Andreas Antonopoulos:

"Your keys, your coins. Not your keys, not your coins."

Andreas Antonopoulos

This refers to the fact that all coins or tokens are controlled by private keys, which are the equivalent of super-secret passwords. When using a centralized exchange, or leaving your funds on a centralized exchange for trading, you are not in true control, so if the exchange goes bust, gets hacked or loses the coins or tokens (in the case of the Mt. Gox bitcoin exchange it was all three), there is nothing the user can do.

Mt. Gox was an acronym for **Magic: The Gathering Online eXchange** and was launched in 2010. In 2013, it was handling over 70% of all bitcoin transactions but filed for bankruptcy in February 2014. Mt. Gox lost almost 650,000 of its customers' bitcoins, issuing a statement that it believed they were stolen and blaming hackers. An independent Tokyo security company, WizSec, concluded that the missing bitcoins where stolen over time since 2011. In August 2015, CEO Mark Karpelès was arrested and charged with fraud and embezzlement of other funds not related to the missing 650,000 bitcoins.

There are decentralized exchanges that provide the ability to exchange tokens automatically, instantaneously, and securely. The technology, usability, and adoption are constantly improving, along with liquidity, so decentralized exchanges are an obvious progression.

Case study – Tenzorum

Tenzorum is developing a multiple-blockchain-secured log in mechanism, with technology to abstract the fact that keys are being used. There will also be support for access recovery. Tenzorum is developing protocols to allow for all of this and more. The aim is to become a general-purpose decentralized key management system that serves as the backbone to support and connect users between decentralized networks and services.

The name Tenzorum has its roots from the word "tensor," which is a multi-dimensional matrix with multiple force vectors to each component. The meaning casted onto it is the concept of pro-freedom and pro-decentralization.

What problem does Tenzorum solve?

When discussing the user experiences and consumer adoption of decentralized technologies, one fundamental interaction all blockchain technologies have in common is the individual's use of keys. The user experiences around key management are the biggest problem with blockchain technologies today.

The lack of user-oriented key management protocols, and the presence of inadequate frameworks to interface with the various blockchain networks, resulted in obscene cryptocurrency losses throughout the year of 2017. Over $225 million was stolen through phishing scams, over $100 million was frozen due to human errors transacting to the wrong addresses, and more than $1 billion was lost due to hacks. Tenzorum believes that:

> *"Keys are the fundamental element of user-experiences on the web 3.0. Today, the mechanism by which users manage and interact with their keys is broken. It is painful and frightening to use Blockchain applications. Tenzorum is set to change that."*

Tenzorum components

The various components within Tenzorum include an ERC20 token that will serve as a medium of exchange to activate core contracts, with a few business logic functions associated to key management services: storage, editing, and recovery of keys. These tasks are intended to be partly supported by a web-of-trust network that has cryptographically verifiable relationships.

Tenzorum Service Node Network (TSNN) will extend the functionality of the project to become a general-purpose key management service network. Access to any external decentralized technology, such as Urbit, Cardano, Nebulas, Bitcoin, and so forth, will be powered by nodes that are being rewarded with tokens according to predefined consensus rules, to perform tasks that support Tenzorum as a self-sustaining public network.

With TSNN, Tenzorum aims to harness staking to establish inclusive governance. This will guarantee the governance of the open-source code base, protocol/user experience features, organizational priorities, growth campaigns, partnerships, and future vision direction.

Tenzorum is looking to create a seamless user experience to interact with keys across multiple blockchains, while not compromising on the security. It's still early days for the decentralized-apps economy, but Tenzorum's hypothesis is that these decentralized services are going to be the next huge wave of disruption.

The protocol layer will interface with existing decentralized networks, such as Bitcoin, Ethereum, and Nebulas, but because it is a protocol or a framework of rules, it can be extended to almost any other blockchain as required.

The Internet of Blockchains

As new blockchains and other distributed ledger technologies emerge, there will need to be a way for them to communicate with each other. There will need to be APIs to help interface between the many chains, otherwise information will be siloed across many disparate systems. This is similar to what we currently see in the health industry, where your medical records often lay strewn across a variety of healthcare providers, such as your general practitioner, your hospital, your physiotherapist, your dentist, your chiropractor, and the list could go on.

Realizing this, technologies like Cosmos and Polkadot are working on creating an interoperable network of blockchains, to allow the transfer of value from one chain to another.

Cosmos

Cosmos is defined as a "decentralized network of independent parallel blockchains, each powered by classical BFT consensus algorithms like Tendermint" (https://cosmos.network/). The first blockchain in the Cosmos network is the Cosmos Hub, whose native token is the Atom.

Cosmos is essentially a network of blockchains. How do these blockchains connect? One way is to connect each blockchain with every other blockchain, but the problem with this approach is that the number of connections grows exponentially with the number of blockchains. 100 blockchains would require 4950 connections according to Metcalfe's law.

What Cosmos actually does is to create Hubs and Zones. Zones connect different blockchains together on a smaller scale, and Hubs connect these Zones together. The different blockchains in the Zones talk to each other using a protocol called **IBC** or the **Inter-Blockchain Communication** protocol. The end goal is that there will be multiple Hubs that can be run by anyone, connecting together multiple Zones.

There is also another language called **ABCI** or the **Application Blockchain Interface**. This is the equivalent of **Amazon Web Services** or **AWS** where all the network infrastructure and consensus algorithms are provided out of a box, so that developers can just focus on creating applications. Tendermint is sometimes referred to as a blockchain engine that can be used to build other blockchains on top of it. Tendermint has been around since 2014, before becoming part of Cosmos.

Cosmos did an ICO in April 2017 and raised $17 million USD (`https://uk.advfn.com/cryptocurrency/icolist/ATOM*`). The technology is still under active development, with ideas such as Basecoin, which is a starter kit (technically called an SDK) to help build other cryptocurrencies or tokens in.

Polkadot

Similar to Cosmos, Polkadot is a networking protocol for connecting blockchains or ledgers. Polkadot is defined as "a heterogeneous multichain technology" (`https://polkadot.network/`). It was built to connect private/consortium chains, public/permissionless networks, and future technological developments. It is designed to enable an internet where independent blockchains can exchange information and trust-free transactions, with the key tenets of scalability, governance, and interoperability.

The development of the Polkadot protocol was led by Dr Gavin Wood, the co-founder and former CTO of Ethereum, founder of Parity Technologies and creator of the Ethereum Parity wallet. Like Cosmos, Polkadot allows the transfer of value across chains but also provides the ability to transfer data through smart contracts from one chain to another.

Polkadot has its own dedicated terminologies, such as Relay Chains, Parachains, and Bridges. Parachains are the equivalent of Zones in Cosmos. Parachains connect to Relay Chains, which are the equivalent of Cosmos Hubs. In other words, a Relay Chain is the glue or central chain that joins all the different blockchains together. Finally, there are Bridges, which allow blockchains within the Polkadot network to connect to blockchains outside the Polkadot network, that do not want to join for whatever reason.

The key difference between Cosmos and Polkadot is that Cosmos is a simpler system and it doesn't require the various blockchains in their Zones to sacrifice the sovereignty of their consensus in order to participate. Polkadot, on the other hand, requires that all the Parachains adopt its pooled consensus to take part in the protocol. Also, by virtue of allowing data transfer in addition to value transfer, Polkadot is a lot more complex, resulting in more development time being required by the team.

Polkadot ran an ICO in October 2017 and raised about $145 million USD with a DOT token (`https://polkadot.market/summary-of-the-polkadot-ico/`). It was a "Spend-All Second-Price Dutch Auction" where the sale was capped, meaning the ICO would close once a certain amount of ETH had been raised. However, the cap changed over time. Initially, it was very high, to make it very difficult for anyone to buy all the DOT tokens and end the ICO.

The "Second-Price" referenced the fact that everyone who participated received the same buy-in price, which was the price the auction ended on. The "Spend-All" referenced the fact that it wasn't a number of tokens being bought but a committed amount of ETH. Therefore, investors would end up spending all their ETH in return for either the anticipated amount of DOT tokens or more, but never less (`https://polkadot.network/auction`).

Other cross-ledger blockchains

There are a number of other blockchain technologies that can interact with other blockchains, such as Interledger, which can be described as a cross-chain atomic swap on steroids. The swap is a token swap across different chains in an atomic fashion, where "atomic" means that the swap will either fully take place or not at all. This ensures the safety of both parties because there is no trusted intermediary.

Komodo, Aion, Ark, Block Collider, and many other projects continue the research in this current field, which can get very technical, as can be seen with some of the terminology used here. The key takeaway is that with all the different blockchain flavors, they will sooner or later need to talk to each other in an ever-increasing networked community of chains.

Governance

Every blockchain community built on a blockchain needs to govern itself. It needs to determine what is allowed and what is not allowed, how the network upgrades, and how to deal with unexpected events. Blockchain governance builds on existing and familiar governance structures, but extends them into a software world by using the likes of smart contracts and transparent voting on the blockchain to make all these decisions.

On-chain/Off-chain governance

On-chain governance takes the concept of traditional governance and "puts" it on the blockchain. Essentially, there is a protocol on how to change the rules around blockchains or decentralized applications. The parties that participate in the governance can be anyone, ranging from token holders and users, to miners and developers.

Take bitcoin's governance as an example. It can be thought of as being governed loosely by a meritocratic process of peer review and rough consensus among its most active contributors.

The most famous example of on-chain governance was on August 23, 2017, when a technology called segregated witness was "activated" or agreed upon. Here, miners could signal their support for or against a particular decision to upgrade the network, and there were rules around what majority percentage was required, and over what time frame the voting had to be conducted as well.

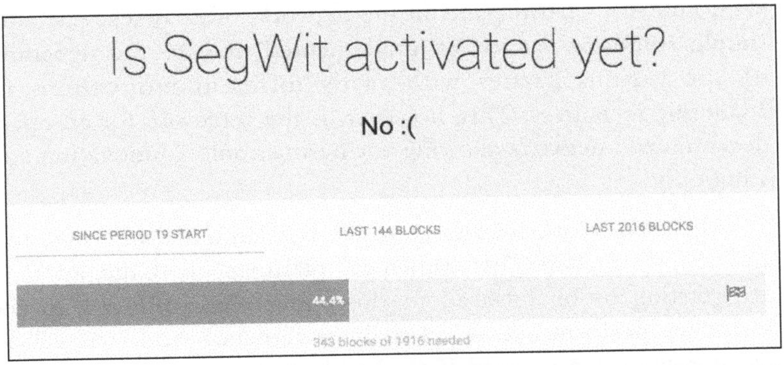

Figure 1: On-chain governance being used in deciding to accept SegWit (https://web.archive.org/web/20170719152619/http://www.segwit.co/)

As an analogy, this is like voting for your local councillor or local city mayor. Taking this concept to the extreme case, Tezos, mentioned earlier in *Chapter 4, Token Varieties,* is making the core protocol and almost everything about it changeable through governance. Users can propose almost any change they want and through voting the community can decide. An on-chain vote occurs, so to speak, and if passed, the update gets promoted to a test network. After a period of time on the test network, a confirmation vote occurs, at which point the change goes live onto the main network. This is what Tezos means when it refers to its concept of a "self-amending ledger."

To give an example, this is very similar to not only having the ability to submit a proposal and voting to make street parking cheaper in your local neighbourhood, but having the ability to change the local bylaws to say parking meters are hereby outlawed and if enough people agree, then the change will be implemented.

The challenge is that governance on the blockchain, or more accurately in a decentralized network, is harder than it looks. With numerous participants in the network, often quick, easy, and simple solutions cannot be implemented, due to the dynamics of the various parties with vastly different motivations or economic incentives. This, however, is the trade-off for an open, decentralized network allowing for permissionless innovation and autonomy.

On-chain blockchain governance is a large and exciting area, and many of these "experimental" platforms that did an ICO are starting to be released to the public. We will start to see how they perform and if on-chain governance works as well as these governance-focused ICOs had hoped. The chances are that most will fail, purely because what looks good on paper doesn't always eventuate in the real world and multiple iterations will be required over time.

The opposite of on-chain governance is off-chain governance. An example includes agreements to implement new features through mailing lists and Bitcoin Improvement Proposals(BIPs). That is, agreement is obtained off the blockchain.

Auditchain

Auditchain is a fascinating concept that provides a decentralized continuous audit and real-time reporting ecosystem for enterprise assurance and disclosure (https://auditchain.com). Auditing is time consuming and labor-intensive with armies of auditors from the "Big 4" accounting firms dominating the market.

The real breakthrough that Auditchain proposes lies in consensus-based attestation and opinions applied and scored by a cohort of auditors, rather than the opinion of a single auditor. The DCARPE™ Explorer provides Streaming Financial Statements™ and AUDT Analytics™ for each reporting enterprise. Subscription revenue to granular and deeper levels of data is shared among the enterprise and the auditors, thereby reducing compliance costs for the enterprise AND reducing conflict; making the auditors truly independent.

No single auditor can provide this kind of assurance to stakeholders. It makes perfect sense as we progress into a digital and tokenized world where the information transacted can and will be tracked (rightly or wrongly), which will naturally then be audited.

Privacy and anonymity

"Privacy is necessary for an open society in the electronic age. Privacy is not secrecy. A private matter is something one doesn't want the whole world to know, but a secret matter is something one doesn't want anybody to know. Privacy is the power to selectively reveal oneself to the world."

– Eric Hughes, "A Cypherpunk's Manifesto", 1993
(`https://www.activism.net/cypherpunk/manifesto.html`)

Ask any individual how important privacy is and you will get the same answer every time: privacy is very important but in a digital age, where we don't have control over our personal information, how do we take it back? In April 2018, this importance was further highlighted in a very public Facebook–Cambridge Analytica data scandal.

An app was created in 2014 called *This Is Your Digital Life* and about 270,000 people were paid to participate. The glitch was that it not only collected personal data from the people who agreed to participate but also the personal information of all the people in those users' Facebook social networks. This led to the accumulation of around 87 million Facebook users' data (https://www.theguardian.com/technology/2018/apr/04/facebookcambridge-analytica-user-data-latest-more-than-thought). Cambridge Analytica obtained the data and used it to profile individuals, in order to target them with personalized political advertisements. This was done to influence public opinion, as explained by Alexander Nix, the Cambridge Analytica CEO:

> *"Today in the United States we have somewhere close to four or five thousand data points on every individual... so we model the personality of every adult across the United States, some 230 million people."* (https://news.sky.com/story/behind-the-scenes-at-donald-trumps-uk-digital-war-room-10626155).

The Cambridge Analytica saga is but one example in a history of infamous data breaches that includes Equifax, Ashley Madison, and Sony, but blockchains and tokens can change all of this. Personal data can be stored on a blockchain that is only accessible by you. You then have the ability to choose who can access this data and for how long. With tokens, you can now also choose how much people can access your data for.

If everything is being tokenized, why not tokenize ourselves? We could tokenize the time we have available or tokenize our personal data. We can then encrypt it and give it or sell it to those who want it or those who need it. These quantum packets of tokens could even be placed on a quantum blockchain, which may not be as far off as many imagine. One particular paper titled *Quantum Blockchain Using Entanglement in Time* even discusses these concepts (`https://techcrunch.com/2018/04/24/meet-the-quantum-blockchainworks-like-a-time-machine/`).

The point here is that the self-sovereignty of data will become a reality, which will naturally create a market of tradable tokenized personal data, and then a bidding war between the global brands. As we trade our personal data, perhaps it won't be as private as we think. Perhaps it will be pseudo-private just like how bitcoin is pseudo-anonymous. We will have ultimate control, but will flaunt it around so much that our data will be everywhere and when a quantum computer with AI has the ability to crack conventional cryptography, it will be the Y2K bug all over again. There will be a huge rush to upgrade all the systems to use new forms of quantum cryptography.

Y2K or the Year 2000 bug: Because many programs represented four-digit years with only the final two digits, there was a concern that the year 2000 would be indistinguishable from 1900 and that computer programs running critical services, such as nuclear power plants, and air traffic control systems, could become compromised. When January 1, 2000, did arrive, the bugs that arose were generally regarded as being relatively minor.

The privacy of cash and coin

Hughes' manifesto explains more on privacy:

> *"Privacy in an open society requires anonymous transaction systems. Until now, cash has been the primary such system. An anonymous transaction system is not a secret transaction system. An anonymous system empowers individuals to reveal their identity when desired and only when desired; this is the essence of privacy."*

Although "A Cypherpunk's Manifesto" was written over 25 years ago, it is still as relevant as ever, particularly in regards to building anonymous systems, defending privacy with cryptography, and freedom of speech being fundamental to an open society. However, there is a movement by various governments around the world to shake things up.

India announced a ban on its largest denominated bills, the 500 and 1000 rupees, the equivalent of $8 USD and $14 USD, in November 2016 (https://www.nytimes.com/2016/11/09/business/india-bans-largest-currency-bills-for-now-n-bid-to-cut-corruption.html). Australia announced that it will be illegal to purchase anything over $7,500 USD ($10,000 AUD) with cash from July 2019 (https://gizmodo.com/australia-bans-cash-for-all-purchases-over-7-500-start-1825946888?IR=T). In France, the maximum payment in cash is €1000. Many other governments around the world are following in the same direction. The reason these governments are attempting to reduce the reliance on a cash economy is to reduce money laundering and tax evasion. Large transactions will have to be done electronically so they can be tracked.

With the slow squeeze on cash, the transition into a digital society is inching closer. Blockchains and cryptocurrencies, such as bitcoin, actually increase transparency. To insure privacy is maintained, it has to be fought for. "A Cypherpunk's Manifesto" highlights a dedicated motivation to ensuring privacy is not lost. Translating the manifesto "Cypherpunk's Manifesto", privacy coins, such as Monero (XMR), Zcash (ZEC), Dash (DASH), Verge (XVG), and many others, continue to fight for the right to privacy and therefore can only continue to grow in the coming years.

Before we jump into more detail about these coins, let's compare privacy with anonymity because they are two different concepts. Privacy is the ability to keep something to yourself. Privacy also is not free, as it takes effort to create and the greater the privacy, the greater the cost. For example, if you don't want people on the street looking into your house, you need to take appropriate steps, such as having curtains or a high fence.

In contrast, anonymity is when you *want* people to see what you do, just not that it's you doing it. The most famous example is Edward Snowden, a former CIA employee who leaked classified information from the NSA. He wanted the NSA's information to be public, but his identity to remain anonymous. A cheeky example:

[

Privacy: You're naked but no one sees you.
Anonymity: You're walking around the city naked but nobody knows your name.
]

This is relevant because some coins enhance privacy and some enhance anonymity, and some do both. In the future, these coins will grow and tokens will also encapsulate these features.

Privacy coins versus coins with privacy features

There is a difference between a privacy coin and a coin with privacy features. Monero, for example, is a coin whose main goal is to achieve privacy. Coins with privacy features implement privacy *as a feature*, such as Dash with coin mixing and Verge with the **Invisible Internet Protocol (I2P)**.

These coins also have what is called "scope of anonymity." Verge, for example, anonymizes only the sender's IP address, while Monero obscures the sender's details and receiver's details, as well as the amount.

Coins with privacy features often provide the user with the option to send transactions in private mode or transparent mode. Privacy coins, such as Monero, force all transactions to be sent privately.

Monero

Monero is a cryptographically private coin by default, meaning there is no option for the user to send transparent transactions like with the other coins. Monero achieves privacy utilizing several techniques, such as **ring confidential transactions (RingCT)** and stealth addresses.

RingCT are designed to improve privacy and security by joining a user's transaction with other older network transactions, such that an observer cannot tell which transaction in the ring is the "real" one. The added advantage is that these other transactions do not need to occur simultaneously with the one that a user wishes to create.

Ring signatures and stealth addresses are used to hide both the sender's and the receiver's address in a transaction. This obfuscation of the addresses makes blockchain analysis virtually impossible. For example, you cannot explore the Monero blockchain or trace any transactions.

Zcash

Zcash offers privacy using a technology called **Zero Knowledge Succinct Non-Interactive Arguments of Knowledge**, or **zk-SNARKs**. Just being able to remember the acronym is good enough to impress your friends!

zk-SNARKs is a mathematical proof proving that the transactional information sent is accurate, without having to reveal what that information is. It also serves to allow for both the verification and the privacy of data at the same time, and is used to encrypt addresses, as well as transaction amounts. However, it is not private by default, mainly due to the inefficiency of the algorithm.

Zcash is a coin where privacy is an option, which unfortunately has meant that currently, according to Zcash's blockchain, only about 3% of funds are shielded or held in addresses starting with "z" (`https://explorer.zcha.in/statistics/value`). The rest are held in transparent addresses starting with "t."

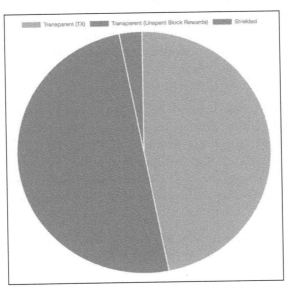

Figure 4: The percentage of private (shielded) Zcash transactions is very low because it is an opt-in and not a mandatory feature

Dash

Dash, a portmanteau of **Digital Cash** and formerly known as Darkcoin, provides some anonymity features but they are opt-in (https://news.ycombinator.com/item?id=14672691). It contains a "PrivateSend" feature, where during the process, your coins are mixed with other coins being sent on the network by special "master nodes." Because of this mixing, Dash is often labeled as not being cryptographically private, but it achieves privacy through mixing.

Dash is also not anonymous in the traditional sense because the transactions can be viewed in a blockchain explorer. It's just very hard to figure out who sent what. Therefore, like Zcash, Dash is a coin with privacy features.

Verge

Verge is not natively private but offers privacy by way of Tor and I2P routing, to obfuscate traffic and conceal a user's IP address when transacting. **Tor** stands for **The Onion Router** and is a network that disguises your identity by moving your traffic across different Tor servers, and encrypting that traffic so it isn't traced back to you. This is known as *onion routing* because your data passes through many layers.

I2P is another network of roughly 55,000 computers around the world (https://en.wikipedia.org/wiki/I2P). It is often called the garlic routing protocol. Each message is a *garlic clove*, with the entire encrypted bundle representing the *bulb*. Each encrypted message has its own specific delivery instruction, with all the *cloves* finding their own way to the end destination.

[**Tor versus I2P**: Tor is time-tested and good enough, while I2P is experimental but has the potential to be much better.]

Therefore, with Verge, all information, including the destination of the transactions and the amounts being transacted, is transparent on the blockchain, and easily viewable by an observer. Moreover, the privacy, traceability, and ability to link transactions and addresses on the Verge blockchain are exceptionally worse than bitcoin because the Verge blockchain contains fewer transactions overall.

Privacy coins will be critical to the future of the technology moving forward. The realization of the ability to track a token back to an owner, identify them and then link them to other coins or tokens will be the impetus to create privacy tokens to protect those who value privacy and anonymity.

Case study – Hedera hashgraph

Formally, hashgraph is known as the consensus algorithm "technology," Swirlds as the consensus platform that implements the hashgraph consensus algorithm, and Hedera as the public ledger that is built on top of the Swirlds consensus platform, that implements the hashgraph consensus algorithm. It is a layered approach because a ledger is a lot more than just a consensus mechanism.

A more simplified version is to think of Hedera hashgraph as being similar to Microsoft Excel, where the first word is the company or brand and the second word is the technology, which in this case is the consensus technology.

The Hedera name

The concept of Hedera stemmed from the idea of the code not forking or having to be pruned in the technical sense. Hedera is a vine and grows, spreads, and interlinks, as opposed to a fruit tree, for instance, which you have to prune regularly. This reflects the fact that information on a hashgraph can grow and spread without having to be pruned. Therefore, Hedera organically suited the concept of the algorithm.

Unless you are in the field of horticulture, you may not have come across the word Hedera. Hedera is actually the genus or type of 12 to 15 species of evergreen climbing or ground-creeping woody plants in the family Araliaceae. In biology, part of the taxonomy goes family -> genus -> species, so here it goes Araliaceae -> Hedera -> 12 to 15 species of ivy plants.

Consensus

In any distributed network, the consensus algorithm is a big deal. Without a secure consensus algorithm to essentially prevent double spending, everything else fails. Within consensus, there is also a distinction between preventing consensus and corrupting consensus.

Every network is susceptible to a one-third attack if it can be split with a firewall. What this means is that if you can break a distributed network into one-third and two-thirds, then what the attacker really needs is just to control one-third of the network to disrupt it and prevent consensus from occurring. This is a very specific attack that every consensus algorithm, that is available right now at least, is susceptible to. Any network susceptible to a 51% attack is also susceptible to a one-third firewall attack.

To take this a step further, hashgraph requires that two-thirds of the network is honest. If more than one-third of the network is being dishonest, then it can prevent consensus for a period of time but it cannot corrupt consensus, meaning that nobody can lie. It may stall the network, but because it will be hard to maintain this, consensus will eventually be achieved.

The idea is that you can prevent consensus with a one-third attack but you cannot corrupt consensus. The only way to corrupt consensus or to tell a lie is to have a greater than two-third control of the network. So, if you wanted to adjust the balance of everyone's wallet and remove the cryptocurrency you just spent and place it back in your wallet, you would have to have greater than 66% control of the network to rewrite history. You could theoretically keep the rest of the network from coming to consensus with just 33% + 1 control of the network. Therefore, two different thresholds have two different effects.

In blockchain, people talk about a 51% attack, so comparing the theoretical threshold for corrupting consensus, it is 51% in blockchain versus 66% in hashgraph. There is also another argument for controlling the blockchain network with a 25% attack, with research done that claims that when using a particular mining attack called selfish mining, only 25% control of the network is required (`https://arxiv.org/pdf/1311.0243.pdf`). In summary, there are different attacks and there are different thresholds for these attacks.

Licensing model

There were a few licensing models that Hedera could have pursued:

- Purely proprietary and closed source
- Purely open source with an open-source license
- Some type of hybrid

If Hedera could have gone with open source it would have, but the argument was that when you accompany open source with financial incentives, it doesn't accomplish all the goals that open source was designed to accomplish. If anything, it prevents a lot of innovation because people get to the point that it is good enough to make money and they stop innovating. Therefore, it made more sense to have an organization that was about the innovation and go for a more controlled hybrid-source approach.

Going with a patented proprietary license model, but with an "open review" model, meant that the source code would be published, so it could be reviewed and potential vulnerabilities could be identified with a reward mechanism or bounty. The other value of this model centers around governance, which allows Hedera to prevent forking, to provide stability in the network, making it more favorable for mass adoption.

Any nodes, however, will be able to get the source code and compile it to ensure that they are running a valid and authentic version of the code. The intent is to embody the spirit of open source and be as transparent as possible.

We know what a 100% proprietary company looks like, such as Facebook, Google, and Amazon, which are very successful, but there are some trust issues to say the least. We've also seen what happens with open source, which usually results in a consolidation of power and forking, which creates instability and thousands of cryptocurrencies. Hedera argues that somewhere in between is the right answer: to create a stable mass market adoptable technology. The patent is there as a defense mechanism to create and ensure the stability of the network.

The network

In some blockchain networks, there is the concept of super nodes or master nodes that have the voting power to form consensus, and regular nodes vote for these super nodes almost like in a democratic government voting system. This is commonly termed "delegated proof of stake."

In Hedera, the public network will start with 39 nodes. The key is that the owners of those 39 nodes happen to also sit on the council and they make governance decisions. The nodes themselves have no additional power over the consensus process compared to any other node. There is a concept called "proxy staking", where any node can create its own incentives to drive end users to your node.

As the network grows, there will be sharding and some of the sharding governance functions will be performed by the 39 council members transparently, but it will not affect consensus. In essence, every node has equal power at the consensus layer, relative to its stake, of course.

The platform

To help visualize the technology, anything that can be done with current blockchain technologies can be done with Hedera hashgraph. Examples include ICOs, micropayments, and even CryptoKitties. This is because the architecture contains a cryptocurrency component, a file storage component and a smart contract component. The compatibility with Ethereum smart contracts was a decision made because of the huge adoption of Ethereum.

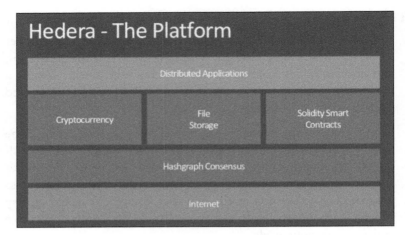

Figure 5: The Hedera platform components

One of the benefits of hashgraph is regarding persistence or the storing of data. In the blockchain world, the whole blockchain, around 200 GB at the time of writing, is required to maintain a full node. A full node is required because each transaction needs to be cryptographically verified against all previous transactions, right back to the beginning of the blockchain or the genesis block. Therefore, blockchains cannot maintain the integrity of the latest block without having a genesis block as a reference, and storing absolutely everything in between.

In hashgraph, instead of securing transactions against an ever-growing 200 GB of history, it is saying that 39 nodes (initially anyway) have confirmed that this transaction is valid and as long as we always have two-thirds of the network being honest and validating every round, we can trust the current round because it was validated against the previous round. So, because of this, hashgraph does not need the entire history to reach consensus.

A valid argument for a blockchain is around immutability, where people cannot lie about the history of transactions that took place because it is imprinted in the blockchain. In hashgraph, all of this can be optionally stored by a node. In addition to this, two-thirds of the network can provide a signature attesting that some event did happen. This is called a state proof in Hedera hashgraph.

Other neat features include multiple payments that can be processed in one transaction, great for splitting the bill or businesses building dApps, and claims that can be added to accounts (think self-sovereign identity) that are signed by an authority and the account owner.

There is also an argument against immutability, especially with GDPR and the right to be forgotten. In blockchains, you cannot forget. For instance, using the distributed file storage concept, illegal content cannot be removed from the blockchain that is potentially being stored on personal computers all around the world. Hashgraph uses the concept of controlled immutability, meaning the user can control what is stored and what is not. From a historical perspective, the network will prove consensus, store it for a period of time, and then discard it, unless it has been explicitly requested to be stored. This way, the user can pay for storage for the next seven years (accounting records for example) and afterwards it will disappear.

Quantum blockchains

To understand quantum computers and their effects on blockchains, it is useful to first of all understand what they are and how they work. Let's start with the basics of how classical computers work. The term *classical* computer is used to describe computers as we know them in today's world.

Classical computer

Everything in the digital world is represented as 0s or 1s, and transistors are used to represent these two states. A **bit**, which stands for **binary digit** is a term used to represent a single binary value. For example, one bit represents on or off. Two bits can represent on-on, on-off, off-on, and off-off.

Transistors representing these bits are getting smaller and smaller, approaching a physical technological limit. This means that each year at Christmas time, the new smart phone you receive will not be twice as fast as last year's model but only half as fast, and only a quarter as fast the year after that. To circumvent the physical limitations, a new technology or paradigm needs to be developed. This is where quantum computers come in.

Quantum computers

In the quantum realm, physics works very differently, to the point where our understanding of traditional computers doesn't apply or even make sense. Quantum computers use the concept of quantum bits or qubits (pronounced *kew bit*), which like their binary counterpart can also be set to a 0 or a 1. However, a qubit can *also* be in any proportion of both states at once and this concept is called superposition. In other words, a qubit can be a 0 *and* a 1 at the same time. Weird right?

Superposition

One qubit can be in a superposition of two states, two qubits can be in a superposition of four states, three qubits can be in a superposition of eight states and so on. For example, if one bit represents a door that is either open or shut, one qubit can represent a situation where the door is both open and shut at the same time, but when observed or measured, it's seen as either fully open or fully shut.

The advantage this brings can be explained by comparing this to a classical computer. In a two-bit system, four states are possible (00, 01, 10, and 11) and four operations need to be performed when evaluating these four states. With two qubits, a quantum computer can evaluate these four states all at once! Imagine what a 50-qubit system can do then!

Entanglement

In conjunction with superposition, another weird and unintuitive property is called entanglement. This is a close connection between two qubits that makes one qubit react to a change in state of the other qubit instantaneously, no matter how far apart they are. This means that when measuring one entangled qubit, it is possible to directly deduce the properties of the other without having to look. Another way to think about this is that tickling one qubit will make the other qubit on the other side of the Earth feel the tickle instantaneously as well.

What can be used as qubits?

There are a number of particles that can be used as a qubit. A single photon (a particle of light) or an electron, for example, can be used to represent 0, 1, or a superposition.

The link to cryptography

One aspect of cryptography relies upon prime numbers. Take the example where a very large integer number, let's call it M, is provided and the goal is to find two factors of M that are prime numbers. In other words, find two other prime numbers that multiply together to get M. It turns out that this is phenomenally hard to do. It is so hard in fact that this forms the basis of encryption. However, what would take billions of years to solve using a classical computer, would take potentially minutes to solve with a quantum computer. This means that the statement that "it is practically infeasible to obtain a private key from a public key" would no longer be true in the quantum world.

The link to blockchains

There are several ways to combat quantum computers affecting blockchains. Firstly, there is research to create quantum-resistant cryptograph. The aim here is to produce private keys in a much more mathematical way, other than with just prime number factorization.

The second method is to create quantum-based cryptography. This is like fighting fire with fire; it will still take billions of years for a quantum computer to crack an algorithm of its own quantum kind. Finally, there is the possibility of creating an intrinsically quantum blockchain, constructed from quantum information over a quantum network. This would be the most ambitious design.

In fact, two researchers from Victoria University of Wellington, in New Zealand, have proposed a new quantum blockchain technology that "encodes a blockchain into temporally entangled states, which can then be integrated into a quantum network for further useful operations (https://arxiv.org/pdf/1804.05979. pdf)." The researchers also show that entanglement in time, as opposed to entanglement in space, plays a pivotal role for the quantum benefit over a classical blockchain. This is a lot to grasp in a sentence, but the main point is that there are researchers contemplating these concepts already, even though we are many years away from actual realization.

The key takeaway from all of this is that while quantum is a threat to blockchain technologies, it would be a bigger threat to the entire security of the internet, and when quantum computing does arrive, a new security paradigm will take over to secure the likes of Web 10.0.

Governments and society

With all the attention from ICOs in the last few years, governments and law makers around the world have woken up to the fact that something has to be done to reduce scams and protect the consumer. The quickest solution is to make the glass slipper fit the existing foot. In other words, we must classify cryptocurrencies and tokens as either a currency, a property/asset, a commodity, or a security (the list goes on) and make it comply with existing rules and regulations.

New rules and regulations will eventually be required but, currently, we are in the tweaking and addendum phase, just like those introduced to handle drones with no-fly zones around airports. The challenge to encourage innovation, yet protect consumers, is a tough balancing act. We are already seeing smaller countries, such as Switzerland, Cyprus, Malta, and Belize, just to name a few, take the initiative and provide more crypto-friendly regulations to encourage investment and innovation, which will help to simulate and grow an economy. A small island country in the South Pacific, called Vanuatu, is even accepting bitcoin as a form of payment for its citizenship program (`https://qz.com/1099475/a-small-pacific-island-will-now-let-you-buy-citizenship-with-bitcoin/`).

> *"Thank you for your enquiry. I can confirm that Bitcoin is accepted as a form of payment for Citizenship Applications. When this story was initially picked up by various news agencies last year it was unfortunately slightly mis-reported that the Vanuatu Government were directly accepting bitcoin - whereas in fact, it is our organization – the Vanuatu Information Centre, which is a Government licensed agent for the Citizenship Program – which accepts Bitcoin payment. We then convert to fiat currency for transmission to the Vanuatu Government."*
>
> *- Vanuatu Information Centre, May 2017*

These smaller island nations have an opportunity to participate in this token economy, raise capital, and create projects to help provide books for schools or more desalination equipment, while existing governments clamber to figure out what is going on and how to play catch up.

Free society

Roger Ver, an early bitcoin adopter and a very vocal advocate of Bitcoin Cash, announced in September 2017 a project called Free Society (https://www.freesociety.com/). The goal is to lease a plot of land from a nation state in an effort to build a libertarian, anarcho-capitalist country. The Free Society project plans to:

> *"Establish a rule of law based on libertarian principles and free markets. We don't see the need to recreate traditional government structures. The rule of law/constitution can be included in the final agreement of the land sale, and will be an extension of the existing contract that will be put in place with the government that granted us the sovereignty. Enforcement will happen through private arbitration, competing court systems, and private law enforcement. It is important to establish a proper rule of law, as our project will set an example for the industry and create an important precedent with governments and the world. We want to make sure the constitution is solid but avoid the inefficiencies of existing government structures."*

Don't rule out an ICO in order to raise capital to help fund this project, as the project has only raised $100 million thus far. To say this is an ambitious project would be a grand understatement, but a true tokenized economy could flourish in an environment like this. Identity tokens on the blockchain, ownership tokens, and cryptocurrencies for payments all sounds like *2001: A Space Odyssey* reborn. Perhaps this is all just a precursor to more futuristic concepts, such as merging blockchains and satellite technology.

Figure 6: Ver's experimental project of creating a "country"
with a central government

As crazy as it may sound, and keeping in mind that it is still early days, there are startups, such as Blockstream (`https://www.prnewswire.com/news-releases/announcing-blockstream-satellite-broadcasting-bitcoin-from-space-300504390.html`) and Spacechain (`https://www.techinasia.com/spacechain-blockstream-blockchain-to-satellite`), which are researching into deploying low-cost, low-orbit, tissue-box-sized satellites into space. Spacechain wants to create an open-source satellite operating system where developers can build and run their own applications, like tracking shipping containers across the ocean or taking photos of Earth.

Spacechain aims to launch its first CubeSat into space in February 2019. This seems overly optimistic but we are in an age of amazing revolution. In fact, the late Stephen Hawking believed space exploration is crucial to human survival:

> *"Our population and our use of the finite resources of planet Earth are growing exponentially, along with our technical ability to change the environment for good or ill. But our genetic code still carries the selfish and aggressive instincts that were of survival advantage in the past. It will be difficult enough to avoid disaster in the next hundred years, let alone the next thousand or million. Our only chance of long-term survival is not to remain lurking on planet Earth, but to spread out into space."* (`https://www.huffingtonpost.ca/2011/11/18/stephen-hawking-space-exploration_n_1101975.html`).

Summary

In this chapter, we put forward arguments that bitcoin is and will continue to the be the reserve currency in the crypto universe because it is the only true decentralized currency that not the SEC nor any other regulatory body can sue, shutdown, or attack. It has this unique equilibrium between the users or consumers of the service, miners who secure the network and the core group of people who look after the code on Nakamoto's behalf.

Bitcoin *is* the killer app, at least for this decade. In the next decade, we will be looking out for that killer smart token, as more and more tokens will be created for everything soon, bringing us to token saturation and then a consolidation. Tokens will become smarter and with the advancement of AI and machine learning, the tokens in our lives will be all managed "automagically" under the covers.

We also outlined that ICOs are going to drastically change, as we've already started seeing, and turn into more traditional securities, but this won't stop the token growth nor the innovation. Distributed ledger innovation will continue to mature and many others will start to gain momentum.

All these distributed ledger technologies, blockchain or non-blockchain, will need to communicate to one another. Inter-chain or inter-ledger communication will happen in order to prevent going full circle back to information being siloed, like the current situation we are in now.

Governments will have a tough time on their hands balancing the push for technological innovation against the need to protect their citizens, and the fight for power and privacy will continue. The end game may be for us to all be in control of data, our money and our destiny, but as we all know, with great power comes great responsibility. Nakamoto has given us a taste of what it feels like to be our own bank. Now it is time to learn how we can take back our identity and potentially the very essence of who we are.

SUMMARY

The journey has just begun

Congratulations for making it to the end of this book. Hopefully you now have a better understanding of the world of Bitcoins, blockchains, and the emergence of this new tokenized economy and in particular, how the ICO craze of 2017 came about.

Let this book inspire you to read and understand further not just about what cryptocurrencies or tokens are but more fundamentally what exactly is money? What is trust in this new digital and decentralized age? Exactly who are the ones playing the tune that we all sing and dance to?

If you are excited about this technology as much as we are and wondering what to do next, pick an area that you are passionate about such as energy, health, supply chain, trading, education, or investing to name a few and learn everything you can about it and how blockchain technologies can and will disrupt it. Bounce ideas with like-minded people and start experimenting because before you know it, opportunities will appear that will allow you to start your own personal journey into not just the technology, but to learn more about yourself and to further grow, develop and learn as an individual.

So what are you waiting for? Learning is doing, so get up, get out, and go get some!

OTHER BOOKS YOU MAY ENJOY

If you enjoyed this book, you may be interested in these other books by Packt:

Mastering Blockchain - Second Edition

Imran Bashir

ISBN: 978-1-78883-904-4

- ◆ Master the theoretical and technical foundations of the blockchain technology

- ◆ Understand the concept of decentralization, its impact, and its relationship with blockchain technology

- ◆ Master how cryptography is used to secure data - with practical examples

- Grasp the inner workings of blockchain and the mechanisms behind bitcoin and alternative cryptocurrencies

- Understand the theoretical foundations of smart contracts

- Learn how Ethereum blockchain works and how to develop decentralized applications using Solidity and relevant development frameworks

- Identify and examine applications of the blockchain technology - beyond currencies

- Investigate alternative blockchain solutions including Hyperledger, Corda, and many more

- Explore research topics and the future scope of blockchain technology

Building Blockchain Projects

Narayan Prusty

ISBN: 978-1-78712-214-7

- ♦ Walk through the basics of the Blockchain technology
- ♦ Implement Blockchain's technology and its features, and see what can be achieved using them
- ♦ Build DApps using Solidity and Web3.js
- ♦ Understand the geth command and cryptography
- ♦ Create Ethereum wallets
- ♦ Explore consortium blockchain

Learn Bitcoin and Blockchain

Kirankalyan Kulkarni

ISBN: 978-1-78953-613-3

- ◆ Understand the concept of decentralization, its impact, its relationship with blockchain technology and its pros and cons

- ◆ Learn blockchain and bitcoin architectures and security

- ◆ Explore bitcoin and blockchain security

- ◆ Implement blockchain technology and its features commercially

- ◆ Understand why consensus protocols are critical in blockchain

- ◆ Get a grip on the future of blockchain

Leave a review - let other readers know what you think

Please share your thoughts on this book with others by leaving a review on the site that you bought it from. If you purchased the book from Amazon, please leave us an honest review on this book's Amazon page. This is vital so that other potential readers can see and use your unbiased opinion to make purchasing decisions, we can understand what our customers think about our products, and our authors can see your feedback on the title that they have worked with Packt to create. It will only take a few minutes of your time, but is valuable to other potential customers, our authors, and Packt. Thank you!

Index

Lightning Source UK Ltd.
Milton Keynes UK
UKHW02f1948221018
330985UK00006B/201/P